COMPLETE BOOK OF THE
BOW & ARROW

COMPLETE BOOK OF THE

OF THE

Stackpole Books

REVISED, THIRD EDITION

BOW & ARROW

G. Howard Gillelan

Bear Archery photography by Bill McIntosh

COMPLETE BOOK OF THE BOW AND ARROW

Copyright © 1977 by
G. Howard Gillelan

Revised, third edition

Published by
STACKPOLE BOOKS
Cameron and Kelker Streets
P.O. Box 1831
Harrisburg, Pa. 17105

*Published simultaneously in Don Mills, Ontario, Canada by Thomas Nelson &
Sons, Ltd.*

Printed in the U.S.A.

Library of Congress Cataloging in Publication Data
Gillelan, G. Howard.
  Complete book of the bow & arrow.

  Includes index.
  1. Archery.   2. Hunting with bow and arrow.
I. Title.
GV1185.G514   1977   799.3'2   76–30484
ISBN 0–8117–2118–3

Contents

CONTENTS

Part I

◉◉◉◉◉◉◉◉◉◉◉◉◉ ◉◉◉◉◉◉◉◉◉◉◉◉◉

The Story on Archery

The History of
Archery

WHAT IS MAN'S oldest sport? It's doubtful that anyone can answer that question with certainty but among the various sport contests in the Olympic Games, the oldest is archery, which apparently had its origins about 50,000 years ago. There is some question about when the first bows were drawn. Some authorities will say only that bows and arrows were in use more than 8,000 years ago. But the late Dr. Saxton Pope, a modern archery pioneer, concluded that the first bowmen were shooting some 50,000 years ago. He based his statement on the fact that arrowheads have been found which were in existence in the third interglacial period.

In its early days, the bow was not an instrument of sport; it was a weapon, a way of life. While the bow certainly is not the world's oldest weapon, it was probably man's first actual invention in weaponry. It seems likely that a rock, a club and a crude spear came first as hunting weapons and as a means of defense against predatory enemies, man as well as beast.

However, these rudimentary weapons could have been in use before man evolved. One can envisage an ape throwing a rock at an enemy, or wielding a club, or even throwing a pointed stick. But it's too much to imagine a lower form of primate bending a branch, securing its ends with a limber strand of vine, and using it to propel sharpened sticks. It seems safe, therefore, to classify the bow as the first weapon developed exclusively by homo sapiens.

It isn't possible to state which group of early men first used the bow, because apparently it was in use before there were any tribal or geographical categories of mankind. Certainly the weapon in a simplified version was a tool of a low form of human. This seems clear since it has been established that bows and arrows were used by aborigines, whose tiny bows were not much more than a foot in length. The arrows, it is believed, were carried on top of the shooter's head, stuck into his thick growth of hair.

Anthropologists and archaeologists are in doubt as to whether the bow was invented by a small group of pre-historic men who, over thousands of years, spread around the world and carried their weapons with them; or whether the bow and arrow combination was an independent creation. The majority of scientists appear to favor the latter view, since advances such as the discovery of the use of chipping flint in fire-making occurred in different places and at different times. In any case, the bow appears historically throughout the world, from the Orient to the Arctic region. It is still used today as their principal weapon by primitive peoples in Africa and in the jungles of South America.

Because it permitted the hunter to attack his quarry from a distance and with some degree of accuracy, the bow was a most important implement in the development of mankind. For the same reason, the bow—greatly improved in later years—was the most important tool in warfare until the introduction of firearms. It may seem like an extravagant opinion, but some historians have stated that through the years the bow and arrow have killed more men than has any other type of weapon.

As time went on, man improved his mental capacity—and his favorite weapon as well. Empires were carved out, to a large extent by archers; civilizations were built and were kept secure by bowmen. In the cradle of world civilization the bow was a tremendously important influence. The Chaldeans, the Hittites and the Israelites depended on the bow. The ancient Chinese had a reputation for using archery militarily.

THE ORIGINS OF MODERN ARCHERY

The most noted of the pre-Christian archers were the Egyptians. At least we know more about their archery, partially because their civilization lasted for almost thirty centuries, partly because they recorded it so well, and also because many of their records are available to us today. Thanks to the diggings of archaeologists, we can now see murals, statues and ancient hieroglyphics that reveal the importance of archery in a culture that flourished longer than any other in history.

In case the modern bowman thinks the slotted plastic nock on the rear end of his arrow is a modern development, he should see an Egyptian arrow in a museum. Although it was made of a reed from the shores of the Nile, and may date back to the time before the building of the Pyramids, the ancient shaft is fitted with a nock made of carved bone that is strikingly similar to the nocks in use now.

The archaeological art portrays chariot-mounted archers in battle and on lion hunts, a shop where leather quivers were produced, and another where bows were made from wood, bonded between layers of animal horn and sinew. The ancient pictorial records show Egyptian kings in combat and in target practice. One king was depicted, possibly by a favor-seeking sycophant artist, as he shot at a thick copper target from the back of his charging steed. The arrows all hit the target and went completely through the metal, "...which had never been done nor even heard of in story," according to the caption on the carving.

The ancient Greeks and Romans — whose civilizations are responsible for so much of our social concepts—were not particularly archery-minded. Perhaps it would be going too far to state that their lack of emphasis on the bow contributed to the demise of their cultures, but it remains as a possibility which must be considered.

The Greek and Roman governments rejected the bow as an important tool of warfare, for reasons which are not quite clear. The Greek generals relied on the spear as the main weapon, despite the fact that on a number of occasions their trusted spearmen were cut down by a rain of arrows from Persian archers.

Using layers of available materials such as animal horn and sinew to strengthen their wood bows, the Persians established an army of bowmen who were feared by all their enemies. The result was that their archers and their weapons played a major part in the advances and downfalls of empires. Although the Roman legions finally adopted bows and arrows as important military weapons, the innovation was apparently too late to preserve their expanded empire.

In later centuries, bows and arrows became dreaded, as swarms of arrows mowed down enemies of Attila's Huns, who were mounted on horses and used short, powerful bows with telling effect. It's possible that one of the reasons for the failure of the Crusades was the skill and equipment of the Turkish archers. Untold thousands of Richard the Lion-Hearted's men fell with arrows in their vitals. Depending on lances and swords and equipped only for close-range combat, the Crusaders were no match for the deadly Turkish bowmen.

The Turks were so advanced in their archery technology that some of their distance-shooting records still stand today. Like the Persians they used laminated bows made of wood cores, strengthened with layers of processed horn and sinew. Their weapons were recurved; that is, when unstrung, they bent backwards. It's astonishing to note that many modern bow designs are based on the weapons of hundreds of years ago.

Few contemporary archery fans realize the contributions made by the Turks to our modern equipment. Instead, we identify our sport with the famed English longbowmen. This may be because the latter are closer to us historically and culturally, while the exploits of the earlier Asiatic archer-soldiers are not so clear. Too, the English used bows to win a number of crucial military engagements. Then, when bows were replaced by firearms as the most effective battle weaponry, the English kept archery alive as a sport of the socially well-to-do.

Today's bows—fairly flat limbs, recurved tips, laminated wood and fiberglass—owe much more to the bowmen of the eastern Mediterranean than to the sturdy English archers who drew their longbows in the Hundred Years' War. The typical old English bow was close to six feet in length, oval or almost round in cross-section, and usually made of solid yew wood.

IMPORTANT INFLUENCES ON ARCHERY

The actual origin of the English longbow is shrouded in the mists of history. Around the Fifth Century the Saxons, emigrating from the lowlands of the continent, invaded Britain. Certainly, they used bows and arrows, and probably introduced them to the wild natives. Dozens of bows as well as a supply of arrows and quivers were found by scientists who unearthed a buried Saxon warship in a Scandinavian bog. Wild Welsh tribesmen are credited by some people with introducing longer bows to other parts of England at about this time.

The Vikings, those fierce sea raiders from Denmark and the Scandinavian peninsula, were also a factor in impressing the early

Some modern bows are not unlike those used by ancient archers of the eastern Mediterranean.

13

inhabitants of the British Isles with the effectiveness of bows and arrows. From 850 to 950 A.D. they swooped into Britain and subjugated the natives. In 1960, a visiting American archer was shown a collection of beautifully-crafted stone arrowheads in Yorkshire, near England's east coast. Assuming that the points were made by American Indians, he was dumbfounded to learn that they had been picked up by a farmer while plowing his land in Yorkshire. After checking with the British Museum, the farmer confirmed the fact that his arrowheads were identical to those used by the Vikings.

Archery played a key role in the Battle of Hastings, in 1066, when the invading Normans were led by William the Conqueror, himself a prodigious bowman. According to the Bayeux tapestry, the defending Saxons at first protected themselves against the Norman arrows by forming a wall with their shields, whereupon the attackers lofted their shafts in a high arc so that the missiles rained down on the enemy troops. This archery strategy apparently was effective. Before the day was over King Harold fell with an arrow in his eye, and the Britons fled the field. It seems likely that the impact of the Norman archers, as well as the victorious William's keen interest in the weapons, were responsible for the high regard of the bow and arrow for hundreds of years in Britain.

The Assizes of Arms, published by Henry II, provided that every man's armor should be left to his heir. Of more interest to archers, the law reflected the stress of the country's leaders on the bow and arrow, stating that all males between the ages of 15 and 60 were required to own a bow and to practice with it regularly.

THE MOST IMPORTANT MILITARY WEAPON

As a formidable tool of warfare, English archery equipment reached its peak during the Hundred Years' War, 1337-1453. It was in the Battle of Crécy in 1346 that repeated showers of English arrows had a telling effect on the much larger French army. Practically half of the French troops, including more than 1,000 mounted, armor-clad knights, were lost. Edward III was in command of the English force, assisted by his son, Edward the Black Prince, who was only 16 years old at the time. The opposing leader was King Philip VI, who depended on a large detachment of mercenary crossbowmen from Genoa. Their weapons were rendered useless when a rainstorm soaked the strings of the crossbows.

While the crossbow was used in the Middle Ages—and is still shot today by a relatively small number of hobbyists—its value as a military arm was never impressive. The crossbows of that era did not have the range of longbows. They had the further disadvantage of being much slower to cock and reload. The most renowned crossbowman was William Tell, the legendary apple-shooting marksman of 14th-Century Switzerland.

The type of armor worn by some of the French knights offered protection against sword blows but could not withstand a well-directed arrow. Some years ago, Dr. Saxton Pope conducted an experiment on a chain-mail shirt, similar to the armor worn in the Battle of Crécy. He mounted the 25-pound shirt on a wooden box and padded it with cloth. Shot out of a longbow from a short distance, Pope's steel-tipped arrow made the sparks fly when it struck the links of steel of the chain shirt. The point penetrated the armor and an inch of wood, then bulged out the back of the shirt.

In 1415, England's Henry V scored a great victory over the French at Agincourt, a crucial encounter in the Hundred Years' War. Though outnumbered 13,000 to 50,000, the well-trained English routed their foe, largely due to repeated volleys of arrows.

Henry VIII, best known for his six wives, was a skilled hunter and archer, and a great respecter of the bow as a weapon of war. Because of Henry's enthusiasm for bows and arrows, he commissioned his old friend and the tutor of his children, Roger Ascham, to set down the formal procedures for bow-handling. The result was a book, *Toxophilus,* the first written description of the steps to be followed in accurate bow-shooting. In one sense, this book was the first manual of arms, since it explained how an archer should properly use his weapon.

One of the most romantic figures to ever draw a bow was Robin Hood. Was this green-clad hero a myth or was there actually such a person? It seems a good possibility that there really was a Robin Hood, leader of a band of outlaws who lived in Sherwood Forest and shot the King's deer. No doubt his men were constantly on the run from the Sheriff of Nottingham, and they probably aided the poor at times. But his exploits obviously were expanded by untold generations of storytellers. As a consequence, the modern conception of Robin Hood should be accepted on the same basis as Johnny Appleseed and Paul Bunyan.

The other group of famous bowmen were the American Indians. Nearly every schoolboy has a vivid mental picture of a near-naked Redskin stalking a deer and skillfully shooting it in the heart with a flint arrowhead. Up to a certain point the picture is as factual as it is colorful.

The truth is that within the limits of their primitive culture the American Indians were fine archers. What must be pointed out, though, is that in most cases their weapons were crude by modern standards. That the first Americans were patient hunters and excellent stalkers, no one can deny. By virtue of their hunting ability, stealth and knowledge of the animals, they were able to get extremely close to the quarry—and this was the secret of their success. Redskins enjoyed the hunt as sport, but it went beyond that: they had to have productive hunts or they and their families would be lacking in food and clothing.

Depending on tribal expertise and location, the archery equipment of American Indians varied from sloppy and comparatively inefficient to durable and—considering their materials and technology—efficient. Regardless of how well the Indian bows rated for efficiency, they did not compare with the performance of the typical English longbows.

Archery Today

THE EVOLUTION OF modern archery is equally as interesting as that of historical archery. The big difference is the influence of a few strong individual personalities on what is now known as the sport of archery.

With the general acceptance of gunpowder and firearms in warfare the bow as a serious military weapon was dead, although Benjamin Franklin had not forgotten the potential of archery in warfare. During the Revolutionary War he made a suggestion to one of George Washington's generals that the Continental Army include archery in its armament. "I would add bows and arrows," Franklin wrote. "These were good weapons not wisely laid aside."

By the 19th Century, bows and arrows were the toys of fashionable young English blades and their ladies. In a similar context, in the United States the country's first archery organization was formed in 1828. The club was the United Bowmen, in Philadelphia, and it is still in existence. Its early members were more interested in exercise and social camaraderie than in promoting archery, so the sport was almost unknown through most of the country.

Following the Civil War, two brothers named Will and Maurice Thompson, took up archery and attracted a considerable amount of interest to the sport. The Thompson brothers were veterans of the war; one of them, Maurice, had been badly wounded in the chest, so much so that a physician suggested they spend most of their time in the out-of-doors. Both Georgians, they decided to camp out in neighboring Florida, at that time a genuine wilderness.

Friendly Indians assisted the brothers, showing them how to make bows and arrows, and how to hunt the abundant game in the region. Having a literary bent, Maurice Thompson recorded their adventures and wrote a book, *The Witchery of Archery*. It covered their hunting exploits and in lyrical terms conveyed their love of wildlife. Because of the romantic depiction of the Thompsons' form of living and their obvious attachment to the bow, the book became a popular success, and country-wide interest in archery was awakened. The National Archery Association was founded in 1879 and held its first tournament that year in Chicago. The first president of the N.A.A. was, appropriately, Maurice Thompson. It is more than interesting to note that at about the same time—the twilight of the era of Indian wars—while many Americans were shooting arrows at bullseye targets, their uniformed countrymen were dodging arrows in the West.

After 1879, archery was better-known, though it still was not a widely-practiced sport. At that time, it was a formal social sport and there was little or no bowhunting. It remained so until several generations later when the bow and arrow re-surfaced as a contemporary hunting implement. Had it not been for a remarkable chain of events involving the right persons being in the right place at the right time, it's possible that archery today would be as dead as the dodo.

In 1911, the last survivor of the Yana Indian tribe gave himself up to the legal authorities in Oroville, California. The Indian's name was Ishi; he was naked, starving and terrified of the whites who had forever erased from the face of the earth the other members of his tribe. Since the Indian had broken no laws and was unable to communicate with his captors, the local lawmen contacted the anthropology department of the University of California. The scientists, realizing that here was a living Stone Age man whom they could study, took him to the university for observation. When he became more "civilized" Ishi was given a minor job at the university museum. It was there that he came to the attention of the previously mentioned Dr. Saxton Pope, a surgeon who also taught at the institution's medical school.

Dr. Pope and Ishi became fast friends. The Indian taught Pope how to make bows and arrows and how to hunt both big and small game. When Ishi died of tuberculosis in 1916, the physician continued and enlarged his interest in hunting with the bow. To the surprise of many sportsmen and naturalists, Dr. Pope, by now an experienced hunting archer, used the bow to take grizzly bears in Wyoming. On numerous hunting trips Dr. Pope was accompanied by his sportsman-friend, Arthur Young. They shot most species of U.S. big and small game, and went on successful hunts to Alaska and Africa. Both men are revered by archers today; the Pope and Young Club, which is probably the most exclusive sportsmen's organization in the world, is named after Saxton Pope and Art Young. The Ishi story, plus some of the adventures of Pope and Young, are set forth in Saxton Pope's book, *Hunting With the Bow and Arrow.*

HOW MODERN BOWHUNTING BEGAN

As the feats of Pope and Young became known, a few other hunters accepted the new challenge and tried bowhunting, but it was still a rarity to see a hunter stalking the deer woods with a bow. During the Depression of the 1930's another great bowman, Howard Hill, kept the archery fires burning through a series of short movie features which showed him demonstrating extraordinary feats with the bow, in exhibitions as well as in the hunting field. It was around this time that another strong personality emerged to influence the sport of archery. This was Dr. Robert P. Elmer, a physician of Wayne, Pennsylvania. His enthusiasm for target archery and his writings on the subject led to the revitalization of the N.A.A. Two other individuals deserve special mention for their contribution to archery theory. Both physicists, Dr. Clarence N. Hickman and Dr. Paul E. Klopsteg conducted research independently on how bows and arrows work. Their findings, arrived at with the aid of modern scientific techniques and equipment, are valuable additions to our knowledge of archery.

In the meantime, bowhunting was beginning to gain new adherents. Wisconsin was the first state to grant a special deer season for archers, in 1934. As word spread around the country that it was actually possible for a modern bowman to bag a deer,

During the Depression, the great Howard Hill made movie shorts of his extraordinary feats with the bow.

Target archers shoot formalized competitive rounds on flat, cleared fields.

archers in other states pressed their game departments for a special season.

A new archery group—the National Field Archery Association—had been started and was rapidly gaining in membership. Organized in 1939, the association consisted of archers who were more hunting-oriented than were the members of the N.A.A. The latter represents target archers, who shoot formalized competitive rounds on flat, cleared areas.

While the early bowhunters were in most cases N.A.A. members, they felt that target archery, with its large bullseyes and repetitive shots, was not the best practice for using bows and arrows on game. With that in mind, they devised the sport of field archery, in which archers shoot from different distances at targets of varying sizes. Originally, field archers used heavier, hunting-weight bows. Their courses, rather than being laid out on a flat, grass-covered tract, were situated in a woodsy setting. In other words, field archery was designed to simulate hunting as far as possible.

The idea caught on in a big way. Soon there were field archery clubs in every state, each of them affiliated with the N.F.A.A. The clubs formed state associations, which worked with their local game authorities to liberalize the archery seasons. Wildlife managers welcomed the idea of bowhunting, because it did not greatly affect the game supply. At the same time, it brought in additional revenue from hunting licenses and offered safe recreation to thousands of people. Today, some states have deer seasons which last for three months or more.

Field archers shoot in a woodsy setting, in typical hunting terrain.

Many of Fred Bear's hunting feats were shown on TV.

The current rise in the popularity of archery owes a great deal to the fact that the sport of bowhunting has achieved legal sanction. In fact, the thousands of licensed bowhunters greatly outnumber the members of archery organizations. The former may not do as much shooting through the year as the club archers, but they nevertheless represent a strong force in the resurgence of interest in the bow and arrow.

Another element which contributed to the rise in archery activity was the use of new materials in the manufacture of archery tackle. Fiberglass, a new development, was found to be an excellent component in bow laminations. Tubular fiberglass arrows were another significant development, while aluminum tubing used in arrow shafts enabled archers to shatter old scoring records. Synthetic materials such as dacron were used to make bowstrings, and proved to be much more durable and efficient than linen strands. With the integration of these new products in the fabrication of bows and arrows during the post-World War II period, bowmen were able to shoot more accurately than ever before.

The popularity of modern bowhunting as a sport was also greatly influenced by Fred Bear, a manufacturer of archery gear. His successful hunts for North American big game were recorded in numerous magazine articles and books. Bear's adventures gained further prominence for bowhunting when his hunts were featured on television shows. He journeyed to all parts of the world that offered challenging game, including Africa and India, where he took an outstanding tiger with one arrow.

Although there had been several archery magazines with limited circulations, bowhunting for some time was not very well-known to the average sportsman. In 1959, *Outdoor Life,* a major fishing and hunting publication, established an archery department. The monthly articles, dealing with all phases of the sport, are read by millions and have been instrumental in luring countless sportsmen to archery. Each year, *Sports Afield,* another sportsman's monthly, devotes a major part of its July issue to archery. *Field and Stream,* the other important fishing and hunting magazine, covers bowhunting, too, with occasional articles on the sport.

In the beginning, field archers approached their sport in terms of heavy bows, while target archers, interested only in precision shooting over longer ranges, used lighter tackle. This led to a split in emphasis between the two branches of archery, occasionally marked by uncharitable feelings between the two groups. Also, by this time target archers had added sights to their bows. This enabled them to set new scoring records.

ARCHERS' DIFFERENCES

A conflict emerged when target archers invaded the field archery tournaments. Their bowsights and lighter-weight equipment gave them an advantage over the field archers, who rejected the targeteers' concept because it was not applicable to hunting practice. The prejudice was based on the fact that adjustable bowsights and comparatively lightweight gear were more suited to attaining high scores than in providing practice for hunting game.

It thus became necessary to set up a special category for "sight" shooters. They were referred to as free-stylers, as opposed to "instinctive" archers. But as the non-sight bowmen became more sophisticated in their aiming techniques, it was apparent that they did not shoot by instinct but were using artificial aiming methods. The differentiation is covered in detail in subsequent sections. (See Basic Archery Form—Aiming.)

Then, in the 1960's, a strange thing happened. Field archery, the sport which had originated as bowhunting practice, was now strictly a competitive game. It lost its emphasis as a training ground for bowhunting and became primarily a tournament activity, with the honors going to the top scorers. As a general rule the best field archers, having discovered that they could shoot higher scores with bows that had lighter draw-weights, reduced the weight of their equipment so that the original idea of field archery as a practice game for hunting archers became—to a large extent—a thing of the past.

Where the early field archers had to estimate the distance from the shooting position to the target, most clubs now announce the exact yardage of each shot. The first field archery courses had brushy terrain, often with tree limbs and trunks as potential obstacles in the shooting lanes. But when the majority of field archers expressed more interest in tournament competition than in simulated bowhunting situations, the trend was toward cleared shooting lanes. In some cases, there are field archery courses laid out in open fields. A number of field archers are interested only in the tournament aspect and do no hunting.

There next ensued an erosion of the resentment which field archers had felt toward target archers. Field shooters began to enter target tourneys, while some club programs became broader in scope and included both field and target archery facilities on their grounds.

INTERNATIONAL ARCHERY

On the international level, until the 1960's, the form of competition had been strictly target archery, a sport started in Britain. Every two years, in a different country each time, the best target shooters assemble for a world championship event, under the leadership of the Fédération Internationale de Tir à l'Arc (F.I.T.A.), which translates to the International Archery Federation. At the 1969 International, held at Valley Forge, Pennsylvania, field archery for the first time was included in the shooting schedule, although on an experimental basis.

This innovation was brought about because of the spread of field archery which, while it had originated in the U.S., was picked up by many European nations through the American Servicemen who took their archery gear with them on duty in Europe. As American field archery fans set up shooting courses in western Europe, local archers were introduced to the sport. Following European pressure on F.I.T.A. to include field in the '69 world championships, the N.A.A.—the U.S. affiliate of the international organization—devised its own set of rules for field archery competition. Though based mainly on the N.F.A.A. formula, the International Field Round uses the metric system in its shooting distances and target sizes. To a veteran archer, the irony of this development is that the N.A.A.—formerly a target archery body—now finds itself engaged in field archery.

Archery in the Olympics is under the aegis of F.I.T.A. and the N.A.A. Archers from the United States dominated the Games, both in 1972 and 1976, when the men's gold medalist was nineteen-year-old Darrell Pace, of Reading, Ohio. The women's gold medal winner in 1976 was Luann Ryon, of Parker, Arizona.

ARCHERY AND YOUTH

To the benefit of archery in general there's another spin-off from the inclusion of the sport in the Olympics. In the 1960's, the N.A.A. hierarchy realized that future U.S. participation in such competition would be enhanced by establishing a training program for young bowmen. Accordingly, the Junior Olympic Archery Development Program was started. Under the terms of the program, the N.A.A. cooperates with any community or civic group which will provide facilities for training young archers. The program has

Many service organizations sponsor young archers' programs.

interested scores of organizations in sponsoring youth groups in archery. It's not unusual now to see service organizations, such as Lions, Kiwanis, Rotary, American Legion posts and even the Salvation Army engaged in running archery programs for the young of their communities.

As a competitive sport for both men and women, archery is also gaining ground in interscholastic and intercollegiate circles. For several decades archery had been popular at some girls' colleges, mostly as a part of the physical education curriculum rather than as a competitive sport. The reasons for increasing attention to the bow and arrow sport on campus are very logical ones. The sport is not a particularly expensive one; it's safe; it requires skill, and it

Archery is becoming more popular as an intercollegiate sport for both sexes.

schools its practitioners in a form of athletics which can be pursued for most of their lives.

The annual intercollegiate archery tourney attracts more shooters each year. A few colleges offer archery scholarships, and there is a growing network of high school and college archery leagues.

Summer camps have for years included archery in their recreation programs. But all too often it has been relegated to some second-string camp staffer with little background in archery and no enthusiasm for instilling interest in it in the campers. At the opposite end of the spectrum is a specialized archery camp, devoted exclusively to the bow and arrow. Formerly Teela-Wooket Archery Camp, in Vermont, it is now The World Archery Center, located in Pennsylvania. In addition to giving interested archers a solid training in the use of the bow, the unique camp has a tough course which certifies its graduates as competent archery instructors in schools, colleges and other camps.

The bow and arrow for years have been prominent in the Boy Scout program. Archery is a feature at most Scouting summer camps and is a sought-after merit badge. Experienced bowmen volunteer their services as merit badge counselors, supervising the boys in shooting and also in making certain parts of their equipment.

ARCHERY IN THE MILITARY AND IN INDUSTRY

There are signs that the military has not completely rejected the bow as an effective instrument of warfare. Although not a weapon that will decimate an enemy unit, the bow has the advantage of silence and for that reason lends itself ideally to guerilla warfare. It was used in a limited way by British Commandos in World War II. Some units of our Special Forces have had training in the use of archery tackle.

A Special Forces trooper with takedown bow and arrows.

Bows and arrows have even been used profitably by industry. Telephone line crews, faced with the problem of getting their wires across deep gorges, have used archery equipment to propel smaller lines across the chasm. These, in turn, were attached to heavier lines and so on, until the men were able to position their cables.

With the growth of industrial recreation programs for employees, archery facilities are not unusual on company grounds. Some firms sponsor teams in league competition, while others enjoy publicity by holding archery tournaments with fat purses for the winners. There have been several cases where firms have subsidized some of the travel expenses of their employees—those who were such outstanding archers that they had won places on the U.S. team in international competition.

But the success of archery in years to come does not depend chiefly on industry and the military. As long as archery enjoys a following among American youth, it is bound to retain—indeed, to increase—its popularity. This, coupled with continued interest in bowhunting and international archery competition, should guarantee a bright future for the sport.

ARCHERY AS THERAPY

Many persons find archery an extremely engrossing activity. For this reason, some psychiatrists and psychologists have found it to be an ideal form of therapy for certain of their patients.

Using one's own muscles to propel an arrow from a bow intrigues many people. To do it well requires a great amount of concentration. This demand for concentration is a factor in freeing the mind of other troubles.

By the same token, archery has been a boon to some paraplegics and others confined to wheelchairs. Shooting a bow not only gives

There are special tournaments for wheelchair archers, who shoot indoors as well as outdoors.

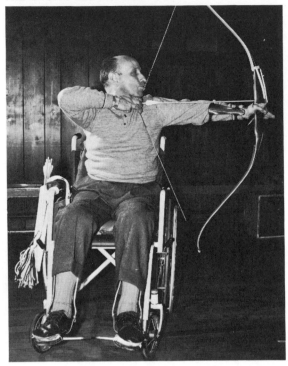

Vernon Kinsey, archer and for many years the owner of Kinsey's Archery Shop, Mount Joy, Pennsylvania. His firm supplies not only arrows, but also a variety of other quality items to archers.

them an opportunity to participate in an athletic activity, but it also provides an opportunity for them to exercise and to use effectively those muscles which they can control, thus building up their self-confidence. An attendant advantage is the fact that it can be enjoyed both inside and in the outdoors.

Commercial Indoor Archery Lanes

THOUSANDS OF DOLLARS have been lost in ill-advised commercial ventures into operating expensive indoor shooting lanes for archers. Also, for the right people who are in the right places, thousands of dollars have been made in the same type business. This branch of archery—still fairly new—has settled down into a

Thousands of dollars have been lost on ill-advised ventures in commercial archery lanes. This is one of many indoor ranges which existed only briefly.

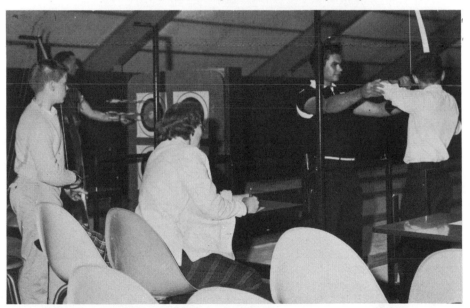

To be successful, a commercial indoor range must be in an area where there is a great deal of interest in archery. It must also have one or more qualified archery instructors.

Automated indoor lanes feature targets that return to the shooting line at the touch of a button.

pattern. The only situation where a commercial indoor archery setup is practical is in a part of the country where archery enthusiasm is high. A few sections in the East are in this category. Michigan and California are other places where commercial archery lanes have been successful.

Logically, the commercial indoor range must be accompanied by a pro shop, manned by knowledgeable archers with a solid line of merchandise to sell. There must also be at least one qualified archery coach, who can assist new archers in buying their tackle and then teach them how to use it properly. The proprietor of the establishment must have a following and the respect of local archers, and he must be a good promoter and businessman.

The most successful indoor archery lanes feature automated targets which return to the shooting line at the touch of a button, whereupon the archers count their scores, pull their arrows and press the button, returning the target to its original position.

The best indoor operations also offer a good stock of equipment, both for sale and rent, and have staffs of instructors capable of giving lessons in proper shooting technique. A big source of income to the indoor archery establishment are shooting leagues, which operate on the same basis as bowling leagues. In fact, the concept of indoor archery lanes is similar to that of bowling lanes, there being, in some cases, archery activities carried on in bowling alleys.

The average charge for an hour of shooting on an automated indoor archery range is about $2. In the case of a beginner, that charge includes basic instruction and the use of archery equipment. When the novice learns the ropes, he can buy a bow and a set of arrows from the range's pro shop.

The Archery Lane Owners' Association is concerned with the business of operating indoor archery lanes. It also oversees the U.S. Archery Congress, which administers archery leagues and the awarding of patches, ribbons and trophies. The address of both organizations is: 1500 N. Chatsworth, St. Paul, Minnesota 55117.

Part II

Archery Equipment

Modern Bows

AS EVERYONE KNOWS, the Wrights' first aircraft bears little resemblance to today's jet planes. There is just as much difference, both in appearance and efficiency, between the weapons of the 12th Century English archers and the bows used now. Indeed, as pointed out at the outset, modern bows are closer in design to eastern Mediterranean equipment than to the English bows, although in other respects our archery culture owes much to the old English bowman. Curiously enough, some of the bows used by American Indians as well as some of the old Turkish bows, are closer to modern construction and designs than to the English bow.

An archer in the army of Henry V had a bow that was in most cases taller than he was. From tip to tip, when unstrung, it roughly described a straight line and was made of wood which was almost round in cross-section. It was called a "longbow," to distinguish it from a crossbow. The latter weapon is mounted on a two-handed frame similar to a gunstock, on which the bowstring is released mechanically instead of manually.

CROSSBOW

The crossbow, somewhat resembling a firearm with a horizontal crosspiece near its forward end, has had a long and interesting history, going back to the Middle Ages. The legendary William Tell, in shooting the apple from his son's head, was supposed to have used a crossbow, which was also known as an arbalest.

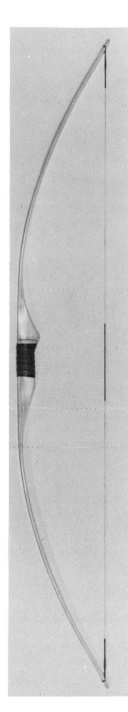

Modern crossbowmen are enthusiastic, but few in number.

A straight bow similar to the type used by the historic English longbowmen.

There are less than a thousand crossbowmen in this country now, most of them enthusiastic and serious in their dedication to the weapon. A few firms produce crossbows but many tournament crossbowmen prefer to make their own—partly because of the challenge, partly because of the sense of accomplishment, and also to satisfy their personal requirements in the weapon's design.

Hunting with the crossbow is not widely popular. Arkansas and Kentucky are among the few states which permit hunting with the weapon. In general, this is not because of any feeling against crossbows by wildlife managers, but more due to a lack of widespread crossbow hunter interest. In at least one state, one which has a law prohibiting hunting with crossbows, the director of the game and fish department once stated that he has no objection to it and that he would consider granting a season were he requested to do so by a substantial number of crossbowmen.

There are a number of speculative reasons why the crossbow, compared to the longbow, has so few followers. It's possible that there's a prejudice which goes back hundreds of years. Perhaps it's because in warfare the crossbow could not match the longbow either in range or rapid fire. It could also be because the crossbow was frowned upon by some key figures in history. The weapon, for example, was once considered so devastating that a 12th Century Pope banned its use under threat of excommunication. Also, some historians maintain that the crossbow was not considered a "sporting" weapon in warfare, due to the havoc it was capable of creating at fairly short ranges.

Like other modern archery bows, the crossbow has been improved by newer materials and advanced design. The bow portion on most tournament crossbows is fiberglass, either solid or laminated, and has recurved tips. The short missiles, called "bolts" or "quarrels," are usually aluminum or fiberglass. The shooters use adjustable sights and built-up cheekpieces on the stocks of their weapons.

Cocking the crossbow has always been something of a problem. After a longbowman takes a shot, he merely reaches into his quiver for another arrow, puts it in position, and draws. The crossbowman must go through a more complicated procedure. At one time, a variety of devices were used, ranging from a stirrup to hold the front end to a ratchet-type crank, or handles which were turned in order to draw back the bowstring. Now, crossbowmen cock their weapons by hand, some of them hooking the front end to a stake in the ground. While using both hands, they haul back on the string far enough to position it. The string is drawn back and secured in a catch on the stock. When the trigger is pulled, the catch releases the bowstring and the bolt is discharged.

Crossbowmen are accepted by the National Archery Association, which puts them in a special division in its annual tournament. Crossbow competitive rounds are explained in para. 13.1-14.0, the NAA *Archer's Handbook* (see references, Part X). While there are at present two national crossbow organizations, the best source of crossbow information is the National Archery Association headquarters, 1951 Geraldson Drive, Lancaster, Pennsylvania 17601.

In 1970, one of the established archery manufacturers introduced a new crossbow. It has the foot stirrup up front for cocking, and it's powered with a metal bow section. Three different types of bolts are available with field points, fish points and broadheads.

 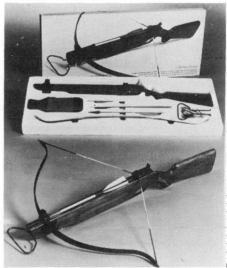

A new crossbow model was introduced in 1970.

LONGBOW

A longbow is not necessarily a bow of exceptional length. Any bow, regardless of its length, can correctly be termed a longbow, providing it's not a crossbow. Some bows favored by hunters are only four feet in length, yet they are classified as longbows.

TODAY'S BOWS

Modern bows and arrows literally are capable of greater accuracy than that of the people who shoot them. Not only is our archery tackle of excellent quality and durability, but the present-day bowman has a wide variety of designs and prices from which to choose.

All bows used by experienced archers today are combinations of fiberglass and wood—two layers of glass on the outside, with a thin core of wood in the middle. Originally, of course, bows were made of wood, in some cases with other reinforcing materials such as the layers of horn and sinew referred to in the beginning section on The History of Archery. Howard Hill's favorite type bow, a few of which are still being used, was made of bamboo, with layers of fiberglass on the face (the surface facing the shooter) and the back. At various times bows have been made of metal, both aluminum and tubular steel, but they did not measure up to the shooting qualities of the laminated fiberglass-wood-fiberglass bows which are so popular today. The most inexpensive modern bows, incidentally, are made of solid fiberglass. Though rugged and practically unbreakable, they are not as smooth-drawing nor as efficient as the glass-wood combination.

Modern, man-made materials constitute a big step forward in bows. No longer are bowmen concerned with the problems which plagued the archers of yesteryear, whose wood bows—usually yew, lemonwood, osage-orange or hickory—had to be treated with tender loving care. Wood bows were subject to breakage at almost any time. Usually, they took a set after repeated use and would react to atmospheric changes.

Newcomers to the sport are often confused by the many types of bows offered for sale. To a large extent this confusion can be traced to the large number of manufacturers and to the specialization within archery. Target archers, whose specialty is precision shooting with arrow after arrow from the same distance, use bows that are different from the weapons preferred by bowhunters. Then there are the field archers, shooting from a variety of distances. Although their sport, originated as practice for hunting, the typical field archer does a lot of shooting in competitive tournaments and thus wants a weapon that is more like that of the target archer than the hunting archer's weapon. Flight shooting—where distance is important and accuracy is unimportant—calls for a different bow design. Still another is the crossbow.

Broadly speaking, there are three types of longbows—straight-

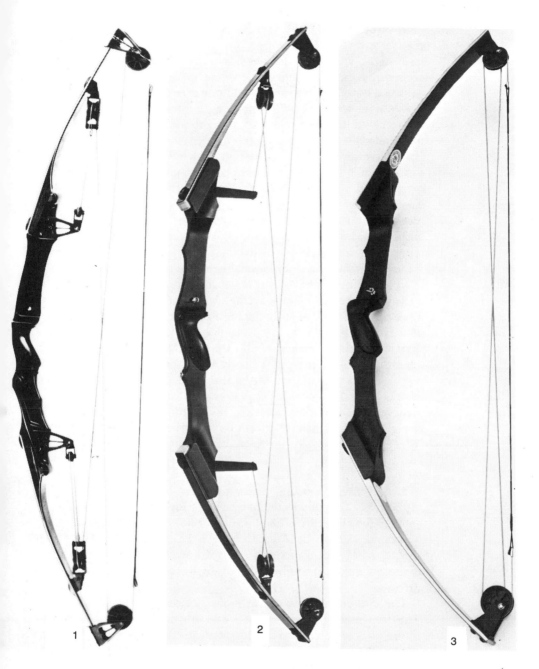

1. A six-wheel compound bow.   2. A four-wheel compound bow.
3. A two-wheel compound bow.

limb bows (also called straight bows), recurve bows and compound bows. A recurve bow is bent away from the shooter at both ends, while the straight bow is not curved at its tips. The compound bow, a fairly new archery development, seems destined to replace the recurve among many experienced archers.

Recurve bows are still being made and are favored by many archers, but just about the only straight bows in use nowadays are patterned after the straight-limb models used by the late Howard Hill. This minority (a few hundred bowhunters against hundreds of thousands of archers) prefers the straight-limb design because of personal aesthetics and a conviction that the straight bow is less sensitive to the archer's shooting errors. The fact is that those who are successful in hunting with straight bows are good archers and skilled hunters, and could do just as well with a recurve or a compound. However, they are individualists who pride themselves on maintaining the straight-bow tradition.

In a given weight, or draw weight (the number of pounds of energy required to pull an average length arrow), a straight bow is more difficult to draw fully than is a recurve. Because of the design of a typical straight bow it is said to be "stacked," which means that the last few inches of the draw require a disproportionate amount of muscle energy. When an archer pulls back a recurve, the required energy is more uniform throughout the draw and thus the bow is smoother to pull. This is mainly due to the fact that the recurved tips act something like two miniature bows, with added energy stored in them. Not only is a recurved bow easier to draw than a straight bow of the same draw weight, it also has a better cast (the capacity to propel an arrow in a comparatively flat trajectory).

The average 45-pound modern recurve has a cast equal to that of the 60 to 65-pound bow of a few decades ago. This is a big advantage for all archers. The bowhunter now does not need to pull a 65-pound weapon in order to have lethal equipment. The target shooter can shoot a moderate-weight bow and doesn't need to elevate so much in aiming, thanks to the flatter trajectory of his arrows.

The compound bow consists of a series of pulleys and cables. The two pulleys on the bow's tips are mounted off-center. Although it's a weird-looking contraption, the compound has a big advantage. Thanks to the mechanical principle of the pulley, the compound is easier to hold at full draw than is a recurve bow of the same draw weight. When the archer pulls the bowstring back

Howard Hill astonished audiences with his spectacular exhibition shooting.

about halfway, the eccentrically mounted upper and lower pulleys turn over. The result is that the second half of the drawing effort is easier to execute. This means that the archer, while aiming, is under no strain to hold steady at full draw, and therefore can aim more carefully.

In some compound-bow models, the weight reduction is as much as 50 per cent. Other compounds have a draw-weight reduction of 30 to 40 per cent. The archer shooting a 60-pound compound must use 60 pounds of energy for the first part of his draw. But at full draw, he's holding the equivalent of only 30 or 40 pounds, depending on the model of his compound bow. Some manufacturers make compound bows that are adjustable; that is, within certain limits, the peak draw weight of the bow can be increased or reduced.

At the same time, the compound produces faster arrow flight, which in turn means flatter trajectory. With a recurve, when the arrow is released, it immediately begins to lose speed as it passes across the bow. An arrow shot from a compound, on the other hand, picks up speed with the second half of the bowstring's forward thrust. Another factor which adds to the arrow's velocity is that somewhat lighter arrows can be shot from a compound bow.

When they first appeared on the archery scene, compound bows were much more expensive than recurve bows. Thanks to research and development, however, compounds now cost about the same as recurves, and the average archer can afford one.

Two types of compound bows are known as four-wheelers and six-wheelers, because they have four pulleys or six pulleys, respectively. Another type of compound has only two pulleys and looks more like a conventional bow.

Compound bows have some disadvantages. The selection of the arrow, including the fletching and the arrow material, is critical. Unless the archer finds the right arrow combination for his compound bow, he may get erratic arrow flight. Some hunting points, because of their shape, are more likely to windplane in flight than with a conventional bow. The compound is widely used by bowhunters and is accepted in field archery tournaments. It is not acceptable in target archery, including international competition.

Compound bows are permanently braced. That's a plus, because the archer need not string his bow before shooting it and unstring it before putting it away. However, if a bowstring breaks, it is not as easy to replace as with a conventional bow.

THE IDEAL BOW

The technical part of archery is surprisingly complex, and even experts admit they're mystified by some aspects of it at times. Understanding the subject fully requires a knowledge of physics, mechanics, aerodynamics and scientific theory, to say nothing of a smattering of history and archaeology. It is not necessary for the ordinary bowman to go too deeply into technical archery and bow design, but he should know something about basic bow shapes and why they are used.

An archer exerts a force of so many pounds while drawing a bow. When the string is released, a certain amount of that force is transferred to the arrow in terms of velocity and momentum. If the bow is a good one, a maximum amount of force will be transferred. An inefficient bow fails to pass on as much force, and the arrow travels slower. So, theoretically, to construct an efficient bow the bowyer (bow manufacturer) must make one that will impart a maximum amount of force to the arrow.

In addition to good cast, the ideal bow must have other qualities. It must be durable so it won't lose its power after repeated use. It must be dependable and effective under a variety of conditions, and it should be fairly attractive in appearance. Another essential feature in bows is somewhat vaguely referred to as the quality of smooth shooting. A bow is not considered to be smooth if it is difficult to draw or if it stacks. Moreover, a smooth-shooting bow will not produce a shocking effect, or kick, on the shooter's bow arm when it is released.

All of these desirable features are related directly to the bow's design and the materials in it. The idea of different layers of materials is not a new one. As previously pointed out, the Turks, Persians and some American Indians employed the composite principle in their bows. While present-day bowyers have borrowed the general idea from archers of the past, there's a different reason for the layers of materials used today. Formerly, the backing of sinew, horn or rawhide was added to prevent the bow from breaking; now, the glass is used to provide greater cast, and the chief function of the wood core is to separate the layers of glass.

Obviously, the glue used to bond a bow's laminations must not only hold the layers together, it must also have great elasticity. The glue used by today's manufacturers is the result of many years of research and experimentation.

The material in a bow must have elasticity; that is, when bent and then released, it must have the property of rapidly assuming its original position and shape. The material must also be capable of repeatedly withstanding great stresses in tension and compression without breaking down. As the bow is flexed, the fibers in the back of the bow are being placed under tension, or stretched. The fibers in the face, or concave surface of the bow, are being squeezed, or compressed. Upon release, these stresses are unleashed with a certain force that's determined by the bow's draw weight, design, and properties of its materials. The material in the bow limbs must be rugged enough to take the strain and stress but must also be light enough to conform to one of the fundamental laws of physics: the lighter an object, the easier it is to move with maximum speed.

It is in this respect that the development of fiberglass has resulted in improved archery weapons. When properly constructed, the fiberglass lamination meets all of the above requirements. In addition, the flat cross-section of contemporary bows, as opposed to the nearly round shape of the old English longbow, is much more efficient in withstanding the stresses of tension and compression.

A reflex bow is one having its limbs bent away from the string when it's unbraced. The theory is that the limbs, when drawn, will have added internal stresses, and, when released, will whip back

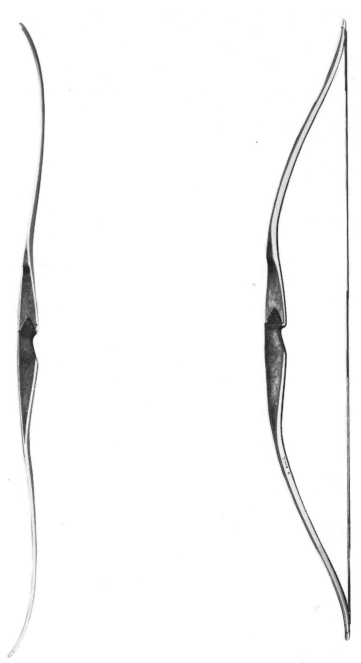

Limbs in a reflex bow are bent away from the string.

toward their original position with greater force and through a greater distance. While this theory works out in practice, it's at the expense of a great amount of kick, or recoil, in the bow-arm.

A deflex bow is slightly bent toward the string when unbraced. Many of our best bows are both reflexed and deflexed, a combination of designs known as duo-flex. The central part of the bow, around the handle riser, has the deflex; beyond the handle riser the limbs are reflexed, and they end with the recurved tips. The effect of this design, theoretically, is to give greater power to the limbs and more stability, or steadiness, to the handle section with a minimum of bow-hand recoil.

As a general rule, target bows have longer, heavier handles than those on the bows made for hunting. Also, the overall length of target bows is longer, some measuring more than 70 inches. Hunting bows, however, are as short as four feet or even less.

NEW ARCHERY CONCEPTS

Most modern bow designers, in their target models, use much longer handle sections than in the past. The rationale for this is based on a number of factors. If the handle portion is longer and does not bend, the limbs are shorter and lighter, and the archer is pulling less mass, theoretically resulting in increased arrow velocity. In the best bows of some manufacturers the handle section varies in size from model to model, while the length of the limbs is almost always the same. Thus, a short bow of about 50 inches may have limbs that are about the same length as a much longer model.

Tournament archers, striving for pin-point accuracy, are concerned with torque, which is the twisting motion which takes place in a bow when it is discharged. This torque is caused by the angular contact of the archer's hand on the bow's grip. Some archers use wrist slings or straps, to counteract bow-hand torque. The bow is gripped very lightly in the fingers. After release the bow is allowed to fall free but is kept from dropping by the leather strap around the bowman's wrist and which is connected to the bow.

Many tournament archers use a straight-wrist grip to offset the effect of bow-hand torque. Instead of the palm of the hand being in contact with the bow's handle, the archer cocks his wrist downward holding the bow in such a way that the only contact is in the web of skin between the thumb and the hand. Although the straight-wrist grip looks awkward and is difficult for some people, it is used by many top tournament archers. Because of the success of this style of grip, bowyers have developed pistol-grip handles which tend to force the hand into the straight-wrist position. Another design feature which tends to offset the effect of bow-hand torque is to build up the grip section of the handle so that it's form-fitting to the archer's hand.

Tournament shooters are also troubled by another problem, which is also a form of torque. This is the movement of the bow caused by vibration. Upon release of the bowstring, the limbs surge forward and—before coming to rest—engage in a series of vibrations so rapid that they're invisible to the naked eye. In a high-speed bow, these vibrations are of such a violent nature that they may affect the direction of the arrow. Bow designers use bulky, heavy handle risers to counteract the effect of the vibrations on the shooter's bow-arm. These large, heavier handle risers are found on most recurve tournament bows.

Another method of cutting down on the effect of the vibrations is the use of weighted stabilizer rods. These are metal rods projecting forward from the bow's handle riser which come in a variety of lengths and weights. Some tournament shooters use only one stabilizer, screwed into a special socket below the grip; others prefer a pair of stabilizers, one below the grip and one above. The majority of top-echelon target archers use stabilizers.

All well-designed bows are made with a center-shot handle. (Also referred to as the sight window.) This is a cutout portion in the handle which gives the archer a clear picture of his target. Some Indian bows had this feature, though it wasn't perfected. An arrow shot from a simple bow points to the left and seemingly must go around the bow to strike the target. This is known as "archer's paradox."

With a true center-shot bow, the arrow points directly at the target. This means that the shaft travels in more of a straight line and loses a minimum of velocity due to initial oscillation. Other advantages of the center-shot feature are that the archer's view of his target is not obscured by a portion of the bow. Also, if he's using a bowsight, the sight will be in direct line with the target.

With the acceptance of the compound bow by most experienced field archers and bowhunters, the matter of bow length is not as important as formerly. In the pre-compound era, longer bows were known to be more stable than short bows, although a number of bow-hunters liked short recurves because of their convenience in brushy terrain and tree stands.

Target archers, since they are not permitted to use compounds

Metal stabilizer rods reduce vibrations of the bow's limbs.

in competition, continue to use bows as long as 72 inches. Bowhunters and field archers are satisfied with the shorter overall length of the various compound models, which range from about 52 inches to 48 inches, although one compound is only 3 feet long.

The standard on which draw weights is based is 28 inches, the length of the arrow of the average adult male archer. When a bow is said to be 40 pounds, and so labelled by the manufacturer, it requires that much energy to draw a 28-inch arrow in that particular bow. In the case of a shorter or longer arrow, the effective variation in bow weight is about two pounds per inch. In other words, if a bow is a 40-pounder and the shooter uses a 26-inch arrow, he draws approximately 36 pounds. At the other extreme, a tall archer who requires a 31-inch arrow will have the equivalent of about a 46-pound bow.

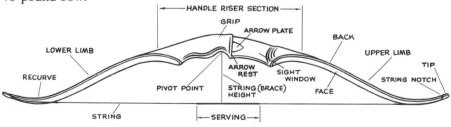

A modern bow and its parts.

Another important specification of bow manufacturers is the string height, or brace height. Sometimes referred to as the fist-mele, from the old English term, this is the space between the bowstring and the point of contact of the bow-hand and the bow's grip. For optimum bow performance in most situations the smart archer follows the bowyer's suggestion on string height. Some archers, because of their particular shooting styles, get improved performance by deviating from the manufacturer's recommendations. They either use a longer or a shorter bowstring, or shorten the string somewhat by twisting it. This, however, is a prerogative that is part of experience; the non-expert should follow the advice of the bowyer.

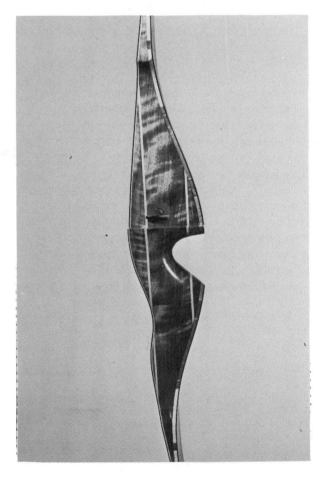

With a modern bow the arrow is drawn across the arrow shelf or the arrow rest. Note pistol-grip handle.

Archers who shoot compound bows need not be concerned about the string height. When they come from the factory, compounds are permanently strung, at the brace height deemed best by the manufacturer.

Not too many years ago, when bows were almost primitive by modern standards, the arrow rested on and was drawn across the upper part of the archer's bow-hand. In a few cases, a small arrow-rest was installed, to support the shaft during the draw and the shooting process. With the introduction of the sight-window, or center-shot feature, the arrow at first was rested on the horizontal surface called the arrow-shelf. In their continuing quest for improvement archers experimented with different types of arrow-rests, in order to give the shaft a smooth take-off as it left the bow.

As a consequence, archers must now decide from a vast selection which type of arrow-rest to use. Some, mostly hunting arrow-rests, are fairly simple. These are intended to lessen the friction and sound when the arrow is drawn and released. Some are merely furry cushions for the shaft, some are adjustable and are made of nylon bristles and some arrow-rests are made from portions of stiff feathers. Arrow-rests for tournament archers are somewhat more

Upper and lower wheels on a compound bow are mounted off-center. When the bow is drawn about halfway, the eccentric wheels turn over and the draw weight is reduced.

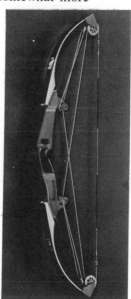

A four-wheel compound bow which can be adjusted for different draw weights.

refined—adjustable and offering less contact surface to the arrow shaft. Most arrow-rests are supplied with adhesive backing for easy installation.

THE LATEST BOWS

Several bow manufacturers produce take-down models, which come in different forms. One type comes apart at the mid-section. In another version the take-down bow is made in three sections—the handle riser and the two limbs. One bowyer who makes this type advertises the interchangeability of his take-down bow. Starting with the basic handle section, available in three different lengths, an archer can equip himself with a variety of bows by buying separate pairs of limbs in different weights and lengths. Many successful target-archery champions, including the 1976 Olympic men's gold medalist, use three-piece takedown bows.

BOWSTRINGS

The bowstring is another part of the bow. Like the bow itself, the string has been improved by modern, man-made materials. Where once bowmen used strings made of linen, the bowstring of the modern archer is made of dacron. It's stronger, longer-lasting, doesn't react to dampness, and requires less strands for a given bow-weight. Bowstrings are made in various lengths, to correspond with the different bow sizes. The number of strands in the string varies according to the bow's weight. With a 25 to 30-pound bow, for example, the string should have 10 strands; a 35 to 45-pound bow requires 12 strands, and so on.

The bowstring has two end loops, both of which are "served," or wrapped with nylon thread to protect them from wear. A section in the center of the bowstring also has the protective serving, since that's where the arrow comes into contact with the string and causes some wear.

Today's Arrows

WHEN A NON-ARCHER or an inexperienced bowman considers archery equipment, his first thought is the bow; the arrows seem to be of secondary importance. The wise archer, however, knows full well that if he had to choose between having a first-class bow and

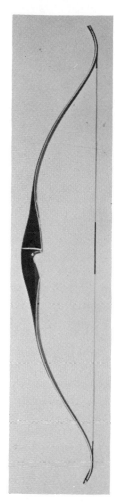

Bowstring has wrapping of thread (serving) at points of wear—both ends and in center.

third-rate arrows or vice versa, he would opt for the very best arrows and the third-rate bow. A good bowman can shoot reasonably well with an inferior bow—as long as he uses top-quality arrows that are matched to the bow. On the other hand, the very best bow will not perform properly, regardless of how expert the shooter, if the arrows are not carefully selected.

The four vital criteria of arrows are length, straightness, weight, and spine (the relative stiffness of an arrow).

If all the arrows in an archer's quiver are not close to the same weight (measured in grains) he cannot expect accuracy. His first shot may be a bit high. On his next shot he'll hold slightly lower, in order to allow for the error on his first attempt. If his second arrow weighs less than the first, it too will strike the target above

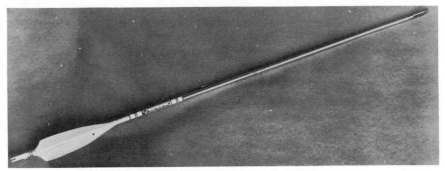

Arrows must be straight and matched in weight.

the bullseye. The shooter, not aware that the cause of his second miss was the variation in arrow-weight, holds lower for his third try. This arrow, somewhat heavier than the first two, hits quite low on the target. With such mismatched arrows, the poor bowman will never reach the point of proficiency that he would have attained with the right equipment. When he knows his arrows are weight-matched, he can make aiming corrections which, all other things being equal, will result in good marksmanship.

Similarly, an archer can't expect uniform accuracy in his shooting if his arrows are not straight. His shot may be executed perfectly but if that particular arrow has a slight bend in it, it will go astray. The frustrated archer, knowing that he was holding right on target, is at a loss to figure out why he missed.

To check an arrow for straightness, make a V with the fingers of the left hand by putting the tips of the thumb and second finger together and bending them in toward the palm of the hand. Rest the front part of the shaft in the fingernail groove. Then, holding the arrow nock in the right hand, give the nock a quick spin with the right hand, while pushing the shaft. If the arrow shaft is not true, it will bounce as it spins and moves across the fingernail groove.

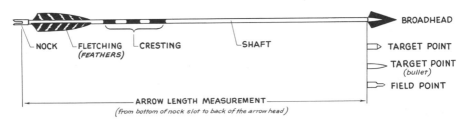

Spine affects the arrow's performance in a different way. When an arrow is released from a bow, the sudden, powerful thrust of the bowstring exerts a tremendous force against the arrow's tail end. This power is applied so quickly that before the arrow's forward end can react by leaping ahead, the shaft buckles in its center. The arrow's first bend, on the horizontal plane, is outward from the bow. In less than the flicker of an eyelash, there's an opposite reaction and the shaft bends to the right, followed immediately by a bend to the left.

The shaft, now beginning its flight, engages in a series of diminishing bends which occur as the shaft attempts to straighten out. These movements are invisible to the naked eye, but are known to exist as a result of high-speed photography.

If an arrow shaft is not stiff enough for a certain bow weight, it will bend too much when shot—so much so, that it can't straighten out completely and will fly erratically. Likewise, the same shaft will not have good flight characteristics when shot from a bow that is too light in draw weight for the stiffness of that individual arrow.

ARROW SPINE

Arrows that are too stiff for the bow will fly to the left; those that are too limber in spine go to the right. This applies to right-hand archers. The deflection is just the opposite for left-handed shooters. (In all further references to right and left-handed archers the explanation is based on a right-handed archer.)

It's obvious then that for optimum accuracy the spine of an arrow must match the weight of the bow. It should be noted that in modern bow designs, thanks to the center-shot feature, the spine factor is not as critical as with earlier bows in which the drawn arrow pointed to the left. Nevertheless, spine is still an important factor in arrows.

An arrow's spine is checked by means of a spine tester, a device with a weight which is applied to the shaft's center. As the arrow bends with the weight, a scale shows the amount of deflection, and the operator can determine which bow-weight is suitable for the shaft being tested.

Owing to the problem of spine, one can't effectively use the same set of arrows in, for example, a 30-pound bow and a 50-pound bow. At the same time, for efficient shooting, the same bow and the same arrows can't be used by a tall, long-armed archer and also by one of short stature. This is due to the arrow-length factor, another important consideration in the archer's equipment.

ARROW WEIGHT AND LENGTH

It was pointed out earlier that bows are rated as to weight by the number of pounds of energy required to fully draw a 28-inch arrow—the length which is suitable for the average adult male archer. If a smaller person shoots the same arrow used by an average archer, a surplus length of the shaft will protrude from the front of the bow.

This is a disadvantage for two reasons. First, the arrow is heavier than it need be for the archer's draw length. This means that in aiming the archer must elevate the bow higher than if he were using arrows of his correct size. Consequently he loses both velocity and the flatness of his arrow's trajectory. Second, there's the matter of spine again. Since the arrows were spined for the archer shooting 28-inch arrows, they will not be correct for the smaller shooter because he is getting less weight (about two pounds per inch) from his draw.

It's also a disadvantage for a long-armed archer to shoot arrows

If arrows fit properly, they do not extend beyond bow.

that are too short for his draw. To begin with, he's not getting the maximum efficiency from his bow, because he is not extending it to the draw length of which he is capable. If he persists in shooting arrows that are too short for his arm, he'll undoubtedly develop bad shooting form.

Finally—but not the least important—the archer with too-short arrows runs the risk of violating one of the archery-safety rules. While he's drawing, with his eyes concentrating on the target, he is not aware of the position of his arrow point. If he should pull the short arrow back to his proper draw length, it would probably drop off of the rear of the arrow-rest. Then, when he releases, the result is trouble. It may be a broken arrow or a broken bowstring. In any case, it's unsafe, it's a traumatic experience for the archer and it can be avoided. An archer's ideal arrow-length depends on his particular shooting style. Some bowmen develop into accomplished archers and continue to shoot arrows of the same length as those with which they began. Other archers experiment with different shooting techniques and change their shooting style, necessitating longer or shorter arrows.

The best way for an archery beginner to determine his correct

For correct arrow length, measure armspread and use chart given in text.

arrow-length is by drawing a special bow and arrow. The bow is very light in weight and the arrow is quite long, with marks on the shaft between 24 and 34 inches. While an experienced bowman is guiding him, the novice draws the arrow back to the desired point. The expert notes the corresponding mark on the shaft and declares that length for the prospective shooter's arrows.

Not all archery tackle shops are equipped with these test bows. So the average archery enthusiast, when he starts in the sport, depends upon another system that works out quite well in the majority of cases. It's based on the archer's armspread. A measurement is taken when the archer extends his arms horizontally. If his armspread from fingertip to fingertip measures about 74 inches, the chances are that he requires about a 28-inch arrow. The chart, approved by most archery manufacturers as a general guide, is as follows:

Armspread	Arrow Length
57 - 59 inches	22 - 23 inches
60 - 62 inches	23 - 24 inches
63 - 65 inches	24 - 25 inches
66 - 68 inches	25 - 26 inches
69 - 71 inches	26 - 27 inches
72 - 74 inches	27 - 28 inches
75 - 77 inches	28 - 29 inches
over 77 inches	30 - 32 inches

ARROW MATERIALS

As in bow manufacturing, modern materials are responsible for major advances in arrows. Originally, arrows were made of natural materials, either reeds or wood. Wood arrow shafts are still used by plenty of contemporary archers, although the trend is away from them. All target archers shoot aluminum arrows, while most field archers use aluminum or fiberglass and hunting archers shoot all three types.

There are several disadvantages with wood arrows, which are made of cedar—usually called Port Orford cedar—from the forests of the Northwest. Wood arrows, by their very nature, react to changes in the moisture content of the air. If not stored properly, they may warp. They're much more subject to breakage than are glass or aluminum shafts. As for spine and weight, man-made materials are more reliable because they are the result of production techniques which closely control their weight and stiffness.

In the days when cedar arrows were used by all good archers, the shafts came in four forms—footed, tapered, barreled and parallel.

Footed arrows are fitted with a section of hardwood on the front end, its purpose being chiefly to strengthen the shaft. Tapered arrows are slightly smaller in diameter at the rear end, while barreled arrows have a wider diameter in the middle than at the two extremities. Parallel arrows are just what the name implies and are the least expensive. The diameter of cedar arrows depends on the weight of the bow. The most commonly used sizes are 5/16-inch and 11/32-inch.

Despite their disadvantages in durability and in weight and spine control, wood arrows are generally recommended for beginners. The reason for this is the lower cost of the wood arrows, combined with the fact that novices inevitably break some arrows and lose a few in grass and brush. After the beginner has mastered the fundamentals of the sport and decides that he wants to delve into it deeper, he usually buys better arrows.

For a somewhat higher price, the archer can get compressed cedar arrows. In these, due to a special process, the fibers of the wood are compressed to a smaller diameter with a greater density. The compressed shafts retain their straightness much better than do ordinary cedar shafts, and they are not as easily broken.

Good cedar arrows cost about $15 per dozen, although unmatched, second-rate ones can be bought for much less. Compressed cedar arrows range from $15 to $25, while fiberglass shafts are in the $20-$30 category. Aluminum arrows cost from $30 to $40 per dozen.

Both fiberglass and aluminum arrows are made of hollow tubing. Weight and spine are controlled by regulating the outside diameter and the thickness of the walls. The manufacturers of glass and aluminum arrows have devised a system of charts to enable an archer to determine the correct diameter of the shafts he should use. To make a selection the bowman must first know his bow weight and his arrow length. He must also consider whether he wants target arrows or hunting arrows, since the two types of arrows have separate charts. With this information he can consult the appropriate chart and arrive at the shaft recommended by the particular manufacturer.

In the case of aluminum arrows, the selection of the proper shaft is somewhat more complex, since the factory turns out several different types of aluminum alloys, each with its own chart. The code numbers applying to aluminum shafting have no relation to those numbers used by manufacturers of fiberglass shafts.

As for making a choice between the two arrow materials, the consensus among experienced archers is that both have their own virtues. Aluminum shafts are comparatively lighter in weight than any other material. The substance is so strong that, although light, it can be used in smaller diameters than glass or wood, even with medium to heavy bows. This, of course, results in flatter trajectory, making them desirable for target shooters, who operate at the longer distances. Aluminum arrows will last indefinitely when shot into nothing but straw targets. When one misses the target and strikes trees, rocks, or even hard ground, there's a chance that the arrow will become bent. The resultant bends, or kinks, are difficult to straighten completely.

Good fiberglass arrows retain their straightness for life. Even when bent to just below the breaking point, a glass shaft will assume its original trueness. They can be broken, but only under conditions of extreme stress. Thus, the bowhunter, who should practice his shooting in rough terrain and who can expect to hit trees and rocks occasionally, likes an arrow that will remain straight.

The latest innovation in arrows is the introduction of graphite and tubular steel as shaft materials. At first, the price of the new arrowshafts was extremely high and the quality was not uniform. But after several top-flight manufacturers became interested in shafts made of graphite or steel tubing, both the price and the quality of the new materials became more competitive with glass and aluminum arrowshafts. In the future, the newer materials may gain wider acceptance.

PARTS OF THE ARROW

The nock is on the tail end of the arrow. It's made of tough plastic and is slotted to fit the bowstring. On most nocks there's a small raised part, running lengthwise. This is called the index and is used to position the arrow correctly on the bow. On wood arrows the index should be in line with the edge grain of the shaft. In other words, the nock index should be perpendicular to the cross-sectional grain of the wood. Nocks come in various colors, of which the lighter or brighter ones are best because the end of the arrow is more visible to the archer. This visibility is important when hunting and also when a bowman is searching for a stray arrow in grass or brush. The inside of the nock is tapered to fit the standard nock taper on the shaft. Wood shafts are sharpened to the proper taper. Glass and aluminum arrows, being hollow, are fitted with inserts, which are tapered plugs that fit into the shaft.

The feathers, or fletching, are just ahead of the nock on the arrow shaft. Their purpose is two-fold: to stabilize the arrow in flight by causing it to spin, thus cutting down on the arrow's wobble in its initial flight; and they give the arrow better balance by off-setting to some extent the weight of the arrow-point. Bowhunters should use larger feathers than those used by target archers, because their arrowheads are larger and offer more air resistance.

For years, the fletching was made of turkey feathers, but they are gradually being phased out in favor of plastic vanes. The vanes, which are still referred to as feathers by many archers, are more durable and are impervious to weather.

The size of the fletching is important. If the feathers are too large, they will cause drag on the arrow or it may make a whistling sound in flight. The shape of the fletching depends on the archer's preference. Some bowmen like the parabolic fletching and others prefer a more angular shape. There are three ways to position the feathers on the shaft. On cheap arrows the fletching is parallel to the shaft. Most arrow-makers glue on the feathers at a slight angle to the shaft, while more expensive arrows are put on in a curved, or spiral position. The direction in which the feathers are angled or spiralled depends on whether the feathers come from the right or the left wing of the turkey. It doesn't matter which side the feathers come from, but all the feathers on an individual arrow must be from one side—either the right wing or the left one.

Most arrows have three feathers, set 120 degrees apart. One of the feathers, called the cock feather, must be in line with nock's index. When positioned on the bow and when the bow is held vertically, the cock feather points to the left. If the cock feather rested against the side of the bow, it would strike the bow as it passed across and a hop would be imparted to the arrow as it left the bow. The cock feather is usually a different color.

There are also four-feathered arrows. The feathers are not 90 degrees apart, but are glued on at 75 and 105 degrees, the wider angle resting against the side of the bow and the smaller angle at top and bottom. Exponents of four-fletched arrows maintain that the two wider-angled feathers on the outside set up a balance equal to the two which are against the side of the bow. Aerodynamically, this reduces the wobbling of the arrow and it gets away faster and straightens up more rapidly in flight.

Test-shooting with high-speed cameras has shown that, indeed, there is a difference in the two types of fletching. Some archers believe that the difference is insignificant, while many experts think the four-fletch covers up deficiencies in an archer's shooting form and in his equipment.

Another form of fletching is called the flu-flu. It consists of untrimmed feathers wrapped spirally around the fletching area of the shaft. In another version of the flu-flu, there are four to six full

Different types of flu-flu arrows.

feathers running parallel to the arrow's longitudinal axis. In either case, the result is a fluffy mass of feathers which offer air resistance. Flu-flu arrows are for shooting at aerial targets, such as birds or squirrels, where the shooter wants his arrow to stop after a brief initial flight.

Immediately ahead of the fletching is the arrow's cresting, a series of painted stripes which serve to identify an archer's arrows. Some arrows are lacquered throughout their length before the cresting is applied. Many bowhunters use dark-painted arrows without any cresting.

Arrow-points vary with the type of shooting. Hunting archers use sharpened steel broadheads; bowfishermen shoot harpoon-like, barbed fish points. For plinking and small game hunting, a popular point is the blunt, which has a flat front surface. Blunts are made of steel, hard rubber or plastic. There are also special bird points with wire extensions and some wire-pronged blunts which will not bury themselves in grass.

The target archer's point is small and light, and is flush with the diameter of the shaft. Field points are heavier and more sharply pointed. Tubular glass and aluminum arrows must have point inserts in the front end. On target arrows the inserts, or plugs, are pointed so that the target point is an integral part of the insert. For field points and broadheads the insert has a five-degree taper, the standard taper for all field and hunting heads. Many bowhunters practice with field points. Before the hunting season they replace the field points with broadheads, using the same arrows.

Some better-quality aluminum and fiberglass arrows are equipped with threaded tips. Using field points, blunts or broadheads which have matching threads, the archer can interchange the points when he switches from practicing to hunting. A number of broadheads are made only with screw-on ferrules to fit these conversion-type shafts.

Quivers
For Every Purpose

THE ARCHER MUST have a quiver to hold his arrows. The type of quiver depends on whether the archer is a target shooter, a bowhunter or a casual plinker.

Target archers usually wear leather quivers held by a belt on the right hip. Since their customary routine is to shoot six arrows or less before advancing to the target to withdraw their arrows and count their scores, targeteers need only a lightweight leather quiver. Some of them use a ground quiver, which is a circular metal framework at the top of a long, thin spike. This is stuck into the ground on the archer's right, and his arrows are simply placed loosely inside the metal ring at the top. Most target archers prefer the hip quiver to the ground quiver, because the latter necessitates bending over to pull out an arrow. With the belt quiver, the archer can continue to stand erect and needs only to reach around and withdraw an arrow.

There's a vast array of quivers for hunting archers. They are covered fully in the section entitled Hunting Quivers, Part VI.

At one time field archers used shoulder quivers, which have a capacity for a dozen or more arrows. Now most field archers use hip or belt quivers, because the large capacity of a shoulder quiver is not needed. The pocket quiver was popular with field archers at one time. Made of leather, it slipped into the right rear hip pocket and held from four to six arrows, enough for an accomplished bowman to shoot a round.

This target archer uses both hip quiver and ground quiver.

A plinker or a roving archer may prefer a shoulder quiver, due to its roominess. He shoots informally and may take a dozen or more shots before retrieving his arrows. For this type archer there are larger shoulder quivers which have divider straps separating two or three different types of arrows—field, blunts and flu-flus. Some shoulder quivers, which were once very popular with hunting archers, have a pocket for the hunting knife and an accessory pocket for a spare bowstring and a file for sharpening broadheads.

Leather Accessories

ALMOST EVERY ARCHERY tyro has had the unhappy experi-ence of having the bowstring slap against the wrist-section of his

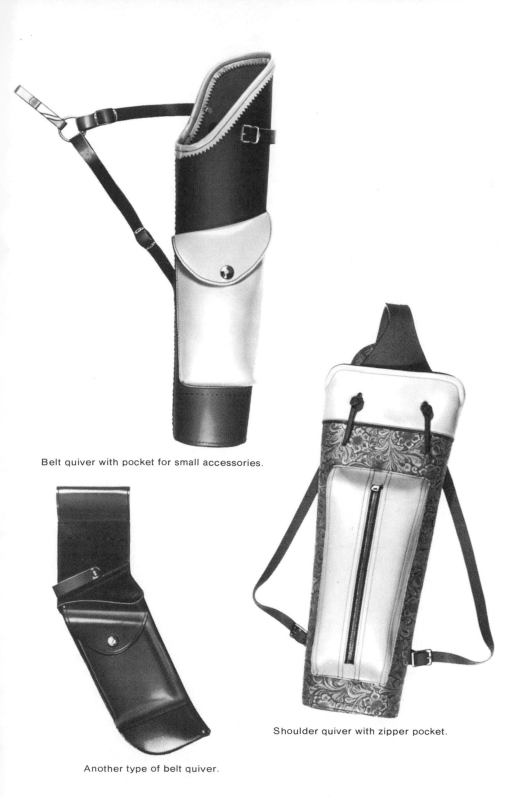

Belt quiver with pocket for small accessories.

Shoulder quiver with zipper pocket.

Another type of belt quiver.

Shoulder quivers have large
arrow capacity.

bow-arm. This is why archers use the armguard, sometimes called a bracer, a stiff leather or plastic pad which is attached on the inside of the left forearm. Some archers develop a shooting style which eliminates the need for an armguard; nevertheless, some of them continue to wear the device for psychological reasons and also to give some protection in case a poor release causes the bowstring to scrape the bow-arm. The bowhunter wears the armguard on the outside of the sleeve of his jacket. The purpose of the armguard in this case is not primarily for protection, but to prevent the loose folds of the sleeve from interfering with the bowstring as it surges forward. There are some 40 different armguard models—costing from $1 to $5—including models that are extra long for hunters and beginners.

On the first three fingers of the right hand—the drawing fingers—archers wear either a shooting glove or a finger tab. This accessory is used by practically all archers for two reasons. One is to prevent the bowstring from blistering the fingertips as it passes over them during the release; the other is to help the archer make a smooth release. While a few bowmen have succeeded in building up callouses on the fingers so that they need no finger protection, the tab or glove is more practical. The string must slide as smoothly as possible over the fingers and this can be accomplished only with a minimum of friction.

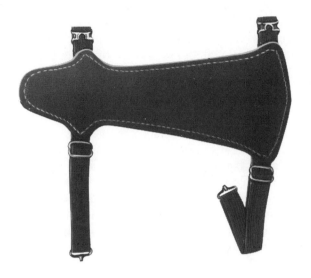

Armguard offers protection from slap of bowstring.

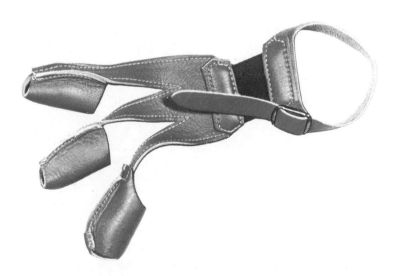

Shooting glove protects fingers from bowstring and makes for a smooth release.

Many archers get good results from thick rubber attachments which are placed on the bowstring above and below the nocking point. Because the drawing fingers come in contact with a surface wider than the bowstring, a tab or a shooting glove is not needed.

Basically, the finger tab is a piece of leather with one or two holes into which an archer's finger (or fingers) is inserted, and a cut-out to accommodate the bowstring. Some tabs are made of leather, some are plastic. In price they run from fifty cents to two or three dollars. The least expensive are simply a strip of leather with the cut-outs. The more elaborate ones are made of thick cordovan leather or calfskin with the hair on the outside. Some have felt pads under the leather to absorb some of the pressure on the fingertips and to prevent the leather from developing a crease from the bowstring. If the finger protection, whether glove or tab, develops a crease from the bowstring, the archer's release is not as crisp as when the string passes over a smooth surface.

An archery glove has three leather (some are plastic) sockets

A matched set of leather accessories.

into which the fingertips are inserted. Connected to these is a strap running across the back of the hand. The strap is connected to an adjustable band, which encircles the archer's wrist. In price, archery gloves range from about $2 to $5. They come in all sizes and are made for both right-handed and left-handed shooters.

In their never-ending search for ways to improve their scores, some archers have come up with various releasing devices, all of which eliminate the need for the glove or tab. Instead of using the three fingers to draw the string, the archer pulls back the string with a release aid. This is hardly a new idea, since the ancient Chinese bowmen used thumb rings, made of ivory, for the same purpose.

Some of the release aids are made of plastic; some actually have push bottons, which the shooter presses to free the string. Several can be described as looping straps, one end of which is secured to the archer's hand. He loops the free end of the strap around the bowstring, grips it tightly with his thumb and draws. To release, he relaxes the thumb, freeing the string. Release aids, when properly used, unquestionably produce a smooth release.

Bowsights—
Increasingly Used

THE USE OF a sight in archery is a comparatively new addition to the sport. A bowsight can be as simple as an ordinary straight pin, or it can be a very complex, precision device. Archers have even used telescopic bowsights as well as an intricate optical arrangement which employed a special kind of eyeglass for the shooter, although the latter never really caught on. Regardless of the variety of bowsight designs, all sights have the same function: when properly adjusted and held on the center of the target, the bowsight helps the shooter to attain better accuracy. That is not as simple as it seems—as will be explained in Part III.

Bowsights were responsible for a schism among field archers. The first field archers, back in 1939, were all hunting-oriented, and they considered their sport a training ground for the hunting field. They thought of the use of a bowsight as effete, unsportsmanlike and impractical. A bowhunter couldn't very well spot his quarry, estimate the distance, and then set his sight accordingly. But it was acceptable on the target archery range, where the shooter could continue to adjust his sight setting until it was zeroed in for the yardage at which he was shooting. On the field archery course it was a different matter altogether, since there the bowmen shoot four arrows from one distance and then advance to the next target, which is a different distance.

When field archery tournaments first evolved, it became necessary to establish two divisions of competition. One division was for the sight-shooters, who were called freestylers, as they are still known. The other division consisted of those who chose not to use bowsights. They were known as instinctive archers, though that term was not an accurate description.

At first, perhaps field archers did rely on their instinct in shooting, in the same way that in football the passer has no accessory to aid him in passing the ball accurately to a running receiver. Nevertheless, as field archers became more sophisticated in their shooting, they devised an aiming method that was based on relating the location of the arrow tip to the target for various distances. First, they had to guess the target distance. Having done that, their training and hours of practice dictated how far above or below the bullseye their arrow point should be held.

Many archers were—and still are—very adept at this so-called gap-shooting technique. A few were able to shoot scores as high as the field archers who used sights, although the consensus was that sight-shooters had a decided advantage. In both cases, the estimation of the range was the key to their success. If the sight shooter figured the distance correctly he could set his sight for that distance. The non-sight shooter judged the distance and knew from experience where to hold his arrowpoint with relation to the target.

However, each 14-target unit on a field archery course consists of a specified mix of target distances and each calls for its own target size. It reached the point where a savvy field archer could look at the bullseye, recognize its size, and be pretty sure what the approximate target distance was.

Another factor which ruffled feelings between the freestylers and "instinctive" field archers was that in tournaments it was necessary to award a separate set of trophies for the winners in the two divisions. This obviously added to the expenses of the organization which was conducting the match. The non-sight shooters felt put upon, especially in many parts of the country where they were in the majority. The freestylers shot higher scores and were sometimes fewer in number, yet they received equal trophies.

During the 1960's most of whatever hard feelings there were between the two factions in field archery melted away. Also, a change took place in the field archery concept. It was no longer considered by the majority as hunting practice, but was thought of as a competition to see who could shoot the best score. And the number of those who use sights has increased, although there are still plenty of non-sight shooters. The important point is that today there is little, if any, harsh sentiment between the two groups. Furthermore, the National Field Archery Association has wisely changed the designation of non-sighters from the unrealistic term "instinctive" to "bare-bow."

Added to this is the fact that an increasing number of bowhunters are using sights. These are not the type of sights on which the archer changes his sight setting before taking a shot. Most of them are multipin sights, in which the shooter has three pins set, as an example, for 20, 30 and 40 yards. Some hunting archers use only one pin, set for about 30 yards. Because of their practice shooting and experience, they know how to elevate the bow at shots longer or shorter than the sight setting.

Miscellaneous Gear

THE LONG LIST of miscellaneous archery accessories is another indication of the great difference in the sport now compared to the days of Robin Hood. Many of these articles are not required by a person who merely wishes to shoot a bow infrequently or on occasion. For the serious archer, however, the use of at least some of these gadgets is almost imperative.

Tournament archers should own or have access to an arrow straightener—to correct bends or kinks which may develop in their aluminum shafts. Likewise, the target archer needs a tackle box, one with enough capacity and compartments to hold a dozen or more arrows and a number of accessories.

A bowstringer (covered more fully under the next major topical head) is considered an important addition by many archers. And, of course, they need some bowyer's wax to keep their bowstrings in good condition.

Since having a constant brace height is a critical matter for the target archer, many use gadgets to check the string height after the bow has been braced. Target archers must choose from a number of different types of bow slings, to prevent them from gripping the weapon too tightly. Also, there are special bow racks for storing the bow at home and other racks for holding the bow safely and securely in a vehicle.

Imagine the amazement of a Sioux brave of a little more than a century ago if he could see a modern target archer. He probably would not even recognize the paleface's weapon as a bow. Here are some of the strange things the Indian warrior would see: a long, shiny weapon with a pair of long brass rods sticking out front; a special rest for the arrow to glide across as it leaves the bow; a strap holding the archer's hand to his bow; a complicated bowsight; a special peephole attached to the bowstring at the archer's eye level; a small attachment on the bowstring which touches the bowman's lips at full draw; a clicking device which sounds off when the bow is fully drawn; a spirit level attached to the bowsight to aid the shooter in holding his bow perfectly vertical—and many more ingenious, esoteric gadgets designed to enable the archer to shoot more accurately than ever before.

While the well-equipped targeteer needs a long list of accessories if he wishes to be a successful contender in tournaments, the bowhunter has an equal amount of gear requisite to increasing his chances on the game trail. These are explained in Part VI.

Care
Of Archery Equipment

IN THE OLD days of wood bows and iron men—who often had to shoot 75-pound bows in order to get decent cast with their heavy wooden shafts—archery devotees had to unbrace the weapon at any time when it was not actually in use. If the bow was kept strung for too long a period, it developed a set and lost some of its cast. The bowman had to unstring his bow at the end of a day's hunt and also when he stopped for a lunch break. It was not unusual for an archer to go into the woods with an unbraced bow. When he sighted game—and not before—he'd string the bow and take a shot—if the animal was still there!

In those days all archers were concerned with the critical stresses of a braced bow. "A fully drawn bow is nine-tenths broken"—was a common expression. According to Dr. Saxton Pope, most archers, regardless of their arm-length, were obliged to shoot 28-inch arrows. If their arrows were longer than that, there was a possibility the bow would break. That was in the 1920's.

The most rugged modern bows are the solid glass models, which are all but indestructible and require practically no care. But few really serious adult archers shoot them because they're so inferior to recurve and compound bows in cast and smoothness of shooting.

Thanks again to the development of new materials and new techniques in archery tackle manufacturing, very little care is needed in the bowman's arsenal. Though it's definitely not recommended, it's possible to leave a strung recurve bow outside for several days in bad weather. That is inexcusable treatment, but it's good to know that a good bow may not be affected by such carelessness. Most archery experts recommend that a recurve bow be unbraced when it's not being used for a long period.

The majority of the established bow manufacturers back up their products with a guarantee. Each bow has its own serial number and is accompanied by a registration card. For his own protection, within a few days after purchase the archer should fill out the card and send it to the company. If any bow failure occurs within six months (with some manufacturers, it's a year) after the purchase date, the company will replace or repair the bow without cost to the owner. If it's between six and twelve months, the repair or replacement will be made at a cost of 25 percent of the original purchase price. From 12 to 18 months the charge goes up to 50 percent and is usually 75 percent thereafter until three years after the purchase. This agreement assumes that the bow's owner has not abused the weapon, thus providing another important incentive for taking good care of a bow.

If the bow changes hands during the two-year period, the guarantee is still redeemable, providing the first owner registered the purchase within ten days after he bought it. In both cases, the archer should write to the manufacturer, stating the nature of the problem, the bow model, weight, serial number and the date of purchase. He will then receive instructions for shipping the bow.

While the problem of returned bows for breakage or twisted limbs was once a major one, it has been reduced substantially. The manufacturers are doing a better job of quality control and archers themselves are more conscious of careful handling when they string their bows.

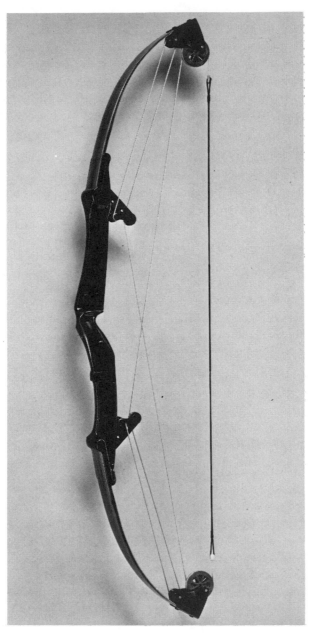

Some low-priced compound bows have limbs of solid glass and can be adjusted for draw weight.

STRINGING THE BOW

Because of the possibility of developing twisted bow limbs while stringing a recurve bow, the stringing operation is perhaps the most important aspect of bow care. Consequently, the bowman should be most careful about not twisting the limbs of his weapon during the bracing operation. Manufacturers will not make good their guarantee if the limbs are twisted due to improper stringing. From time to time the weapon should be checked for twisted limbs. With the bow braced, place the lower tip on the ground a few feet in front of you and hold the other end at waist level. When you look at the string it should be aligned with the bow's centerline throughout its length.

There are three standard methods of stringing a bow. The newest and best involves the use of a bow-stringing device. The most traditional method—which goes back to the time of the straight-limb bow—is the push-pull technique. The third way to string a bow is called the step-through method.

Before stringing the bow, the archer should secure the lower bowstring loop in the grooves of the lower bow tip. This can be done with a rubber band, placed only a short space from the end of the loop, so that it won't interfere with the movement of the string. It's much better to use a rubber bow-tip protector. This is a tight-fitting rubber sleeve which holds the bowstring loop and also protects the bow's lower tip.

In the step-through method of stringing a bow the string's upper loop is detached from the bow and held in the archer's left hand. The right hand is placed on the bow's upper limb in such a way that the palm of the hand is against the back, or concave, surface of the recurve. The curve of the bow's lower limb goes over the outside of the archer's left ankle. The archer then puts his right leg between the bow and the string, with the bow's center section against the outside of his right thigh, or hip. The left heel is raised, keeping the lower bow tip away from the ground or the floor. The right hand presses the upper tip inward or to the left, while the left hand moves the upper bowstring loop toward the upper tip. When the tip moves close enough, the archer slips the loop over the bow tip and into the string grooves. When he's sure the loop is properly seated in the grooves, he relaxes the pressure on his right arm and the bow is braced.

To unstring it, the same procedure is followed in reverse. Most right-handed archers follow the above when using the step-through method but some find it more natural to use the opposite hands. When the bow is unstrung by this method, the upper string loop can be held by slipping it under a rubber band wrapped around the bow's upper limb near the tip. There are also commercially-made string keepers which serve the same purpose.

A string keeper is not needed with the push-pull method, because the upper bowstring loop encircles the bow loosely instead of being free. The archer grasps the bow at the handle with his right hand and pulls, while pushing away with the left hand. The bow's lower tip, with the lower string loop securely in position, is held against the inside of the instep of the right foot. The archer should be careful not to let the bow tip touch the ground or the floor but should place the tip in the hollow of the inside instep just above the sole of the shoe. As the left hand pushes, it also slides up the limb until the upper loop can be slipped into its grooves.

The push-pull method is safe for the bow but can be hazardous for the bowman, since the upper limb may slip from his hand and whip back to crack him on the skull. This can happen also if the upper bowstring loop is not securely seated in the bow-tip notches. In fact, there have been some reported cases of archers suffering eye damage as a result. Another objection is that this procedure may be difficult for a person with short arms and a heavy bow.

The step-through method, while safe and easier on the archer, may result in a twisted bow limb if the maneuver is not performed properly. The string must be held in alignment with the bow and the bow's center should be placed against the archer's thigh so that equal pressure is applied to the bending of the bow limbs. Only the ball of the left foot should be on the ground. The raised heel, pointed outward, helps to keep the string in alignment with the bow.

Using a bow stringer is practically foolproof from the safety angle as well as good protection for the bow. An inexpensive bow stringer can be carried in the pocket. One model is simply a foot strap with a little leather pocket for the bow's lower tip. Another consists of two elements which fit on the bow's tips and a length of braided nylon cord. First, the string is attached to the lower bow tip, with the upper loop around the bow's upper limb. After slipping the bow's tips into the two ends of the stringer, the archer simply places his foot on the cord and flexes the bow. The tips bend as the archer pulls his bow upward, sliding his upper bowstring loop into position.

The push-pull method of stringing a bow.

This is how one type of bow-stringer is used.

The step-through method of stringing a bow.

As pointed out previously, a compound bow is permanently braced, so the above instructions do not apply.

HANDLE WITH CARE

Archers with recurves should pay attention to the manufacturer's recommendations as to draw length. Some models are not intended to be drawn more than 30 inches, while some bowyers state that their products may be safely drawn even by a bowman with exceptionally long draw.

Compound bows are made for individual draw lengths. For a 28-inch draw, the upper and lower pulleys are a certain diameter. With longer or shorter draw lengths, the pulleys are a different size. This is a point which must be considered by an archer buying a second-hand bow. It's important that the compound be set up for his particular draw length.

Sometimes the glass in a bow's limbs develops small fissures, or cracks. Usually, these are not genuine defects but are confined to the finish on the bow's surfaces. The cracks probably do not indicate a breakdown of the glass fibers, but if there's any doubt it's wise to check with a good dealer or bowyer.

While it's not necessary to baby a good bow it does no harm to wipe it with a dry, soft cloth after it has been exposed to rain or snow. Occasionally, give it a coating of good furniture wax, which should be well rubbed in. Mud and grit should be wiped off, too, especially around the bow's nocks. Don't store the bow by standing it on end in a corner. It's much better to hang it by the end or to place it on a rack with two supports for either limb. The bow should be stored in a clean, dry place which is not subject to heat or severe changes in temperature and humidity.

Never leave a strung bow locked in an auto with the windows closed on a hot day, as this may loosen the laminations. After putting a bow in an auto, before shutting the doors, make absolutely sure that the bow tips are in the clear.

The string requires very little attention, but it should be waxed occasionally with the special preparation that is available from dealers. If the serving becomes worn at the nocking point the string can be reversed. Any fraying of the string or loose strands is the signal to put on the spare string, previously broken in, which the archer should carry with him at all times.

The breaking of a bowstring is one of the most unforgettable experiences in archery. One moment the archer is at full draw, con-

Don't put a strung bow in a closed car on a warm day.

centrating on his aiming. Suddenly there's a shocking explosion directly in front of his face. The trauma is bad enough for the archer, but even harder on his bow. Formerly there was a good chance of a bow fracture when the string broke. Now, not many bows break when the string parts suddenly but the strain on the limbs is severe. It's difficult to estimate the life of a bowstring. This depends on the amount of shooting the string is subjected to as well as the care it's given.

When not in use arrows should be kept in some type of container, or at least in the quiver. Surplus arrows should be kept in their original boxes, which have supports to keep them straight. This applies particularly to wood arrows, which require much more careful handling than fiberglass or aluminum arrows. If not stored properly—in a cool, dry room and with bracing supports to hold them straight—they become warped and impossible to shoot accurately.

A typical example of the toughness of glass arrows is the time a bowhunter shot one at a deer. He missed the animal, but his arrow struck a tree trunk. Not wanting to create a disturbance in the woods, the bowman didn't bother to recover his arrow. The following year, while hunting in the same place, he found the arrow, still in the tree, still intact and still shootable. The broadhead point was a bit rusty but the shaft was perfectly true and the fletching was in good shape.

That fletching had been treated with a special waterproof spray, available at all well-stocked archery dealers. If untreated feathers become wet from rain or snow, they lose their stiffness and don't do their job of stabilizing and balancing the arrow. Droopy, soaked feathers, however, can be revived by steaming them over a boiling vessel.

Archers should check their plastic arrow nocks once in a while, especially after one arrow strikes another in the target and after a wild arrow ends up in trees or rocks. When a nock shatters, the archer's shock is almost as severe as when a bowstring breaks.

To pull an arrow from the target, don't just grab it and haul back on the shaft. Grasp it at the spot where it emerges from the target and pull straight back.

Making And Repairing Archery Tackle

THERE ARE FOUR basic reasons why some archers make all or some of their tackle. The first one is, of course, to economize. Another is that some people are handy with tools and enjoy tinkering. Some bowmen appreciate archery more if they shoot

To remove an arrow, grasp it close to the target and pull straight back.

With the right tools, arrow-making is not difficult.

their own hand-made weapons, much like the fisherman who gets added pleasure when he catches a big trout with a home-tied fly. The fourth reason is that many bowmen are so particular about their tackle that they insist on custom-made equipment.

The average person should think at least twice before attempting to build his own laminated bow. The person who has the best chance of success is a skilled do-it-yourselfer who has a well-equipped workshop and is handy with tools. Even then, he won't have an easy time turning out a bow that's comparable with a moderately priced factory model.

It's possible to buy a partly assembled bow at a reduced price. The bonding of the laminations and the rough shaping of the bow have been done at the factory, leaving the amateur bowyer the job of smoothing out the rough edges and applying the finish.

It is estimated that less than one percent of archers make their own bows. An even lower percentage makes the easiest article to make in the archer's kit—the bowstring. The reason, apparently, is that a good bowstring is not expensive—about $2 for the very best, and they will last for a long time with the proper treatment. Therefore, the average bowman does not need to replace his string for one or two years or perhaps even longer.

In order to make a bowstring, it's necessary to buy a supply of dacron thread, some wax and a string server. This represents an investment of about $6. In addition, the archer must either make or buy a bowstring jig, which costs between $5 and $10.

Many beginning archers take a terrific financial beating in lost and smashed arrows. That's when they get the urge to economize by making their own arrows. Later, as their shooting skill develops, their arrow mortality rate goes down. A dozen arrows lasts them a longer period and the incentive for arrow-making disappears.

Arrow-making is not difficult, thanks to some very useful tools. It does take a certain amount of experience, though, to develop the necessary know-how. The time involved in learning how and then in producing arrows, combined with the investment in special tools and raw materials, makes it questionable whether arrow-making for the average bowman is really practical. This is especially so when one considers that the cost of a dozen arrows is reasonable and that they'll last for quite a while.

First, let's consider the raw materials—shafts, points, nocks, feathers, cement and lacquer or paint. In order to save money the amateur arrowsmith is obliged to buy his materials in large quantities. This means that, unless he uses up a great many arrows, he'll have a large inventory of raw materials.

When the materials are bought in smaller quantities, there is no substantial savings. As an example, take the components for building a dozen fiberglass target arrows. Here's what is needed: one dozen raw glass tubes, one dozen target points, one dozen nock plugs, three dozen feathers and one dozen nocks. The combined cost comes to about $25. Compare that figure to the retail price of a dozen factory-made glass arrows—in the neighborhood of $30. One large mail-order archery firm offers complete arrow-building kits, containing the raw materials for making one dozen arrows. The prices extend from about $8 for cedar arrows to around $25 for glass.

It's hardly worth it, when you consider that the amateur must have a fletching jig, which can run from $15 to more than $25. Cheaper models are available, but the better ones are necessary for

In order to make arrow-making pay, the raw materials must be purchased in large quantities.

It's difficult for an individual to compete against mass production, as shown in this cluster of fletching jigs.

turning out quality products. In making a dozen cedar arrows the components cost less, but the archer needs some additional equipment, such as two different tapering tools for the ends and a special dipping well for coating the shafts with lacquer.

Regardless of whether arrow-making is profitable for an individual, it's a good idea for every archer to have the tools and some background in the technique. Then he'll know what to do when it becomes necessary to make minor arrow repairs. Good professional arrowsmiths can replace damaged feathers and broken nocks and points, but if the bowman can manage the job himself he'll save some trouble and expense.

Part III

Archery Form
And
Technique

How To Shoot

THE RIGHT CHOICE of a bow is important for all archers, but for the beginner it is absolutely imperative that he be properly equipped. If he tries to learn with the wrong bow and inferior arrows he'll be off on the wrong track. After that he may become discouraged and turn into an archery drop-out. Even if he continues in the sport, he'll never develop into a good bowman unless he's lucky enough to come into contact with an experienced archer who can diagnose and correct his shooting faults and the deficiencies in his equipment.

Many questions should be considered by the prospective archer. Is he a youth who thinks he may enjoy trying a new sport? Is he a mature individual who is looking for a new type of recreation? Perhaps he's a deer hunter who has always used a rifle and now wants to try the challenge of hunting with a bow. Does he have access to a well-equipped archery shop? Are there any indoor archery ranges in his locale? Does he know an experienced bowman who can guide him? Does he know the location of the nearest archery club? How much money is he willing to spend on his first venture into archery?

These are some of the pertinent questions which confront the person who is thinking of trying archery and they have a direct bearing on his future success in the sport as well as his enjoyment of it. Regardless of which of the above categories an individual is in, the same general principles apply in the beginning.

HOW TO START IN ARCHERY

Ideally, the archery beginner should have a close friend or a relative who is conversant with the sport. If so, he'll have the best chance of success in learning to shoot a bow well. His advisor can help him with the selection of his starting tackle and can also teach him how to use it. Without this connection, the beginner is at a distinct disadvantage.

Assuming the embryo bowman has no close associate to guide him around some of the pitfalls, the next step is for him to locate an archery specialty shop. If he's lucky enough to have such an establishment within a reasonable distance of his home, he'll have a big advantage over one who lacks such a facility. In most parts of the country there are general sporting goods stores which deal in archery equipment. In too many cases the archery departments of these stores are staffed by people who are not qualified to advise a beginner on which bow and which arrows to buy. Furthermore, it's

The beginner should have a friend or relative who can coach him.

unlikely that such a store has a wide variety of tackle from which the beginner can choose.

The ideal place for a new archer to equip himself is a shop which specializes in archery tackle. The owner is usually an archer himself and stocks several lines of good bows and hundreds of arrows in various materials and spines. If he's a good businessman he'll be interested in making a steady customer of the archery newcomer. Consequently, he won't attempt to take advantage of the beginner's ignorance. He may even have a selection of good used bows, by which the new archer can save some money on his first expenditure.

It's helpful, too, if the archery dealer has a target, either indoors or outside. Then it's possible for the buyer to check-shoot two or more different bows before deciding which one to buy. At the same time the owner of the shop can give him some instruction in proper bow-shooting procedure.

A commercial indoor range provides an excellent opportunity for the expectant archer to get his start. A typical indoor facility has a number of target lanes, at least one qualified professional coach and a full line of equipment for rent or for sale. Thus, the novice will be able to feel his way and, while doing so, will come in contact with other archers. Some will be beginners with the same problems as his own. Some will be veteran bowmen who will be glad to pass on a certain amount of their knowledge and expertise. There, too, the beginner can get a line on the location of the nearest archery club.

THE FIRST BOW

The draw weight of the first bow is vitally important. If the neophyte archer is overbowed with a weapon that is difficult for him to draw with ease, he's in trouble right at the start. He'll develop bad shooting habits which will be difficult to overcome later. He won't be able to get consistently accurate shots. The next step is that he becomes discouraged, convinced that he's just not cut out to be an archer.

What the archer should bear in mind at this point is that shooting a bow is not a test of strength but is a skillful act of coordinating the muscles and the mind. If necessary, there's plenty of time in the future to change to a heavier bow—either for hunting or for tournament use.

The beginning archer is *learning*. He's using his mind and his muscles in a new set of circumstances. If he must struggle to draw the bow and strain to hold it back during the aiming process, he develops bad shooting habits which will be difficult to cure later. He'll be concentrating more on the draw and the hold than on the other aspects of shooting an arrow from a bow. The result is that he's handicapping himself in learning the proper archery form.

Let's assume a beginner is not extreme in age, size and financial condition. He should start shooting with a low or medium-priced bow, made by an established manufacturer, and not exceeding 40 pounds draw weight at the maximum. Regardless of his stature and strength, it would be best if he learned with a lightweight weapon of 30 to 35 pounds.

The archer must remember that this is his first bow and that its purpose is to serve him during the early stages of his archery career. As his ability develops and improves and his archery interests become enlarged, he can buy a better-quality bow which may be heavier in draw weight and has a better cast. On the other hand, if he is merely a casual archer, the first set of tackle will be satisfactory in the future. At the start, though, he should have a bow that he can draw without much conscious effort.

The first time a person draws a bow, even a fairly lightweight one, he may have some difficulty in getting it fully drawn and holding it there. This is expected, due to the fact that his archery muscles have not yet been broken in. After buying the new bow and shooting with it for a few days or weeks, his muscles gradually become conditioned and the bow can be drawn easily. One good general guide in deciding on an individual's best starting bow weight is a weapon that he can hold at full draw for about 10 seconds.

The brand-new archer should not be confused by the wide range of bow lengths. The extremely short ones are popular with some hunters, although by no means all of them. The extremely long ones—70 inches or more—are for tournament archers. A good medium length is in the 60 to 66-inch range.

Opinion is generally divided among archery coaches as to whether a beginner should start with a compound bow. There are those who insist on a novice learning to shoot with a recurve, because the compound is more complicated. On the other hand, the weight-adjustment feature on some compound bows makes them practical for a new archer. One model, for example, can be easily adjusted to draw weights of 35, 50, 55 and 60 pounds. The beginner can learn to shoot at the lowest draw weight and increase the bow's poundage, if he wishes to, as he progresses in proficiency.

THE FIRST ARROWS

For the bowman's maiden effort, cedar arrows are perfectly acceptable, providing they are made from first-quality shafts, are straight, weight-matched, correctly spined and fletched properly. Fiberglass shafts are better, but the average beginner is better off starting with wood shafts because of the high arrow mortality rate in the initial part of the archer's training. For the same reason it would be foolish to go to the extra expense of aluminum arrows, which the beginner would not appreciate anyway. The arrows should be pointed with field or target points. For the correct length, rely on the advice of a qualified dealer or use the chart in the section, Arrow Weight and Length, Part II.

While the above recommendations are for those of average size, age and means, there are other types of beginners to whom a different set of recommendations may apply. One example is a schoolboy who has had to save from his allowance or spare-time job, in order to buy his archery tackle. For him, the answer may be a solid fiberglass bow and some cedar arrows, matched in weight and spine as closely as his limited pocketbook will permit.

ACCESSORIES

Instead of a shooting tab, the archery student should start with a glove. It's easier to adjust to the string and less troublesome to learn to use than the tab. For the beginner, a glove with fingers of stiff cordovan leather is easier on the fingers than is one with softer, more pliable leather.

The best armguard is the simplest one. If the shooter finds that a regular armguard does not extend up his forearm far enough to protect him completely from the slap of the bowstring, he should buy one of the beginner's armguards which have an oversized section. When the archer's form improves, he'll no longer need the extension on the armguard. The surplus portion can then be cut off, leaving a normal-size armguard.

Most archery experts agree that the beginner's quiver should be the belt type, or hip quiver. It can be attached to the belt of a man, or he can use a special belt for the quiver, as is the preference of lady archers. The quiver should have a capacity of about one dozen arrows.

The three leather accessories—glove or tab, armguard and quiver—will probably be replaced later, as the archer acquires more knowledge of bow-shooting. Since they are the least expensive items of the archer's gear, he usually should not be too concerned about the cost of buying better accessories when his archery interest increases.

Another accessory is important—something to shoot at. What kind of target he uses depends on the archer's special circumstances. If he's unusually fortunate he'll have one of the following: an archery club's target range within easy reach of his home, an archer-neighbor with some type of target setup, or a commercial indoor archery range close to his home. If he's blessed with any of these facilities, he'll be getting a superior archery indoctrination, because he'll be able to shoot often.

Many people, however, don't have such shooting layouts close to their homes. To make up for this lack, many archers have backyard targets. It's not necessary to have long-distance shooting. The important thing is to have an easily accessible target where the bowman can shoot a few arrows in the morning and evening. While long-range practice shooting is in some cases desirable, in this case the vital point is that the archer—especially the beginner—can shoot often. This helps him with his form and his accuracy, and the frequent shooting keeps his archery muscles in shape.

If the bowman's basement affords sufficient space and headroom, he can set up a target indoors. Here again, the distance is unimportant, because the main purpose is to have a place where one can shoot regularly so as to keep the archery muscles in condition and the shooting eye sharp.

For both indoor and outdoor practice there are several types of targets — or, rather, target backstops. Two or more tightly-compressed bales of hay or straw are good arrow-stoppers. They are used on most field archery courses, as are commercially processed bales of excelsior. The regulation target backstop in target archery is the 48-inch straw matt, a tightly-woven material made especially for this purpose. Matts come in smaller sizes, too, and are available in most archery shops.

Several kinds of modern synthetic materials also are used as target holders or backstops. They hold up fairly well after repeated use and have the virtue of being lightweight and thus portable. Some of these are made of tough, spongy materials and another is made expressly for broadhead practice.

ARCHERY SAFETY

The archer, particularly the new one, should be most careful about the area behind his target backstop. It must not be a place where people or animals are likely to wander. It should be free of brush and high grass, both of which make it difficult to locate arrows which miss the backstop. An excellent backstop is a vertical or near-vertical earth bank which is free of stones.

Prior to doing any serious shooting with his new bow, the archer should acquaint himself with the safety rules in archery. Most of these involve simple common sense, such as being sure that the shooting lane to the target is clear of people and obstructions. A bow is a potentially lethal instrument and should be handled accordingly at all times.

Never point a drawn bow at anything which you don't wish to shoot. The string may break or slip from the fingers. In either case the arrow takes off.

Never shoot at a target—living or inanimate—unless you're sure there is no one in front of it or behind it. Watch for obstructions such as trees in the target lane. The arrow may ricochet and damage people or property.

Never shoot an arrow straight up to see how high it will go, because you don't know where it will land when it comes down.

Keep archery equipment in good condition. Cracked arrows, bad nocks and frayed bowstrings may cause trouble.

If you're a bowhunter, treat your broadheads with great respect.

THE NOCKING POINT

Most experts agree that it's desirable for the beginning archer to install a fixed nocking point on his bowstring. The nocking point is a spot on the bowstring at which the arrow-nock is placed. Its importance is very much similar to the rear sight on a rifle. If a rifleman is shooting with a floating rear sight — that is to say, a rear sight which is not fixed and which may be moved with each shot — it follows that he cannot expect close groups on his hits on

Don't shoot an arrow upward.

target. The archer, by the same token, must have a definite point on the string for positioning the rear of his arrow.

While one would think that the arrow should be nocked at a 90-degree angle with the string, it has been established with modern bows and arrows that the most effective position for the nocking point is approximately 1/8-inch above the 90-degree point.

To determine this spot on the string the bowman must use a T-square or a similar device. If a draftsman's T-square is not available, one can use a newspaper or magazine, folded across the bowstring in alignment with the arrow's position on the bow at the arrow-rest. Having thus arrived at the 90-degree mark on the string, the archer makes a mark with a soft pencil or a pen on the bowstring. The arrow-nock should be positioned 1/8 inch above this point.

To install the nocking point, some archers wrap the string at this point with dental floss or fine thread, holding it secure with several coatings of household cement. There's a possibility that repeated use will cause the nocking point to slip, in which case the whole purpose of the nocking point is defeated. To prevent any slippage, some archers use a needle and run the thread through the bowstring while it is being wrapped into place.

Instead of the hand-wrapped nocking point there are a number of different commercially-made nocking points. Some are made of rubber or plastic material and are placed on the bowstring at the spot where the nock is to be positioned. Many archers prefer only one nocking point, placed either over or under the nock, while others like two nocking points, one over and one under the arrow-nock.

The nocking point serves two functions. It allows the bowman to place his arrow-nock on the string at the same spot on each shot. It also affords him a means to nock his arrow consistently without actually looking at the string when he places his arrow in position. This, of course, is more important to a hunting archer than to a target shooter.

WHICH EYE?

Before making a final decision on buying a bow, an archer must determine whether his right eye or his left eye is the dominant one. It's a simple matter to ascertain which is the dominant eye. Hold a pencil or an arrow tip in line with a distant object, looking at it with both eyes. When you close or cover the left eye and the object is still in alignment, the right eye is dominant. If the reverse is true, the left eye is the stronger one.

In most cases those with a dominant right eye should shoot a right-handed bow and vice versa, although there are instances where the opposite holds true. As a general rule, the person who is right-handed but who has a dominant left eye should start with a left-handed bow. The opposite applies also, but as is the case so many times in archery, there are exceptions. Not infrequently a right-handed archer who experiences problems in his shooting has switched to a southpaw bow. Despite having to learn to shoot almost from scratch, many bowmen who have changed hands find the alteration to be beneficial.

Basic
Archery Form

ALTHOUGH ARCHERY HAD for thousands of years figured prominently in the hunting and military activities of both Eastern and Western civilizations, it was not until the reign of England's Henry VIII during the Sixteenth Century that a prescribed procedure for shooting the bow was set forth in writing. At the suggestion of the rotund ruler, a scholar named Roger Ascham analyzed the requirements of correct bow shooting and produced the first archery book—*Toxophilus*. The title derives from the Greek and signifies a devotee of archery.

Modern bow fans are often referred to as "toxophilites." Interestingly, Roger Ascham was the tutor of King Henry's daughters, Elizabeth and Mary, both of whom were later to play important roles in British history. One cannot avoid astonishment at the fact that the scholar who tutored one of Britain's greatest monarchs, Elizabeth I, was the same man who first recorded the necessary steps to archery success.

Furthermore, Ascham's precepts, after more than 400 years, are still the basic standards for anyone who hopes to become proficient in archery, although some refinements have been added to his formula in recent years.

Ascham recognized that the key to success in bow shooting depends on consistent archery form. His analysis convinced him that an archer goes through five separate steps in shooting an arrow from a bow. If the shooter masters the five steps and executes them in exactly the same manner with each shot, it follows that he will be a good marksman with the bow.

THE COMPONENTS

Roger Ascham's five traditional components of archery form are: Standing, Nocking, Drawing, Holding, and Releasing. Modern archers have added two components—aiming and the follow-through—although these may be interpreted as part of the original five elements. Aiming is one of the steps in holding, while the follow-through is the final part of the release.

Having been outfitted with the proper accessories, a nocking point, a good set of arrows and a bow which is not too heavy to be drawn without much effort, the archer is ready to begin his first shooting session.

THE STANCE

The stance, while perhaps the simplest of the components to master, still requires some attention. It involves more than the placement of the feet. First, both feet should be parallel, angled in a direction perpendicular to a line to the target. They should be spread comfortably, so the shooter has good balance, with the weight distributed equally on both feet. The head should be held erect, facing the target. The archer's left shoulder should be facing

Note difference in stance of these two archers. Both are experts who prefer to shoot compound bows.

The wrist sling enables the archer to use a loose grip. With a light hold, the strap prevents the bow from falling after the release.

the target. All these instructions, of course, are based on the requirements of right-handers. Those who shoot left-handed bows should follow the opposite procedure.

Gripping the bow is considered a part of the stance. Actually, it's more critical than the simple matter of assuming the correct stance. The grip should be firm but relaxed. Some bowmen say you should hold the bow in the same way you'd grip a suitcase handle. Others describe it as the way you'd shake hands with another person.

The bow should be held firmly, but without tension. A tight grip tends to throw the bow off to one side upon release, resulting in bowhand torque. This is why so many tournament shooters use wrist slings. Another way to learn the loose, firm grip is to attach a cord loosely to the bow and the archer's wrist.

Instead of the bow handle pressing against the ball or the heel of the bowman's hand, it should press against the web of flesh between the thumb and the index finger. Today's bows have a form-fitting pistol grip which greatly facilitates using the proper grip. The wrist should be held straight, in line with the forearm.

After he has mastered the correct grip, the archer must hold the bow handle exactly the same way and in the very same place on the bow on every shot. Any deviation results in a lack of uniformity in the archer's shooting.

NOCKING

Before the arrow is nocked, the bow, in the left hand, is held at waist-level, parallel to the ground, with the string close to the archer's body. The right hand withdraws an arrow from the quiver. Holding it by the nock, the archer places his arrow on the bow just above, or to the right of, his left hand. He then revolves the arrow until the cock feather is straight up, or at right angles to the bowstring. The nock index—that little ridge which is in line with the cock feather—will be facing up also. The nock groove is then placed on the string at the nocking point.

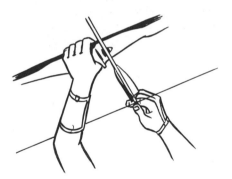

Arrow, with cock feather upright, is placed
on bow in this way.

THE DRAW

The first three fingers of the right hand are used in the draw. The index finger is above the nock and the other two fingers below it. The string presses on the creases between the first and second joints of these fingers. At this point the arrow is drawn back an inch or two, so that the string will be under tension. The arrow can be maintained in this position by holding it with the index finger of the left hand. The finger is curled around the shaft, keeping it under the tension of the bowstring.

These three fingers are used in the draw.
The index finger is above the nock, the
other two fingers below the nock.

In the next step, the bow is raised to a vertical position at shoulder height. The archer begins to draw it, at the same time freeing the left index finger from holding the shaft. The finger now joins the other fingers of the left hand, loosely holding the handle.

Almost all beginning bowmen have one difficulty during the draw: the arrow slips off the arrow rest and drops to the left. To counteract this, the novice makes the mistake of canting the bow more by moving the upper bow limb to the right. The proper way to prevent arrow drop-off is to keep the drawing fingers as straight as possible while the string is being pulled back. What causes the shaft to move to the left is the curling of the drawing fingers. This is illustrated by holding a pencil between the right index finger and the next finger. With the pencil held at arm's length simulating an arrow, the hand is brought back to the face, the two fingers being held straight and stiff. There is no lateral movement of the pencil. However, if the fingers are curled inward during the simulated draw, the pencil moves to the left.

The draw is accomplished by pushing with the left arm and pulling with the right arm, the shoulders doing most of the work. Contrary to the belief of non-archers and bowmen who don't know the fine points of the sport, the muscle power of the proper draw comes from the shoulder and back muscles. The two arms are something like attachments to the shoulder muscles. The bow arm—the left one—is merely a rod that holds the bow at arm's length. The right arm can be considered a long lever with a hook on its end, powered by the back and shoulder muscles. That does not mean, however, that the arm muscles are not employed in the drawing of a bow. The arm muscles are used, along with the pectoral muscles. But most of the power, assuming the weapon is drawn correctly, comes from the shoulders and back.

In getting the bowstring back into shooting position, the archer extends his left arm, points the arrow toward the target and focuses both eyes on the bullseye. The bow's upper tip is canted slightly to the right, at about the one o'clock angle. Later, the archer may wish to devote his attention to target archery, in which case he will hold the bow straight up and down. If he becomes primarily a bowhunter, he will continue to cant his bow to the right, perhaps even beyond the one o'clock position. In either case, it's important for him to maintain uniformity, holding the bow at the same angle each time he shoots.

HOLDING

At the completion of the draw, the bowman's right hand comes to rest at the anchor point, another extremely important element in the draw. The anchor point can be likened to the rear sight on a rifle. If it's not constant, the arrow will not be pulled back to the same spot and through the same distance on each shot. A variable anchor point, like a shifting rear sight on a rifle, can't be expected to produce accurate shooting.

Most field archers and bowhunters anchor with the right index finger pressed firmly against a particular spot on the right side of the face. Some of them use the right corner of the mouth as the anchor point; others prefer to anchor on a point higher on the cheek. Target archers use a lower anchor, usually with the right index finger pressing against the underside of the chin. The arrow is given more elevation this way, since its rear end is lower. Bowhunters prefer the higher anchor because it enables them to look almost directly down the length of the arrow shaft.

Whichever type of anchor an archer uses, he must be absolutely consistent, with no variation in the anchor point.

When the bow is fully drawn, the archer's left arm is straight, although some archers bend the left elbow slightly. Either way, the left arm is relaxed. The right forearm is relaxed and the right elbow is raised to shoulder height. The stance is comfortable, with no tenseness in the legs. The right hand is pressed snugly against the anchor point. If the arrow is properly fitted to the shooter, when fully drawn its tip will be just forward of the arrow rest, but not projecting out in front of the bow's front surface. In the case of hunting arrows, the broadhead extends beyond the front of the bow.

There's much more to the hold than simply keeping the bow fully drawn until the release. The hold is another very critical link in the chain of archery form. It's during the hold that aiming takes place. Even though the latter may be executed flawlessly, the shot

Although this bowman is shooting on a field archery course, he uses a target anchor. Note difference in second photo, in which the girl uses a high, or field, anchor.

These two photos of the same bowman were taken at different times. Notice how his anchor, bow hand, bow arm and right elbow are exactly the same in both pictures.

The bow arm may be either bent or straight, but it must be uniform and relaxed.

won't be a bullseye if the hold is not done well. The hold is also the true test of whether an archer is overbowed and whether his shooting muscles are conditioned.

When the weapon is too heavy or when the archery muscles are not in good shape, the bowman may fall into some bad habits while holding. One of these is called creeping—the unconscious tendency to permit the drawing hand to ease forward a fraction of an inch just before the release. Creeping can be a difficult fault to cure mainly because the archer isn't aware that he's doing it. An archer who lets the arrow creep is not getting the full power out of his draw and he upsets his aim at the same time. Overcoming the habit requires a great deal of concentration and will power.

Snap-shooting, although it can also be considered a part of the release, is another problem frequently encountered by archers. This unfortunate habit is generally involuntary and can best be described as letting the arrow go before the aiming step has been completed. It's usually but not always one of the results of being overbowed.

One of the advantages of the compound bow is applicable in the holding process. Because the archer is holding a lesser weight than the bow's peak weight, he should have no difficulty in maintaining a steady pull for a careful, deliberate aim.

AIMING

Explaining how an archer should aim is like telling how a great quarterback can regularly connect on passes to a teammate who is weaving a deceptive pattern through the opposing secondary defense. Part of it is form and the ability to coordinate mind and muscle, but a large part of it is practice—not merely repeated shooting sessions, but practicing while concentrating on each and every move.

There are three aiming methods in archery—instinctive, gap-shooting and shooting with a bowsight. Which is best? It depends on the individual's eye-mind-hand coordination, on his temperament and attitudes, and on the type of archery which attracts him.

Strictly speaking, the term "instinctive," as it is applied in this connection, is a misnomer, since an instinct is something with which humans and animals are endowed at birth. However, because no one has come up with a better descriptive word, the term must be accepted.

A true instinctive archer—and there are very few of them who

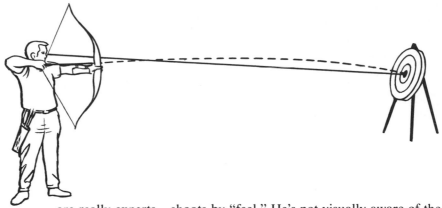

are really experts—shoots by "feel." He's not visually aware of the elevation of his arrow tip in relation to the target. He looks at the bullseye, concentrates intensely on the spot, and releases when he believes he's elevating correctly. Some instinctive archers make no attempt to figure the target distance. Like a baseball outfielder making a throw to second base, his accuracy depends on his practiced judgment plus his coordination. The good instinctive shooter must have excellent coordination and must put in many hours of practice. As in all aspects of quality archery, his form must be good.

Most barebow field archers use the gap system, a technique which also requires much practice and a high level of coordination. The gap-shooter figures the yardage to the target, draws, then checks the alignment of his arrow tip. If he estimates the target to be 50 yards away, he knows from experience with his particular tackle that he'll hit the bullseye by holding his arrow point directly

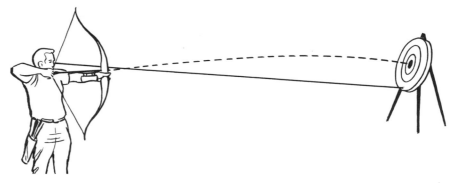

In gap-shooting, or point-of-aim shooting, the bowman visually aligns his arrow tip with a point on, above or below the bullseye, depending on the range.

on the target's center. At 25 yards he knows from training how low to hold his arrow tip in relation to the bullseye. When the target is more than 50 yards away, the archer knows how high to hold his arrow tip above the bullseye. Through his shooting experience he can determine the gap between his arrow point and the target's center. Obviously, his form must be consistent and he must devote many hours to practicing.

For most tournament-type field archers and all target archers, a sight is as much a part of their tackle as the bowstring is. It's not an accessory, it's a part of the bow in that type of archery. Indeed, one manufacturer produces a bow on which the sight is a built-in, integral part of the weapon. Where the absolute maximum in accuracy is desired—as in top-level tournaments—a bowsight is imperative. This does not mean that shooting with a bowsight is easy. On the contrary, it calls for the same requirements as other aiming methods—good form and plenty of practice.

THE RELEASE, OR LOOSE

After holding and aiming, the archer is finally ready to let go with his arrow and he comes to another critical step in the bow-shooting process. Some veteran archers must work regularly on improving the release and on not allowing bad habits to develop.

There's more to the release, also called the "loose," than merely freeing the drawn arrow. The last portion of the aiming process is directly related to the release; the arrow should not be loosed until the aim is exactly right.

The release also involves the final stage of holding. When the bowman is at full draw and has his arrow aimed where he wants it, he slowly increases the tension of the hold by means of his shoulder muscles. At the precise moment, he relaxes the drawing fingers of his right hand. The release must be smooth. The string must not be jerked and the right hand should move straight back rather than to the outside, while the arrow glides smoothly from the fingers.

The various release aids, popular with many tournament archers, simplify the release by making it smoother.

THE FOLLOW-THROUGH

The follow-through is simply the holding of the same stance and position after the loose. The only change in the shooter's position should be in his right hand, which comes back slightly after the arrow is released. The bow arm is held at exactly the same level as

Note perfect follow-through in these two photos.

during the hold. A costly bad habit is lowering or raising the bow arm while releasing. A bowman with good form looks like a statue as he maintains his position until the arrow strikes the target.

SELF-ANALYSIS

In order to be proficient in archery, the shooter must be able not only to analyze his errors, he must also know how to go about correcting them. This is another reason why the tyro should have the assistance of an experienced archer. The beginner has to cope with a multitude of strange actions and has to think of numerous things to do and not to do while sending an arrow on its way. As a consequence, it's difficult for him to know whether he's doing one thing wrong, or whether his lack of accuracy is due to a combination of mistakes. When he misses the target by a wide margin, he may simply chalk it up to his overall inexperience and keep plugging away, repeatedly making the same mistakes. His coach, if he's a good one, is able to recognize the faults of the new archer and can explain how to correct them.

The experienced bowman knows there's a definite reason when his arrow fails to connect. He starts by reviewing each element in his form. If he can't pinpoint the problem, he may call on another archer to watch him shoot. Permitting the arrow to creep forward a tiny bit is often difficult to detect, as is a slight drop or rise in the bow arm. One archer, unable to decide where he was erring, had a member of the family make motion pictures while he shot six

Having another archer watch is sometimes a good way to detect deficiencies in archery form.

This archer analyzes his shooting faults by means of a movie camera.

arrows. When the processed film was viewed, he discovered that he was creeping. It was almost imperceptible, but just before releasing he'd fallen into the habit of unconsciously easing up a trifle on his draw.

The first thing the archer should strive for is to group his arrows as closely as possible. Even though they're not all in the target's center, as long as they're clustered fairly close together, the shooter knows he's on the right track. On the other hand, if his hits are scattered all over the target face, identifying the mistake is difficult.

SHOOTING PROBLEMS

If his arrows uniformly strike above the bullseye, the bowman knows that a certain set of mistakes are responsible. He checks his nocking point to make sure it hasn't shifted downward on the bowstring. He inspects the brace height and also makes sure he's not overdrawing. On his next shot he checks to make sure he hasn't lowered his anchor point or raised his bow hand at the instant of release.

In the case of a low group of arrows, he knows either he's creeping or lowering the bow arm or not making a full draw.

When a veteran bowman has trouble with his arrows all going to one side of the bullseye, he looks for another set of symptoms. Possibly an alteration in his stance is the cause, or it could be attributed to gripping the bow too tightly or holding the bow's handle in a different spot. All of this pre-supposes that the arrows are properly spined for the bow and that they're straight and matched in weight.

Uneven groups can also be the result of varying the elbow position of the left arm. If the left elbow is held too far to the right, or bent inward, the shooter is likely to have the string slap his forearm excessively. Thanks to his armguard, he may not suffer any sting but the seasoned bowman knows that something is wrong in his form when this occurs.

Sometimes, arrows seem to weave violently just after they come off the bow. Archers describe this as flirting or fishtailing. The causes of the problem are numerous. One possible cause is jerking the bowstring away from the face while releasing. Or the trouble could be in the arrow rest or in curving the drawing fingers around the bowstring. Another possibility is the right index finger pressing down on the arrow nock during the hold and loose.

FREEZING

By far the most difficult shooting problem for archers to correct is freezing. This ailment has several manifestations and is something which sooner or later afflicts almost all serious archers after they've been in the sport for a while. Freezing is psychological in origin, although it can beset an otherwise stable individual. In its most common form it prevents the shooter from holding directly on the bullseye. In spite of the fact that he wants to aim at the bullseye, he lines up perfectly on, let's say, the three o'clock position of the target. No matter how hard he tries, he can't manage to move the arrow slightly to the left, where it will be centered on the bullseye. Then one of two things may happen. The bowman becomes so frustrated and so tired of holding that he releases out of desperation, scoring a perfect three o'clock hit. Or, if he is finally able to move his arrow tip to the left, he can't make it stop at the bullseye but allows it to drift over to the nine o'clock spot. Freezing appears to be unique to archery and has been the cause of hundreds, perhaps thousands, of people giving up the sport in disgust.

One well-known bowman had the freezing bug so critically that he considered dropping out of archery. But shooting the bow meant so much to him that he made up his mind to exert his will power and somehow cure himself. He tried dry-firing—drawing an arrow and holding it on the target without releasing. It didn't work. Each time he came to full draw and had the arrow lined up fairly close, something triggered his release and the arrow was shot involuntarily. He tried drawing the bow without an arrow in place and holding an imaginary arrow on the bullseye. That didn't work either. As soon as he drew and looked at the target, some uncontrollable mechanism released the bowstring without an arrow. Fortunately, his bow was not damaged.

He finally hit upon a cure, but only after some painful hours of effort. The bowman used an oversized bullseye and stood about four feet from his target. He aimed at the center and drew, determined to hold for several seconds without releasing until he knew the arrow was aimed correctly. On the first few attempts he released prematurely and involuntarily. But by calling on all his will power and forcing himself not to release, he managed to hold on center and then let down the bowstring slowly without shooting. He repeated the same procedure for a half-hour, then unstrung his bow and quit for the day. By doing the same thing day after day for about a week, the frustrated bowman was at last able to move back to 30 yards and hold his arrow on target without releasing. His patience and perseverance served him well, because he managed to beat the freezing habit, although that type of treatment is not necessarily effective for all archers.

There have been some cases where serious archers, determined to continue in the sport, were able to conquer their freezing habit by changing from right-handed to left-handed shooting. This necessitates buying at least one new bow, plus the effort of learning to shoot all over again. But, surprising as it may seem, the change of hands has often resulted in the elimination of freezing and in the individual becoming a better all-around archer.

Tournament archers, both field and target varieties, use a simple device called a clicker, as a means of defeating the freezing problem. The clicker is a thin strip of flexible metal attached to the left side of the bow just forward of the arrow rest. Before the archer draws, he places the clicker over his arrow, so that it presses against the shaft. He comes almost to full draw, leaving a portion of an inch of his arrow shaft in front of the clicker. The archer aims carefully, holding on the bullseye. When he's satisfied that he's holding on center, he increases his draw, activating the clicker. As the shaft moves back, the springy metal clicker snaps back against the bow's surface. The slight sound of the clicker is enough to trigger the archer's reflexes and he releases.

The Beginner

IF THE NOVICE bowman intends to go into target archery, there's no question about it—he should learn to shoot with a sight on his bow. If he plans on becoming a field archer, it depends on whether he leans toward the barebow division or the freestyle division. In the latter case he should certainly start with a bowsight. For the casual archer, it's a toss-up.

The embryo bowhunter is a bit different. He should start without a sight and hope that he'll develop into a genuine instinctive shot. If he can hunt with a minimum of mechanical aids, he'll be better off. If he doesn't have the remarkable coordination of a real instinctive bowman and if he's willing to devote many hours to acquire the expertise of gap-shooting, he should not learn with a sight. Otherwise, he should cut his archery teeth with the aiming device.

Some archery coaches like to start all new shooters with a sight, even though the bowman may not want to become a sight-shooter. The idea is that while learning, the beginner need not be concerned with the problems of windage and elevation and can address his complete attention to developing his form. For the same reason, some champion barebow field archers sometimes put on bowsights temporarily and practice with them. That way, they don't have to worry about aiming so much and they can concentrate on correcting faults in the release, the bow arm, the anchor or other difficulties in their form.

To some extent, the same applies to point-of-aim shooting. This simply means placing an object on the ground between the archer and the target in such a way that when he holds his arrow point on that particular spot, the arrow will strike the bullseye. For their point-of-aim, some archers use a highly visible object such as a golf ball. The placement of the point-of-aim must be worked out by trial and error for a given target distance. Some people refer to gap shooters as point-of-aim archers, because they align the tip of the arrow with a point below or above the target.

There are literally dozens of bowsights on the market, but a simple one—good enough for experimenting—can be made of inexpensive household materials. All that's needed is a strip of cork or balsawood or adhesive tape and a round-headed straight pin. The strip is put on the surface of the bow facing the target (the back of the bow), just above the arrow rest. The pin is inserted so that the head protrudes on the bow's left side, in the center-shot section or the sight window. By shooting repeatedly from one distance and moving the pin in and out, up and down, the archer can have it set for that particular range.

Having established this location of the pin, he can draw a line on the strip and write in the yardage. If he wishes, he can move to another distance and by the same process determine the pin location for that distance. As he moves farther away from the target, the pin is moved down. If his arrows group to the right of the bullseye, he shoves the pin into the strip more. When his groups go to the left, he pulls the pin out a bit. In other words, the sight pin is moved in the direction of the error.

Of course, it would be better for the archer to buy a mechanical sight, but if he wants to improve with a temporary installation, the simple pin here described is adequate.

It's only human nature for a beginner to want to hit the round spot in the target's center. In reality, at the early stages of an archer's development, accuracy is almost a secondary consideration, the much more important thing being the development of good form. It's awfully difficult to impress the beginner with this seeming paradox, but if the proper form evolves, the accuracy will take care of itself.

Again, this points up the benefit of the sight. Let's say the archer is shooting from 20 yards and his sight is adjusted for that distance. When he shoots, he is absolved of the aiming step. Not that it's easy to hold the pin on the target, but it eliminates one step. Then the beginner can concern himself with his stance, his shoulder muscles, his anchor, release and follow-through.

The beginner should not start with a small target, as this archer is doing.

The first series of arrows shot by a beginner should be taken from a distance no longer than 20 to 25 feet, at a target that's larger than usual. This practically guarantees that the shooter will hit the target somewhere. Therefore, he's not troubled by arrow loss. More important, he doesn't need to devote his attention to making good hits and he can think more about his stance, hold and release, because the aiming part is taken care of. It's only natural that he'll want to hit the bullseye, but he needn't work too hard to do that if he's close enough and if the bullseye is large enough.

SHOOTING WITH A SIGHT

As in all types of archery, a high degree of concentration is necessary in sight-shooting. The bow is held at arm's length and the sight pin is aligned on the bullseye. Both eyes should be open and focused on the target, instead of on the sight, which is seen by the

Note archer's relaxed grip on bow, bowsight on front of bow, steady hold with both eyes open.

The two photos show how the right hand comes back slightly, and the archer holds his position after the release. This archer is using a wrist sling, so that he won't grip his bow tightly. His sight is mounted on the bow's inside surface.

archer's secondary vision. Holding as steady as possible, the archer tries to keep the sight pin on center. That's far from being as easy as it may appear.

From that point on, the sight-shooter follows the same steps as does the barebow shooter. He concentrates on his bow arm and its steadiness. He makes sure the elements of his form are right, including his anchor and that he has a full draw. Continuing to hold on target, he tenses his back muscles and releases smoothly. He must guard against letting the right hand creep forward. This is accomplished by slightly increasing the pull with the right hand, while relaxing the fingers on the bowstring. Following the release, the right hand comes back a bit and the position is held until the arrow strikes the mark.

The Advanced Bowman

TUNING THE BOW

In advanced archery circles, tuning the bow is very important. A precision bow, like some types of firearms and hunting knives, is not ready for the individual when it comes off the production line. It must be tuned in to the shooting technique of a particular archer.

The seasoned archer knows that he must do some experimenting with a new bow. By trial and error, he must determine the best nocking point for his particular shooting style. It may be a quarter of an inch lower or higher than it would be for another archer, and it may be a bit different than it was on his old bow. It's the same with the string height, or brace height. Usually, the manufacturer allows a certain amount of leeway on this score. Within those limits, the advanced archer should shoot with different string heights in order to establish which is best for his personal shooting style.

The arrow rest, too, is an individual matter. A certain type of rest may work well for one archer, but not for another. The adjustable arrow rests must be altered to suit the individual shooter. Again, the only way the archer can find which is best for his individual form is to experiment by taking many shots with different arrow rests.

TOURNAMENT TENSION

At the advanced level of archery, the problems are intensified. A tournament winner is supposed to know all the answers to shooting prowess, but those who are honest with themselves know that the deeper they get into the sport, the more they must know. Their personal temperament and emotional status are important influences.

One competitive shooter may come out of nowhere and dazzle the archery world by zooming to the top with a spectacular tournament score in a national match. The next year, he may be a has-been. At the same time, there are some who are steady, serious contenders year in and year out. Any one of them may take the top national honors one year, only to drop back to fourth place the following year. But he still manages to stay among the top ten. Why the difference between the two types—the flash in the pan and the steady contender?

No one can answer that question. However, there are a few possible explanations. At that level of competition, practically all of the best archers are just about equal in ability. Determination and competitive desire are important considerations, as is the case with champions in any sport. Physical condition is a factor, too.

Age doesn't seem to matter greatly in archery competition on the top stratum. One year a teenager may become a national champion, or even world champ. The next year, he may be shot down by a much older archer. There's really no firm explanation. One could argue that the youngster has fewer emotional hangups than does the older shooter, who may be facing a family crisis or financial problems. The reverse can apply also. The young archer may be frustrated with the difficulties of youth, while a more mature shooter may be secure and emotionally stable.

In any event, the top shooters, in order to stay on top, must have a remarkable ability to concentrate on shooting the bow. This is clear to anyone who has observed the champions in action. Between shots, they're a study in concentration, standing statue-like while they prepare themselves mentally for the next shot. They're going through such obvious turmoil that the average archer almost wants to thank his lucky stars that he's not up there on the shooting line fighting it out with the champions.

A top-level contender must concentrate on every move he makes. More than one champion has described his shooting cerebrations more or less in these terms, as he talks to himself during each shot: "How's my stance? Better check it. Am I drawing the way I should? Is my anchor in the right spot? What went wrong on that last shot? I mustn't forget to aim carefully and take my time. I can't let any distractions influence my next shot. People are staring at me, flashbulbs are popping, cameras are grinding. I must steel myself to ignore these things. I've got to make a smooth release this time or I'll blow the whole match."

EXPERIMENTS IN FORM

The typical target archer anchors under his chin. The bowstring may touch his nose or intersect the middle of his chin. His head is erect and his bow and body are exactly vertical.

By contrast, the average hunting bowman anchors at the corner of his mouth or higher on his cheek. His bow is tilted slightly to the right and his head is bent somewhat toward his bow hand.

Many experienced archers have experimented with innovations

Target archer—anchor point under chin.

This field archery champ has an exceptionally high anchor.
Note his loose grip and the way he cants his bow.

Notice wide stance, angled feet and body bent at the hips. Archer is Steve Lieberman, who has been successful with unorthodox shooting form.

in their shooting form, sometimes successfully. Some change the stance, so that their feet are quartering the shooting lane, instead of standing perpendicular to it. One archer improved his scores by thrusting his left leg forward and pressing the bowstring against it, but that doesn't mean that the same change in form would help every archer. Another switch is to position the cock feather so that it faces the bow, instead of facing to the left, away from the bow. Some get good results on short shots by placing the three drawing fingers under the nock. Another radical change was adopted by some archers who use different nocking points for different yardages on the field archery range.

These innovations in archery form are undoubtedly effective for some archers. The average bowman, however, should stick to the prescribed formula. These different experimental techniques show that bowmanship is a highly individual undertaking. But before experimenting in different interpretations of archery form, the archer must discipline himself on the accepted procedures. For most archers, advanced or otherwise, the wisest course is to stick to the established elements of form.

Part IV

Target Archery

Target Archery
As An International Sport

MUCH OF THE importance of target archery and its U.S. organization, The National Archery Association, lies in the sport's European roots. Because of archery ties to the Old World, the N.A.A. is the official U.S. representative of archery on the international level. Field archery is gaining popularity in other countries, but the target type of archery is the basis of most international bow competition and that's why the N.A.A. takes on an international character.

There are regional competitions between different countries on both sides of the Atlantic and also in Asia. But the most impressive is the World Championship Tournament held every two years in a different nation and supervised by the International Archery Federation. Because of its French translation, Fédération Internationale de Tir à l'Arc, the organization is usually referred to as FITA, which is the way it's pronounced.

There are 45 member nations in the International Archery Federation. They are: Australia, Austria, Belgium, Cambodia, Canada, China, Czechoslovakia, Cuba, Denmark, Ireland, Finland, France, East Germany, West Germany, Great Britain, Holland, Hungary, Indonesia, Italy, Japan, North Korea, South Korea, Luxembourg, Mexico, Mongolia, Monaco, Morocco, New Zealand, Norway, Philippines, Poland, Portugal, Puerto Rico, Rhodesia, Singapore, South Africa, Spain, Sweden, Switzerland, Turkey, United Arab Republic, U.S.S.R., U.S.A., Venezuela, and

The U.S. ladies' team puts on an exhibition prior to an international archery tournament.

The U.S. men's team during competition in an international archery tourney.

Ray Rogers, a part-Cherokee from Oklahoma, has been U.S. national champion and world champ.

Yugoslavia. Not all of them shoot in the FITA World Championship match, but many of the countries do participate.

The 1969 International was held at Valley Forge, Pennsylvania. For obvious reasons, countries like Cuba and Red China did not enter teams. However, for the first time, the Soviet Union sent a team, which made a surprisingly good showing, especially in view of the fact that the U.S.S.R. had been involved in competitive archery for only a few years. York, England, was selected for the site of the 1971 World Championships. The 1973 International was in Grenoble, France, the 1975 in Interlaken, Switzerland and the 1977 in Canberra, Australia.

In this contest, a double FITA round is shot. In each round ladies shoot 36 arrows at 70 meters (76 yards, 1 foot, 7.90 inches), 36 arrows at 60 meters (65 yards, 1 foot, 10.20 inches), 36 arrows at 50 meters (a little over 54 yards), and 36 arrows at 30 meters (a bit over 32 yards). The FITA round for men consists of 36 arrows at

90 meters (almost 100 yards), 36 arrows at 70 meters, 36 at 50 meters, and 36 at 30 meters.

As in all international sports contests, the metric system is the standard. At the two longest distances, the target for both men and women is 122 centimeters (48 inches) in diameter; at the shorter distances, the target size is 80 centimeters (31.5 inches).

Arrows are shot in groups, or ends, of six arrows. The ten scoring rings are valued 10-9-8-7-6-5-4-3-2-1. A perfect single round is 1440 and 2880 is a perfect double round. Gold medals are awarded to the first-place lady and to the first-place man, and to the three members of both the winning ladies' and men's teams. Silver medals are given for second place and bronze for third.

In recent years the U.S. has dominated the World Championships. Although the Americans don't make a clean sweep of the team championships and the individual championships, they are in the majority when the awards are presented. There are several reasons for this. First, we now have more archers in this country than any other country. Second, our archery equipment is the best. A great many of the foreign shooters use U.S.-made tackle. Those

The men's shooting line at an international archery tournament.

Here, lady archers from three different countries are shown at an international match.

who don't, use bows and arrows which are obvious imitations of ours.

The N.A.A., in order to raise some of the travel expenses for sending the U.S. team to the biennial International, sells souvenir pins to its members and to other interested people.

The organizational structure of the N.A.A. is based on the nine-man Board of Governors, who are elected to office and represent different regions of the country. The chairman of the board serves as president of the association. The executive secretary and treasurer, who draws a salary, is selected by the board. N.A.A. dues are $5 annually, which includes a subscription to the organization's publication.

Going back to the time when the FITA match was held every year, here's a list of past world champions.

Year	Location	Ladies' Champion	Gentlemen's Champion
1931	Lwow	Janina Kurkowska, Poland	Michel Sawicki, Poland
1932	Warsaw	Janina Kurkowska, Poland	Laurent Reith, Belgium
1933	London	Janina Kurkowska, Poland	Donald Mackensie, USA
1934	Bastad	Janina Kurkowska, Poland	Henry Kjellson, Sweden
1935	Brussels	Ina Catani, Sweden	A. Van Kohlen, Belgium
1936	Prague	Janina Kurkowska, Poland	Emil Heilborn, Sweden
1937	Paris	Ingo Simon, Gr. Br.	G. DeRons, Belgium
1938	London	N. Weston-Martyr, Gr.Br.	Frantisek Hadas, Czech.
1939	Oslo	Janina Kurkowska, Poland	Robert Beday, France
1946	Stockholm	P. Wharton Burr, Gr.Br.	Einar Tang-Holbek, Denmark
1947	Prague	Janina Kurkowska, Poland	Hans Deutgen, Sweden
1948	London	P. Wharton Burr, Gr.Br.	Hans Deutgen, Sweden
1949	Paris	B. Waterhouse, Gr.Br.	Hans Deutgen, Sweden

Year	Location	Ladies' Champion	Gentlemen's Champion
1950	Copenhagen	Jean Lee, USA	Hans Deutgen, Sweden
1952	Brussels	Jean Lee, USA	Steller Anderson, Sweden
1953	Oslo	Jean Richards, USA	Bror Lundgen, Sweden
1955	Helsinki	Katarzyna Wisniwoska, Po.	Niles Anderson, Sweden
1957	Prague	Carole Meinhart, USA	O.K.Smathers, USA
1958	Brussels	Sigrid Johansson, Sweden	Stig Thysell, Sweden
1959	Stockholm	Ann Weber Corby, USA	James Caspers, USA
1961	Oslo	Nancy Vonderheide, USA	Joe Thornton, USA
1963	Helsinki	Victoria Cook, USA	Charles Sandlin, USA
1965	Vasteras	Marie Lindholm, Finland	Matti Haikonen, Finland
1967	Amersfoort	Marie Maczynska, Poland	Ray Rogers, USA
1969	Valley Forge	Dorothy Lidstone, Canada	Hardy Ward, USA
1971	York (England)	Emma Gapchenko, USSR	John Williams, USA
1973	Grenoble	Linda Myers, USA	Victor Sidoruk, USSR
1975	Interlaken	Zebiniso Rustamova, USSR	Darrell Pace, USA

Archers who shoot in the International must be strictly amateur. It's the responsibility of a nation's FITA affiliate—the N.A.A. in this country—to see that its team in the International consists only of amateurs.

Formerly, there were three archery matches between the United States and its neighbors—Canada, Mexico and Bermuda. Because of the increasing archery interest in Central America and South America, the former matches have been replaced by the Championship of the Americas, which attracts archers from the United States, Canada, Mexico, Puerto Rico, Brazil, Colombia and Costa Rica. Held during even-numbered years so as not to conflict with the International, the Championship of the Americas takes place in a different nation each time.

How To Join
A Target Archery Club

THE BEGINNING TARGET archer, for many reasons, should join a club. If one is interested in affiliating with a target club and does not know how to go about it, a letter to N.A.A. headquarters

Mexican and U.S. ladies' team during a two-nation archery tournament.

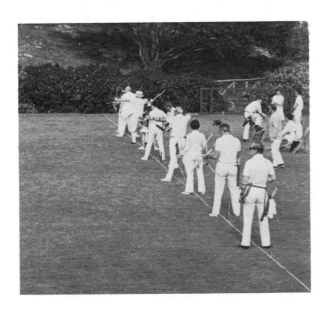

The shooting line at a U.S.–
Bermuda archery match.

(1951 Geraldson Dr., Lancaster, Pennsylvania 17601) will produce the location of the nearest club. The national organization also provides information for those who wish to form a new club.

Once a new target archery club has been started with a nucleus of a few interested archers, a suitable shooting place must be found. One possible location is a public park. It's usually quite accessible to a majority of the membership, and park officials can usually be counted on to cooperate, since their basic function is to provide public recreation. In some cases, sportsmen's clubs have shown interest in adding archery to their activities and are willing to install target ranges on their grounds.

School and college athletic directors are sometimes willing to permit target archers to use one of the institution's playing fields. Still another possibility for the location of the range is a community-minded industry which has some unused ground adjacent to its plant.

In all of these cases, interested bystanders will likely be attracted to archery as a result of watching the shooters in action. Some of them will be potential members of the club.

RANGE CONSTRUCTION

It's extremely important that the target archery range is laid out to conform with N.A.A. standards and thus qualify as an official target range. The club may then be affiliated with the N.A.A. In this way, the club will be able to hold tournaments that are recognized by the national organization.

Here's one example of the advantage of having a standard range which is N.A.A.-approved. If a tournament is properly registered with the N.A.A. as a Six-Gold shoot, qualified participants are eligible for the coveted Six-Gold pin. To win the award, an archer must shoot a perfect end. (An end is a group of arrows. In target archery an end usually consists of six shots, after which the arrows are scored and removed from the target. In field archery, the usual end is four arrows.) In target archery when all six arrows in the end hit the yellow bullseye, called the "gold," the archer makes a Six-Gold. If the club has not paid the required $3 fee to have the shoot registered with the N.A.A. as an official Six-Gold match, the archer is not eligible for the award. (In addition to the Six-Gold pin, the N.A.A. offers other awards to archers who make exceptional scores.)

THE TARGET ARCHERY RANGE

Following are the N.A.A. instructions for the correct range layout, as well as information on the official target.

It is important to provide a maximum distance of 100 yards. The range must be reasonably flat. There must be a 30 or 40-yard distance behind the target line as a safety factor. This distance may be less if there is a hill or bunker 15 or 20 yards behind the targets which will stop misses and ricochets.

A minimum distance of six yards must be allowed behind the shooting line. This is divided equally into a shooting area and a tackle or bench area.

The width of the range is optional. The wider it is, the more targets it will accommodate. Each target will accommodate a maximum of four shooters, so one can readily see that the width of the range and the number of targets it will handle are important, particularly if the club wishes to accommodate many archers in tournaments. Regulations specify that targets must be spaced five yards apart (plus or minus one yard).

The archer must shoot toward the north. A variance of 45 degrees from due north is allowed. This rule, covering the direction of the range, is made to minimize glare of morning or afternoon sun.

Figure 1 shows the layout of an archery range. Note that the corners are perfect 90-degree angles. The best way of laying out these angles is with a transit. A 100-yard steel tape will also be useful. Usually a university engineering department or the local park department will assign a student or workman to help with this surveying problem. The procedure is as follows:

1. Lay out the target line between two stakes.

2. Take a 90-degree angle from one stake and at exactly 100 yards drive a third stake.

3. From the third stake take another 90-degree angle and drive a fourth stake. This procedure will produce a perfect rectangle.

It is an easy matter to lay out lines parallel to the target line at distances of 30, 40, 50, 60 and 80 yards from the target line. These will be shooting lines for the respective distances. The original 100-yard line will be the shooting line for the 100-yard distance.

Where the range will be a permanent one, the shooting lines can be laid out with rock salt. The salt will kill the grass along the line, and the markings will be permanent. Regulations specify that the

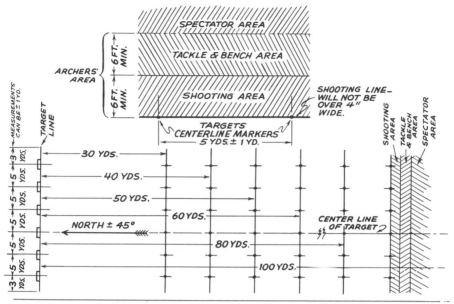

LAYOUT OF AN OFFICIAL ARCHERY TARGET RANGE
Figure 1

shooting lines shall not exceed a width of six inches. If it is not to be a permanent range and such markings across the field would be objectionable to others using the range, mark the end of each shooting line with stakes that are driven flush to the surface of the ground. A day or so before a tournament it is an easy matter to then mark the lines with lime or whiting. The use of the customary lime or line marking wheel speeds up and simplifies the marking. Even in the case of permanent salted lines, the appearance of the range is improved if the lines are whitened the day before a shoot.

To complete the official range, mark the center of each target on all shooting lines. Stakes are often used. For example, in Figure 1, the first target is three yards from the end of the target line. A stake is driven three yards from the end of each shooting line. The center lines of the other targets are marked in a similar manner.

This now forms a marked range suitable for all target rounds except the FITA, or International round. The shooting distances in the International round are 90, 70, 60, 50 and 30 meters. When needed, temporary stakes are used to mark these distances.

127

TARGETS

On a permanent range it is most economical to construct permanent targets. These can be made by stacking four bales of straw (or compressed hay) sideways and binding them tightly together. Figure 2 shows the layout of an official stationary archery target. Note that these stationary targets must have a 12 to 18-degree slant. This angle is plainly shown in the diagram. On the non-permanent or temporary range, targets may be portable ones. Figure 3 shows the layout of an official portable archery target. These 48-inch targets are most satisfactory; they may be purchased from any archery dealer. Most clubs use a one-wheel or two-wheel cart to carry the targets and the target stands to the firing line. Portable targets should never be rolled along the ground; rolling does considerable damage to the target. When targets are stored, they should be laid out flat. Standing them on edge will damage them.

Many clubs merely construct several permanent practice targets on their ranges. The permanent butts should be erected several lanes apart. This layout gives additional safety during practice, and it is then a very easy matter to add additional portable targets to the line.

Figure 4 shows an ingenious target height and angle gauge. This simply-made gauge serves to insure that all portable targets on the line at a tournament are set at the proper angle and height above the ground.

The gauge consists of an upright bar to which an angled arm is attached by a cross bar at the top of the upright, the lower end of the angled bar being attached to the upright in such a position that the proper angle is attained for alignment of the target. These three pieces are fastened together rigidly with screws to insure that the angle and the vertical measurements remain constant.

To insure accuracy in using the gauge to check the targets, a bubble level is fastened to either the upright bar or the top cross piece. This level should be positioned so that the bubble is centered when the upright bar is held plumb.

The upright is marked off in inches measured from its lower end, which rests on the ground when the gauge is being used. The height above ground of the target center is specified as 15 degrees, halfway between the angle limits. This bar could be so constructed that the angle could be varied within the specified limits, but in the interest of simplified construction, it is positioned rigidly at 15 degrees.

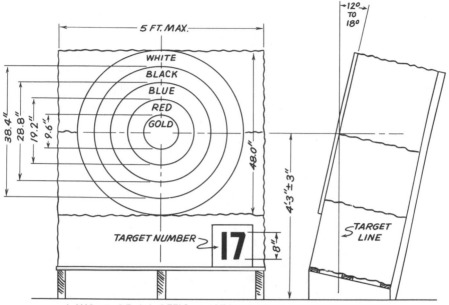

LAYOUT OF AN OFFICIAL STATIONARY ARCHERY TARGET
Figure 2

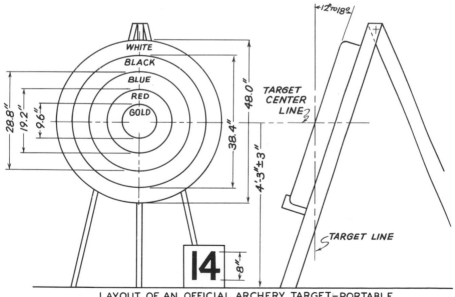

LAYOUT OF AN OFFICIAL ARCHERY TARGET–PORTABLE
Figure 3

Most clubs use carts to carry targets to the line.

In use, the angle bar is placed against the target face with the lower end of the upright in contact with the ground and so held that the level-bubble is centered. The target center is checked against the inch marks and the angle is checked against the angle bar. Necessary corrections are readily made by moving the stand legs so that the target conforms to the gauge.

The gauge is made up of lattice strip, ¼-inch thick and 2½-inches wide. The upright consists of two such strips, 60-inches long, with both the cross bar and the angle bar held between the two strips of the upright, sandwich fashion. Filler strips are put in the open spaces to add rigidity, and the whole is nailed and screwed together firmly. The level is set into the upright and held in place with small screws and epoxy glue.

The regular use of such a gauge would greatly simplify setting up a target line and would insure that the targets are all at the official angle and height. In addition, when all targets are aligned exactly the same, the appearance of the field is greatly enhanced.

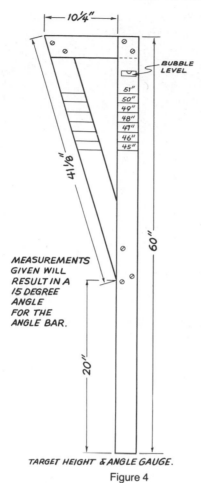

TARGET HEIGHT & ANGLE GAUGE.

Figure 4

Sometimes, when a number of portable targets are stored, fire regulations require that they must be fireproofed. The following solution will serve this purpose and is easy to apply:

9 oz. sodium borate (borax)

4 oz. boric acid

1 gallon water

Spray this solution all over the targets and allow them to dry. For winter storage of targets, the storage room should be well vermin-proofed. Mice, squirrels or rats can ruin targets in a few weeks.

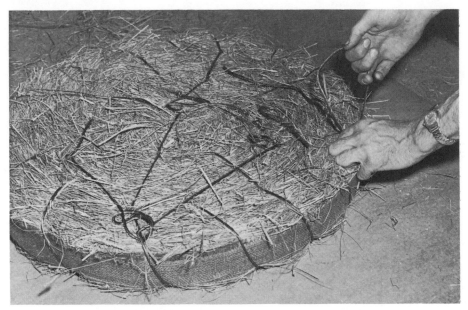

Target matt should be treated, to make it fireproof and vermin proof.

The club should appoint a Range Master who, with his committee, will be responsible for the upkeep of the range, storage of targets, etc.

(This information reproduced through courtesy of *The Archer's Handbook,* the official rulebook of the N.A.A.)

N.A.A. Rules, Regulations And Rounds

WHILE THE N.A.A.'S rules are not terribly complicated, they are somewhat lengthy, because every detail must be spelled out in order to avoid any disputes. For some important excerpts from the N.A.A.'s *The Archer's Handbook,* see Part X.

FLIGHT SHOOTING

There are some other forms of archery competition which seldom come to the attention of that segment of the public who are not

Flight shooters use highly specialized tackle and shoot for distance rather than accuracy.

bow-and-arrow fans. One of these is flight shooting, a contest in which the shooters compete for distance instead of trying to score bullseyes. Flight shooters use highly specialized tackle—short, powerful bows and slim, undersized arrows. The number of serious flight shooters is limited (less than 100) but they are constantly experimenting with different bow designs. Thanks to their efforts, archers have been able to loft their arrows well over 700 yards.

In 1970, Harry Drake, the dean of flight archers, set a new distance record. Shooting in the freestyle class (lying on his back, his feet raised and against the bow's limbs, pulling the string with both hands), Drake shot an arrow more than one mile.

Clearly, flight shooters need an expanse of flat land where the atmosphere is dry and there are no humans likely to be wandering about. Because of this, there are not many places where this branch of archery can be carried on. At one time the flight contest was a part of the N.A.A. National. The shooting took place at dawn on the runway of the nearest airport. This proved to be impractical; so now the National Flight Championships are held in an isolated stretch of wasteland, most recently at the Bonneville Salt Flats in Utah. They are still sanctioned by the N.A.A. A new flight record was set at the Flats in 1976 by Bruce Odle, shooting in the unlimited class. Odle used a hand-held recurve bow, specially designed by Harry Drake, to shoot an arrow 1,077 yards, 3 inches.

ARCHERY GOLF

Another rather esoteric form of bow shooting is archery golf. It's just what the name implies. Archers make their way around a golf course. Distance shooting is a requisite on the equivalent of the drive in golf, and accuracy is imperative when the contestant reaches the green. Archery golf is limited in scope, its main area of interest being in the Cincinnati, Ohio, area.

In 1975, in a special match at the Martingham Golf Club, St. Michaels, Maryland, an archer defeated one of the top golf pros in the East. The bowman was George Mann, a retired diplomat who once defeated the best golf pro in Israel. In the 1975 contest, Mann beat Tom Smack, the Martingham pro, by one stroke, or shot.

INTERNATIONAL FIELD ARCHERY

The N.A.A. now finds itself in the field archery end of the sport. Field archery has been growing in many of the other FITA-affiliated nations, some of which petitioned the Federation to include the field sport in its International match. Since the N.A.A., not the National Field Archery Association, is the U.S. affiliate with FITA, international field archery is the responsibility of the N.A.A.

The first FITA field tournament was conducted at the 1969 International, in the U.S. The second one was held in Wales, in 1970. After that, the International Field Archery Championships take place in even-numbered years, while the FITA target matches are in the odd-numbered years. As is the case with this country's target archery team in international competitions, the field archery team is selected by means of a tryout tournament. In some other countries, the teams are selected by the nation's archery leaders, instead of shooting their way to a position on the team.

For FITA field archery rules, see Part X.

Hardy Ward, the 1969 FITA champ, shows rock-steady form as he aims.

For a change of pace, some archers enjoy archery golf.

Junior Olympic Archers

ONE OF THE most effective N.A.A. projects has been the Junior Olympic Archery Development program. It was started to generate interest in the Olympics. The leadership realized that the future of U.S. archers in the Olympic Games depends on the introduction of more young people to the sport, and then their development as archers. The program has brought countless youngsters to the sport, and has also resulted in many parents becoming archers themselves.

The program is quite broad in scope, in that it takes in every possible organization which may be interested in working with the nation's young people. Virtually any adult organization can sponsor a J.O.A.D. club. This includes the service clubs, such as Lions and Kiwanis; it also embraces outfits as diverse as the American Legion and the Salvation Army. Local Y.M.C.A. groups are welcome to participate in the J.O.A.D. program, as are schools, Boy Scout troops, church groups and community improvement associations. It's not even necessary for the organization to have an active archer among its membership. If no qualified bowman is available to guide the young archers, one can be provided.

If any organization is interested in sponsoring a Junior Olympic club, the first step is to apply to N.A.A. headquarters, the address of which is given elsewhere in this section. After the simple initial requirements are satisfied, the club becomes an official J.O.A.D. affiliate.

The Junior Olympic concept has been so successful that there are now thousands of young people who are seriously interested in shooting bows and arrows. It's inevitable that some of these boys and girls will emerge as future contenders in international competition. As evidence of the success of the J.O.A.D. program, Darrell Pace, a J.O.A.D. alumnus, won the gold medal at the 1976 Olympic Games. He also won the World Championships in 1975. Among those who don't develop into possible Olympic material, many will shoot on school and college teams and a substantial number of them will remain serious archers for years to come.

Archery In Schools And Colleges

BEGINNING IN THE late Sixties, there has been a steady growth in competition among high school and college archery teams. At

The N.A.A.'s Junior Olym-
pic program has introduced
countless youngsters to
archery.

Some of these young archers may represent the U.S. in future Olympics.

both levels, the amount of interest is dependent upon the ability and enthusiasm of the archery coaches. Two of the important centers of interscholastic archery are in the states of New Jersey and New York where the small upstate town of Greene is extremely archery-minded. Cincinnati has long been a hotbed of archery interest at all age levels. Culver, the famous military school in Indiana, has for some years had an archery team which competes with other schools and clubs. Each year Culver holds an invitational tournament which is well attended by many young archers. Another popular interscholastic event is the N.A.A.'s Annual Mail Tournament.

Schools compete in mail matches, as well as in shoulder-to-shoulder contests.

TEAM MEN	SCORE
SAN BERNARDINO	5535
MT. SAN ANTONIO	5519
PIERCE	5500
BRIGHAM YOUNG	5441
PALOMAR	5439
SHORELINE COMM.	5140
CITRUS	5118
CERRITOS	4674
GLENDALE	4500

The top men shooters in an intercollegiate tourney.

Although more colleges were represented, these were the leaders in a recent intercollegiate championship archery match.

Archery in schools is growing, as shown in these scenes from a military school.

Target archery is increasingly finding a place in college athletics across the country, to the point where a few colleges offer archery scholarships. The sport is strongest in California and some Southwestern states, but is rapidly spreading to other areas. Texas A & M sponsors an annual intercollegiate match, in which five Texas colleges and one from Lousiana are represented. Numerous Eastern colleges are involved in archery. There is an annual collegiate tournament in New York State, and New Jersey has an annual college division championship tourney.

Clothing And Special Equipment for Target Archers

U.S. TARGET ARCHERS traditionally dress in white when shooting in a tournament. The neatly-dressed shooters present a very attractive spectacle against the green background of the field. The large multi-colored targets add a note of color to the overall view.

Note fine form and loose grip of Rose Svarc, an All-American archer.

Most target archers use belt quivers.

Some target shooters wear chest protectors—leather pads covering one side of the chest and held by a strap around the shoulder. Its purpose is both to protect the chest from the bowstring and to hold in the loose folds of a blouse or shirt.

The majority of targeteers use belt quivers; some of them prefer the ground quiver. The latter has a circular metal ring at the top, connected to a long spike which is inserted into the ground. The arrows are placed loosely in the upper ring, their points on the ground. One advantage of the belt quiver is that the shooter does not need to bend over when he takes an arrow from his quiver.

The arrows and accessories are transported in a large tackle box, which holds at least a dozen arrows, as well as spare articles. The archer may also have hanging on his belt a container of white powder, similar to talcum powder. The powder is sprinkled on the glove or tab to reduce the friction when the bowstring slides across the leather during the release. Some target archers also have on their belt or quiver a large tassel made of yarn. This is used to wipe the arrow shaft if it happens to miss the target and go into the ground. Binoculars or a spotting scope mounted on a tripod are used so that the archer can see exactly which target ring his arrow hit on the longer distances.

The target archer's arrows are aluminum, with tiny plastic vanes instead of feathers. His bow is equipped with a multitude of special gadgets, all intended to help his accuracy. He has either one stabilizer, sticking out in front of the bow, or two of them, mounted on the limbs. His arrow rest may be any one of the numerous models designed to let the arrow pass smoothly from the bow. Of course,

Target archers usually transport their arrows and accessories in large tackle boxes.

there's a bowsight on his weapon, perhaps supplemented by a peephole sight attached to the bowstring at eye level. The sight may also be equipped with a spirit level (so that the archer knows whether he's holding his bow in a vertical position) or a small optical prism (to help in aiming). Many target archers use a "kisser," a small attachment on the bowstring at mouth level. The archer knows his anchor is correct when the kisser touches his mouth. Usually, the target archer's bow is equipped with a clicker and a bow sling.

Many of these accessories are used because of the target archers' special shooting technique, explained in Part III.

Part V

◉◉◉◉◉◉◉◉◉◉◉◉◉◉◉◉◉◉◉◉◉◉◉◉◉

Field
Archery

Field Archery
and the N.F.A.A.

THE GROWTH OF field archery and the development of the National Field Archery Association was never envisaged by the little band of hunting archers who started the sport back in the Thirties. They approached the game as hunting practice. They wanted natural terrain, just like in actual hunting. They also insisted on shots from different yardages, since shots at game are from varied distances.

As they shot with one another, human nature made them want to compete with each other in a friendly way to determine who was the best shot. This led in turn to a system of scoring and targets, and amiable challenges between groups of hunting archers. Indirectly, that's how field archery began. As the idea grew, the N.F.A.A. was formed.

At first the fledgling organization consisted mostly of chartered field archery clubs. There were also some independent members, especially in sections where clubs had not yet been organized. Today, the N.F.A.A. is structured as a federation of state field archery associations, with about 1,500 affiliated clubs.

Regular members of the N.F.A.A. are affiliated with a local field archery club, which in turn is part of its state association. Regular members pay $10 N.F.A.A. dues, in addition to their local club dues. That includes a subscription to the official N.F.A.A. publication, *Archery* magazine. Associate members pay $5 annual dues, which includes the magazine but not the right

Field archery started as practice for bowhunting.

N.F.A.A. is a federation of state field archery associations, which in turn are composed of field archery clubs. Here, a club officer gives instructions to shooters before a tournament.

Field archers dress casually for shooting around the course. Note two-wheel compound bow.

Field archery is a sport for the whole family.

to shoot in N.F.A.A. tournaments. There is also a Bowhunter membership, with dues of $5 per year. Of that, $2 goes to the N.F.A.A. Bowhunter Defense Fund. Bowhunter members not only receive the magazine and personal liability insurance coverage up to $25,000, but are eligible for N.F.A.A. bowhunting awards. Many bowhunters and archery organizations contribute to the Bowhunter Defense Fund, which is designed to help counteract the numerous, well-financed antihunting organizations.

COMPETITION AND THE FIELD ROUND

The basic form of competition is the field round, which consists of two 14-target units. Four arrows are shot at each target, so that 112 shots are taken in the round. To complete a round, the archer

These archers are shooting a field round, the basic unit in field archery competition.

moves progressively from target to target, in the same way a golfer moves from one hole to the next.

In 1977, the N.F.A.A. converted its targets to the metric system, and the former target sizes and scoring have been changed. The black and white targets now have a number of scoring rings, whereas formerly there were only two scoring rings, which counted 3 and 5. Under the new system, a hit in the black bull's-eye counts 5, an arrow in the white intermediate area scores 4, and a hit in the outer black ring adds 3 points to the score. There's a Professional class in field archery, in which the targets are scored 5, 4, 3, 2 and 1.

A standard NFAA field archery target. An arrow in the black center scores five. A hit in the white ring counts as four points, while the outer black ring scores three.

AWARDS

At recognized tourneys, N.F.A.A. members may win a 20-pin award by scoring a 20 on one of the targets. Other N.F.A.A. awards are: the Art Young Big Game and Small Game Awards (covered fully in Part VI), the Compton Medal (for those who have made exceptional contributions to the sport) and the Order of the Bone (a booby prize for bowhunters who have made amusing mistakes).

In a field round, the shooting distances run from about 80 meters to about 7 meters. The shorter distances are shot at a 20-centimeter target face and are called "bunny shots" by some field archers. The longer the distance, the larger the target. At the longest ranges, the targets are 63 centimeters in diameter, or a bit over 24 inches, which was the size of the premetric target.

A standard 14-target unit contains the following target sizes, four arrows being shot at each: 20, 35, 50 and 63 centimeters. The shooting distances are mixed up, so that the archer does not shoot all four arrows from the same distance.

Obviously, a proper field course—one which is approved by the N.F.A.A. for conformity and safety—must include a fairly large

In the Hunter round, the scoring rings are not visible from the shooting line.

Targets in the Animal round simulate various types of animals.

Field archers also shoot indoors in winter.

acreage. In most parts of the country, where typical deer hunting is in woodsy terrain, field archery courses are laid out correspondingly. Where the hunting takes place in arid, desert-like areas, the courses are situated in similar terrain.

In addition to the field round, field archers shoot the hunter round and the animal round. Other forms of competition—not as popular as the above three, but still sanctioned by the N.F.A.A.— are the N.F.A.A. International Outdoor round, the Flint Indoor round, the newer N.F.A.A. Indoor League round, and the American round (under the same basic rules as in the N.A.A.).

BATTLE CLOUT

When competing in the Battle Clout, archers shoot at a target that is laid out on the ground with chalked rings. The shooting distance is 200 yards and the bullseye is 12 feet in diameter. The four outer rings are six feet apart. A total of 36 arrows are shot, in ends of

Freestyle field archers change their sight settings before starting on a new target.

six. The scoring is nine for a hit in the center, and 7-5-3-1 for the outer rings. The unique thing about the Battle Clout is that the competitors' arrows must weigh at least 425 grains each, and they must be tipped with broadheads. Owing to the long yardage and the difficulty of finding a long, flat area that's safe enough for lofting broadheads through the air, the Battle Clout is not shot as often as some archers would like.

HANDICAP SYSTEM AND RULES

In competition, field archers are rated under a handicap system which is supposed to allow all archers to compete on a more or less equal basis. The details of the handicap system are given in the section on N.F.A.A. rules (see Part X).

Throughout most of its history, the N.F.A.A. has been plagued with conflicts over its rules and regulations. As field archers became more sophisticated and extremely competition-oriented, some of them devised unorthodox shooting techniques which were considered both devious and unfair by some of the other field archers. For example, in the barebow division (as opposed to the freestyle division, in which archers use sights) some bowmen marked their bows with small dots or lines which were in reality sighting aids. Other points of controversy were string walking (using different nocking points for different distances) and the three-fingers under technique (in which the shooter draws with all three fingers under the arrow nock). Still another serious disagreement arose over the use of release aids. As a result of so many devious attempts to win trophies and to thwart the rules, the N.F.A.A. rulebook is a rather complex maze of regulations.

But all serious field archers should have a copy of a booklet called the 1976 Constitution and By-Laws of the N.F.A.A. It is available for $2 from the organization's headquarters, Route 2, Box 514, Redlands, California 92373. Some of the more important regulations in the N.F.A.A. booklet, appear in Part X.

Part VI

Bowhunting— A Still Growing Sport

The Bowhunting Challenge

HUNTING ATTRACTS MORE archers than does any other branch of bow shooting. There are only about 5,000 U.S. target archers affiliated with the N.A.A., and the N.F.A.A. represents less than 50,000 field archers. No one has compiled any reliable figure for the total number of hunting archers but it must be a substantial number. There is some type of bowhunting in every one of the 50 states, while the state with the largest number of licensed bowhunters, Pennsylvania, annually fields more than 200,000 archers in its deer woods.

All species of North American big-game animals have been taken by bowmen but the deer is by far the most popular target. One reason is this species' availability. Not only are deer widely distributed throughout the country, but their numbers are increasing in general. Thanks to enlightened game management programs there are more deer now than there were in the days when the only bowhunters were Indians.

There are four types of deer in the U.S.—whitetails, mule deer, blacktail deer and Coues deer. There's also the diminutive Key deer, a tiny creature native to Florida. They're not hunted because they were so few in number that they became practically extinct.

In addition, there is the sika deer, a small Asiatic species that is a member of the elk family. A few sikas were imported as pets by private landowners about 50 years ago. The animals escaped into the wild and are steadily increasing in number. Sikas are hunted

Whitetail buck was shot by an archer on a national wildlife refuge which is open for bowhunting only.

only in Eastern Virginia and on the Eastern Shore of Maryland, where they have increased to the point of presenting a predation problem on local farms.

Of all types of U.S. deer, the most prevalent is the whitetail, which, with good wildlife management, is capable of thriving in sections that are surprisingly close to human concentrations. The mule deer is a larger animal and is found farther to the west in more open country, while the whitetail can manage almost anywhere. The blacktail is mostly confined to the northwestern part of the U.S. and the little Coues deer makes his home in a limited area of the Southwest.

All North American deer are elusive and cunning. Fairly abundant in their native habitat, deer are challenging to hunt and an ideal species of big game to test the skill of bowhunters. In fact, among those archers who have hunted other, more glamorous game in North America as well as in Africa, the consensus is that for archers the sportiest, most challenging big game animal is the whitetail deer.

Bowhunting is strictly a short-range method of shooting game. An arrow is capable of killing from a distance of 200 yards or more, but no archer—not even the best ones—can consistently count on making accurate hits at extreme ranges. Surveys have shown that most deer taken by archers are shot from no more than 35 yards. Some are arrowed from 60 yards or longer, while some deer are shot from only a few feet. In most cases, though, the animals are shot from about 20 to 30 yards. The short-range shot requirement, coupled with the fact that a deer is a very wary, clever animal, are factors which lure so many sportsmen into hunting with the bow.

HOW A BROADHEAD ACTS

A broadhead-tipped hunting arrow with razor-like cutting blades is a deadly missile. But to be effective, it must sever a vital organ—the heart, lungs, liver or one of the major blood vessels. The broadhead finishes the animal as a result of hemorrhage. Unlike a rifle bullet, which carries a great amount of shocking power, the well-directed broadhead does its job by inducing blood loss.

Consequently, the hunting archer must see the animal clearly enough and closely enough to aim for a vital area. This rules out

Mule deer buck was taken by a bowhunter in Utah.

long shots and shots at running game. The only bowhunter who should take a shot at a running animal is one who has put in many hours of practice at fast-moving targets.

At one time there was some criticism of bowhunting on the mistaken grounds that it was inhumane. There is, of course, a certain amount of game loss, just as there is in any type of hunting. However, the sincere, well-schooled bowhunter is willing to spend many hours in tracking down his game after a hit. The shots are so few and far between in most areas that the archer exerts every opportunity to recover his game. In some states the game managers have made post-season surveys of the deer regions. Wildlife men check the woods after the bow season and again after the firearms season. In every case their surveys show that for every hundred hunters there are less wounded and unrecovered deer following the archery season than after the firearms season.

The bowhunter should know the limitations of his marksmanship. If his practice shooting indicates that he's unable to shoot fairly tight groups at a 30-yard target, he must discipline himself accordingly and not allow himself to be tempted into taking longer shots.

BOWHUNTING ATTRACTIONS

Many sportsmen get into bowhunting as a result of their participation in field archery. The opposite is true, too: many bowhunters join field archery clubs because they want to get some shooting practice to help them in hunting. Thousands of gunners have joined the ranks of the bowhunters, some of them giving up hunting with guns altogether and some of them enjoying a double hunting season by using both weapons in seasonal turn. There are a number of attractions for gunners in bowhunting in addition to the greater hunting challenge. The archery season begins earlier in the fall and in most states it lasts longer than the firearms deer season. In one state, for example, the archers have a three-month season, while the gunners have only about 10 days. Another attraction in most states is the fact that archers are permitted to shoot either bucks or does, whereas gunners must confine their shots to bucks.

Still another attraction for gunners to try bowhunting is that it's generally an easier matter for a bowhunter to secure permission from a landowner to hunt on his property. A typical landowner does not as readily object to having archers on his place, whereas he may not want to run the risk of having high-powered rifle

Many bowhunters take up field archery to get practice for the hunting season. Here's a tough target on a field course in a natural setting.

bullets flying about. That brings up one more attractive angle of bowhunting—the safety factor. Bowhunting accidents, although they do occur sometimes, are quite rare. Since the bowhunter must be close to the game and must see it clearly, there's virtually no chance that he'll mistake another man for an animal.

Finally, there's the unique challenge of bowhunting. Where a gunner with a scope-sighted rifle can register a hit on a deer from a distance of several hundred yards, the bowman must first have the animal practically in his lap. This requires a great deal of hunting skill as well as expertise with the weapons. Hence the bowman finds his hunt more thrilling because of the challenge to try to get close to his quarry.

A large number of two-season hunters in states like Pennsylvania go afield during the earlier bow season and limit their hunting to bucks, which they'd much rather shoot than does. If unsuccessful during the archery season, they can go out again during the firearms session. Their self-imposed restriction as to hunting bucks only is based on the rationale that they don't particularly want a doe and the knowledge that if they get one during the bow season, their hunting for the year is finished. Consequently, they prefer to limit their hunting to bucks so they can enjoy a longer hunting season.

In quite a few states the authorities require the purchase of a special archery license, over and in addition to the cost of the regular state hunting tag. Many archers don't object to the extra charge because they enjoy hunting with the bow so much that they're willing to pay for the privilege. Some of the leaders in the archery field approve of the surcharge because it provides an accurate tally on the total number of bowhunters, thus revealing whether interest in the sport is increasing. Archers believe, too, that the extra fee obviates any complaints from gunners who may resent the longer hunting season of the bowmen. The special archery license also discourages some of the casual, disinterested hunters who may buy a bow and hunt without really knowing how to use it properly.

A few states, notably Colorado, have "either/or" seasons, which require a hunter to use either a rifle or a bow. Since there's no crossover with the two weapons, dual-season hunting is not legal.

Elements of Bowhunting

NOT TOO MANY years ago, a survey was made among some of the nation's top bowhunters in an attempt to establish in what priority they rated the important elements in bowhunting. Those all-important elements are: the choice of the hunting ground, which also includes the hunter's familiarity with the area; his knowledge of the game's habits; stalking and tracking ability; efficient equipment; and marksmanship.

Aside from the fact that these expert hunting archers all agreed on the basic elements, there was not much uniformity in their approach as to the order of importance of the elements. However, a majority figured that overall hunting ability comes first, that any bowman with skill in that direction can make up for deficiencies in marksmanship. In other words, an exceptionally good archer— one who can shoot six-inch groups from 60 yards—is no match for the bowman who knows his game and the terrain and who is an accomplished stalker-tracker. The latter, thanks to his ability in the hunting field, is able to get shots from 20 yards, a range from which an average archer can easily hit the mark.

BOWHUNTERS' GENERAL PROBLEMS

Due to the extreme excitement and tension, there's a lot more to drawing a bead on an animal— large or small— than on a lifesize target (*see* text, Practice for Bowhunting). Many bowhunters, vet-

Knowing the precise moment to shoot is a knack that comes only with experience.

erans and novices alike, have a tendency to shoot at the whole animal instead of aiming at a vital spot. One reason is the pressure of the hunt; the other reason is that the bowman may be too accustomed to lining up on a lifesize target. At least one experienced hunting archer, when he's about to draw on an animal, reminds himself mentally to "pick a spot, pick a spot, pick a spot."

Another problem that plagues many bowhunters is knowing the precise moment to shoot. This is a knack that comes only with experience and sometimes not even then. It doesn't necessarily hold that the hunter should shoot the instant he sees his target in bowrange. He should first glance around to see if there are any other deer in the vicinity. There may be a better trophy moving in or there may be another deer watching the bowman, ready to give the alarm when he raises his bow to shoot. While the archer must not hesitate too long, he must consider whether by delaying the shot briefly, he may get a closer shot or one from a better angle.

BROADHEADS

One thing that all experts agree on is the importance of the bowhunter's broadheads.

There are about 50 different broadhead designs on the market.

As a rough but educated guess, it's probable that about six of those different designs are responsible for 80 or 90 percent of the big game animals slain by archers. The archer's broadhead should weigh the same as his practice points; 125 grains is about the average. Some broadheads are heavier, in which case the archer's practice points should correspond in weight.

The choice of a broadhead is a decision which the bowman must make for himself. One archer may swear by one type head; his hunting companion, due to differences in his individual shooting style, may find that the same broadhead flies erratically for him.

When the archer does not have a smooth release, some broadhead designs have a tendency to windplane—to sail off on unpredictable tangents, even though the shooter's aim is perfect. Other things that cause windplaning are crooked arrows, improperly spined shafts and heads which are not correctly mounted on the shaft. There's an easy way to tell if the broadhead is not perfectly true on the shaft. With the point resting on a block of wood and the arrow held verticallly, the archer spins the arrow by revolving it between the palms of his hands. At the same time, he watches the point where the shaft and the head are joined—the rear edge of the broadhead's ferrule. If the head is not mounted straight, a wobble appears at this point when the arrow is spun with the hands. If the head is not on straight, it must be removed and be re-seated.

Some broadheads are perfectly flat, with two blades or cutting edges. There are also three-bladed and four-bladed models. Some are basically two-edged broadheads, but have a slot into which thin, razor-like inserts are fitted to convert the point to a four-bladed head. The archer can use it in its two-bladed form for his practice shooting; then when he's ready to hunt, he slips the insert blades into place. Some bowmen believe that a two-bladed broadhead, having less resistance, provides better penetration qualities. Other archers contend that multi-blade heads are better because they have extra cutting edges.

The newest broadhead design consists of a bullet-shaped point which is slotted for the insertion of thin, razor-like blades. Made by a number of manufacturers, the razor-insert broadheads come in three-, four- or six-bladed variations. The advantage of this type of broadhead is that it provides sharp blades, even for the bowman who is unable to unwilling to put keen edges on conventional broadheads.

Aside from the flight characteristics of the different broadheads, the other most important consideration is the degree of sharpness at the head. This is something on which all bowhunting experts agree: that the broadheads must be razor-sharp. A broadhead with keen edges offers better penetration, more cutting capability and will slice through tough organs which would deflect a dull head. The steel in some broadhead brands is too hard to sharpen well; the steel in others is so soft that it will not retain its sharpness. The best ones are those which take a keen edge and hold it. Ideally, the blades should be keen enough to shave the hairs on the back of the hand.

A mill file is used by most bowmen to sharpen their hunting points, while some finish the sharpening job with an oilstone. A large, heavy mill file can be used in the home or hunting camp, and a smaller one for touching up the blades in the field. It's easier to clamp the broadhead in a vise while filing it. Otherwise, the arrow can be gripped with one hand, placed on the shaft just to the rear of the head. Each blade should receive three or four swipes on one side, then the same number on the opposite side. Opinion is divided as to whether the file should move from rear to front or vice versa. The important thing is to hold the file at approximately a 20-degree angle to the blade. A needle-point should be avoided, in favor of a chisel-type point, which will be better able to glance off bones rather than becoming embedded in them. At the end of each hunting day, the bowhunter should check the sharpness of his broadheads and go over them with his file, if necessary.

Bowhunting Methods

THERE ARE FIVE basic ways to go about hunting deer with archery tackle: stalking (and still-hunting), driving, standing, hunting from a blind and hunting from a tree. With the possible exception of the last-named method, the direction of the wind as well as its intensity is of the utmost importance.

While many experienced gun hunters are aware of the importance of the wind, there are others—perhaps in the majority—who give little or no attention to the wind. In their type of hunting, it's often not a serious factor in the success of their hunt. But it's just the opposite with the hunting bowman. Wind direction may mean the difference between success and failure. When there is no wind but only air currents, the direction of the moving air is extremely important. The rifleman, with his long-range weapon, can often overcome this problem. But the bowhunter must be constantly on the alert—not only to determine the prevailing breeze, but to be aware of shifts in the direction of the wind.

Deer, and most of the other big-game animals, have an extraordinarily sensitive olfactory apparatus. They can pick up human scent from long distances and immediately head in the opposite direction. They have equally acute hearing, so that the slightest unusual sound will send them off at a frenzied run. While this is not too relevant to the hunter with a weapon-capability of several hundred yards, the bowman must depend on not being detected— neither by smell nor by sight nor by sound. Consequently, the wind and wind direction plus sight and sound play important roles in the bowhunter's methods.

STALKING AND STILL-HUNTING

The first bowhunting method—stalking—is often the most interesting but not the most productive. Generally, it's recommended only for those mid-day hours when deer are not usually on the move. Also called still-hunting, it means moving around in the woods, stepping stealthily into the wind, perhaps seeing small game or following a set of fresh deer tracks. Sometimes the roving archer discovers a hidden crossing which may have gone unnoticed; sometimes he gets a shot. More often, stalking means pushing deer out 100 yards ahead, frequently unseen.

The bowhunter who is still-hunting moves slowly and quietly, stopping for a ten-minute period when he comes across a likely looking spot, such as a well used game trail or a place where there's a profusion of fresh droppings and tracks. When he stops he places himself strategically behind a tree or some brush, always with the wind direction in mind. Fo obvious reasons, he doesn't rest in an open area and he doesn't expect any game movement from downwind. His hope is that he'll pause near a deer run and that a buck may come by from the upwind side. When there's no action after a reasonable interval, he moves on, continuing in a slow, quiet walk.

If he sees a deer that is some distance away, he can attempt the most challenging and rewarding part of the bowhunter's art—a deliberate stalk on a deer. One step on a brittle twig underfoot or a slight puff of wind from the wrong direction will ruin everything.

In stalking, or still-hunting, the archer moves slowly and quietly.

There are exceptions, of course, sometimes so vivid that an archer may be led to think that stalking is the most effective technique. For instance, it's possible to almost step on a deer when you move upwind very carefully during a strong windstorm. Even when moving downwind, the noise of a gale in the trees will smother human sound, and the wind's force will often dissipate a man's scent.

Here are the comments of one experienced bowhunter during a strong wind:

"You're really in luck if you're able to spot a feeding deer from afar during a strong fall blow. The most successful stalk I ever made was under just such conditions. It was 2 p.m. on a sunny October day in northern Michigan, and the wind was a deafening roar in the treetops. While heading for my blind, I spotted a deer feeding half a mile away along a cleared strip.

"I slipped into the woods and just about galloped in the direction of the animal, knowing the brush would cover my movement and the wind would prevent any sound from carrying. Making a right-angle turn when I figured I'd covered the right distance, I came out within 15 yards of the woods' edge and could see the deer 30 yards away, still feeding.

"The mistake that followed has been committed by thousands of bowhunters. I was overanxious and failed, in my haste, to realize that I could have crept to the very edge of the woods and shot the buck at 15 yards. Overwhelmed by the success of the stalk, I feared that he would detect me. So I hurriedly released my arrow from inside the woods and was rewarded by having it deflected by a small oak branch.

"Though the stalk worked out in this case, it was only due to the terrific force of the gale and that particular stretch of terrain."

DEER DRIVES

Driving deer—in the sense that many firearms hunters use massed drivers—is not very suitable for bowhunters. It should be resorted to only when the cover is nearly impenetrable. Even in the tangled swamps of the South where it's legal to use hounds to force deer into the open or across a cleared trail, bowmen seldom use the drive system.

If there are enough hunters present and they have the feeling that at least one smart buck is hiding in a large thicket or wood, it may be feasible to try a drive. If organized by an experienced huntsman, the drive may flush one or more deer. But they probably will not present a decent shot for an archer, because they'll be traveling like antlered rockets coming off a launching pad. That's the main drawback with driving in the archery-deer season—the driven animals usually are moving too fast to afford realistic shooting with a bow.

When a drive is used by archers, the standers should be placed carefully and spaced at strategic points. The drivers should move slowly, making as little noise as possible. In this way, if a deer is moved out, there's a fair chance that it won't be terribly alarmed and thus may give a reasonable shot to one of the standers.

One example of a practical driving situation would be a wooded tract surrounded by cleared land. With the standers located around the perimeter and with the wind direction ever in mind, the drivers proceed quietly through the woods. Another example of a place where driving is practical is a long, narrow island in a river or lake. With the standers waiting on the upwind end of the island, the drivers move very slowly and cautiously. Normally, the deer are reluctant to take to the water. As long as the drivers take only a few steps and then pause for a few minutes, the deer will not likely move too rapidly ahead of them.

STANDING

With this bowhunting method, the archer stands (or sits) at a strategic place and waits. It's recommended for bowmen who don't have the time to set up a more permanent blind and for those who are hunting an area on a transient basis. If he's located near a good trail, if there's enough brush to offer some amount of concealment, and if he remains still, there's a good chance that the bowhunter will get some shots this way.

BOWHUNTING BLINDS

Far more satisfactory than taking a stand, there's the technique of hunting from a blind. It's most effective, of course, during the first three hours after dawn and in the last three hours before darkness falls. While there have been cases where blind hunting pays off during the middle of the day, it's usually best to stalk at that time.

Trying to outwait and outwit a wary game animal by hiding behind a screen of brush for hours can be quite frustrating. Sometimes it's very dull, and the confinement is difficult for some archers to cope with. But in spite of the frustration, using a strategically located and well-built blind is the most successful bowhunting method.

Location and construction are both important but location is critical. No matter how effectively the blind conceals the bowhunter and no matter how well-built it is, an archer will not shoot any game from it unless it's within good bow range of the quarry. Regardless of how many deer are in the vicinity, the blind site must be chosen to take advantage of the prevailing wind. Otherwise, there's not much point in the bowman even stringing up his bow, because he won't have an opportunity to draw it on game.

The bowman can't expect the deer to make a beeline immediately to the feeding area directly in front of a carefully-selected blind. It may take the animal a while to work into the shooting zone. You may spend hours watching some deer browse or graze 60 yards away or waiting for one to come down a trail near your stand. Be patient and have confidence. If the bowhunter conducts himself properly by being quiet and motionless, and if his blind is in the right spot, he'll get off a shot eventually.

Even though you give sufficient attention to wind direction, it's possible that an unexpected air current will waft the unmistakable human scent to the deer, which are noted for valuing safety first and food second. In this regard, here's an experience which happened to a veteran bowhunter:

"One season I was hunting as a guest from a blind on the wooded edge of a long grain field about 200 feet wide and with woods bordering the far side. It was an ideal setup. The fall breezes would whip down the length of the field and sweep my scent away from the blind. My second day there was windless, although there were shifting air currents. A doe minced out of the woods directly across from me, followed by a large fawn and then a buck. As the animals chewed away at the tender shoots, I was so sure they would feed within arrow shot that I could almost smell deer liver sizzling in the skillet. I was trying to make up my mind whether to cook bacon or onions with the liver, when the buck suddenly streaked back toward the woods along his approach trail. He didn't raise his head to sniff the air or hesitate in any way. He just went.

"In a few seconds, the doe followed—less frantically, I suppose, because of the fawn, which continued to feed. The doe reappeared and almost forcibly herded the reluctant youngster back into the woods.

"I hadn't moved a muscle during the whole affair. Since I'm sure the deer didn't see or hear me and there was no wind, I'm convinced that some subtle air current carried my scent to them. A rifleman could have flattened that buck as soon as he showed, but I had to wait and hope that he'd graze close enough for me to make a good hit."

That experience shows that no matter how careful the bowman is in selecting his blind location, an unexpected puff of air can upset his plans.

Before deciding on the location of the blind, the archer should scout the hunting area for deer sign. Look for heavily-tracked areas in which the footprints and droppings are fresh. Orchards, watering places and salt licks are usually reliable, but make sure the sign is plentiful. Some bowhunters distribute a dozen or so apples in front of their blinds. This may attract some deer and it will also give you an indication as to whether the animals are feeding in your area.

If there's a heavy mast crop, you should see numerous tracks around oak trees where deer have been eating acorns. In good deer country, pasture land and cultivated fields of wheat, rye, corn, soybeans and some other crops are generally studded with fresh sign.

There's a drawback in having a blind on the edge of a large field, even if the sign is abundant. Because of the tract's size, deer can wander and feed all over the field without coming within range of your blind. Often, good deer trails are found at the corners of a field. If so, the blind should be situated at the wooded edge of the field near a well-tracked corner. In very large fields, the deer trails are not confined to the corners, however. The bowhunter's scouting trips before the season will reveal the trails which are most used. Don't make the mistake of assuming that one hunting spot will be productive season after season. Deer may change their feeding patterns, depending on changes in the feed conditions as well as on the availability of water. There was once a case where there was plenty of feed on a particular farm where the deer herd had been building up year after year. Then, for no apparent reason, the bowhunter who had been using the farm found that the deer population was absolutely nil. He found out later—too late, because he hunted it for several days without seeing a deer—that a pack of wild dogs had driven the deer from the farm.

Try to find the main feeding and watering areas, the trails leading to them and the bedding grounds. Before the hunting season starts, try to spend at least one morning and evening in the area. Note the prevailing wind, and try to figure out the best spot for the blind accordingly. It should be placed where it will seem perfectly natural. Don't locate it directly in the middle of a feeding area or directly on a trail. It should be 20 or 30 yards from where the game is expected to appear.

It's important to have an easy passage to the blind. Since the bowhunter will figure on entering his blind well before daylight, he must be able to walk to it in the darkness with a minimum of commotion.

In approaching the blind, avoid walking on ground that may be used by deer. Don't follow deer trails when going to your blind, and stay away from the area directly in front of your blind. You won't be spreading your scent where it will alarm the deer later.

It may be necessary to have two or more blinds, so that you can adjust to changes in the wind and variations in the feeding habits of the deer. When you arrive at your blind and find the breeze coming out of an unusual quarter and blowing from the blind to the deer area, you're through hunting unless you have an alternate blind site. In some places and at certain seasons deer may have separate morning and evening feeding areas, and prolonged dry spells will change their watering habits. Here again, you have the answer if you have more than one well-located blind.

If you go to the same hunting ground every year and consistently get shots from a certain spot, it may be a good idea to make a permanent blind there. Aside from adding some fresh brush to the blind each season, you won't have to do any work on it prior to hunting, and the deer will accept the blind as a normal part of their habitat after a while. Before counting on your permanent blind, though, make a pre-season visit in order to make certain that the deer have not changed their pattern of movement for some reason.

It's a wise bowhunter who sets up his deer blind well in advance of the season. Obviously, this can't be done when the archer plans to hunt in a distant state. On occasions, it's possible to build a blind in the middle of the day and be able to get shooting from it within four hours. Those are exceptions, however, where conditions just happen to be just right. It's much better to have the blind built a week or so before it's used. Even better is the blind which is built a month or more prior to the start of the season. The problem there is that the early feeding habits may not be in force two months after the blind is built.

The blind should be as unobtrusive as possible. The bowhunter should take advantage of existing cover and look for rock formations, brushpiles, windfalls and other objects that can be used for natural blinds. By adding branches here and there in the right spots, the hunter can set up an effective ambush without a great deal of trouble.

A clump of trees growing close together can be used as the foundation for a deer blind. Fill in the gaps with brush so that the blind looks perfectly normal to the game. The materials in the blind should be native to the area and should be arranged so they won't attract attention by looking unnatural. When you cut branches, stick the fresh-cut ends into the ground or rub dirt on them so they don't stand out against the background.

A few years ago one Michigan bowhunter built a very natural-looking blind in this fashion. Most of the trees still had plenty of leaves at the time. With an ax, he lopped off a pile of popple boughs. After jabbing the white, newly-cut ends into the ground in a circle at the base of a tree, he was all set for the next morning's hunt.

He had been in his blind the next day for about an hour when a spike buck approached from behind and began browsing on the leaves and twigs of the blind. The bowman, seated on a stool, tried to find an opening in the blind through which to loose an arrow, but he couldn't raise his bow for the shot, because the deer was only two feet away and the flicker of an eyelash would have sent the animal off in a panic. Still, something had to be done, or a portion of the blind would have been eaten away to reveal the anxious archer.

After about five minutes of uncertainty, the bowhunter inched his arrow back across his bow. That was too much. The little buck leaped straight up in surprise and then streaked for cover. The bowman's only chance, which he wisely passed up, would have been a desperate shot at a running deer.

In addition to a machete for blind-building, a pocket-size ball of binder twine is handy. The twine is of a neutral color and can be strung between tree trunks or stakes driven into the ground. Boughs can be leaned against the twine all around, sticking the cut ends into the ground. The blind's silhouette should be kept as low as possible. If necessary, use a small spade to dig a pit in the center. You can then sit on the ground with your feet in the pit. This makes it more comfortable during what may be a long wait.

Camouflaged netting stretched around the trunks of three or four trees makes an effective blind, but some brush is usually needed to break the straight outline of the top edge.

A bowhunting blind should be large enough so that you can move about and stretch your legs. To maneuver your bow you may find that you need more room than you think at first. Clear the ground of dry leaves and twigs which might make a noise when you shift position. At the same time, raise your bow in a simulated shot to make sure there are no overhead branches which might interfere with the weapon.

Veteran bowhunters, once established in their blind, take a few practice shots to make sure that everything will be in order when the big moment comes. Also, they pace off the yardage to various landmarks around the blind, so that they can estimate the distance when a deer appears. This should be done, if possible, before the season starts, so as not to have so much human scent around the blind.

BOWHUNTING FROM A TREE STAND

In the strict sense of the word, a tree stand is not a blind, but the tree's branches serve the same purpose as the concealment of a blind on the ground. The tree stand is in some ways the most effective bowhunting method. It puts the bowman on a plane where deer do not normally look when they're checking out potential danger. At the same time, the hunter's scent is carried on a higher level and is not often picked up by a game animal on the ground.

It must be stated, though, that there are some disadvantages in hunting from a tree. Tree stands are illegal in a few states. Many landowners and most foresters don't like the idea of hunters driving spikes into tree trunks and sawing off branches that might interfere with the archer's bow-handling and his view of the quarry.

Most tree stands are considerably more confining than a ground blind. They're difficult to shoot from without a good bit of special practice from the elevated position. They usually provide a more limited shooting sector for a hunting archer. Climbing a tree is not easy for many hunters, although it's not necessary to be much more than 10 to 12 feet above ground level.

There's the problem of safety, too. Each season, a number of tree hunters lose their footing and tumble to the ground. Broken

Many tree stands offer a limited sector for shooting with a bow.

173

bones are not uncommon. A few years ago, a Pennsylvania archer, hunting alone, somehow fell from his perch and landed on his own broadheads, causing fatal lacerations. He managed to make it to his car but after driving a short distance en route to a hospital, he collapsed and died from severe loss of blood. Because of the number of serious accidents, many bowhunters who have had some experience with tree stands use a rope or some type of safety harness to prevent falls.

When the bowman has a permanent hunting setup where he is reasonably sure of getting some shots, he can construct a long-term stand. Some of these are made with heavy lumber and include wide platforms as well as ladders, all camouflaged or painted with flat, dark-colored paint. To cater to the numerous hunters who use tree stands, several firms produce specially-made stands which can be moved from one area to another as required.

Regardless of whether the archer shoots from a stand behind some brush or from a blind or from a tree stand, he must not overlook the problem of disposing of human waste. The call of nature must be answered at times but the ground around a blind or a stand must not be fouled. If so, the game won't come near, even if

Some tree stands are constructed for long-term use.

Some tree stands are designed for temporary use.

the hunter is situated on a good deer trail or a choice feeding area. The use of a strong deer scent helps under such circumstances, but it's not the complete answer. While a few bowhunters go so far as to use skunk scent to disguise human odors, the vast majority of successful hunting archers find that such an extreme measure is both undesirable and unnecessary.

SAFETY FOR BOWHUNTERS

Any archer's appreciation of the safety factor is important to both himself and the sport he enjoys so much. In the hunting field, the usual archery safety rules apply (see Archery Safety, Part III) but there are additional precautions required, because the bowhunter is using weaponry designed to kill instead of merely to hit inanimate targets.

There have been very few hunter fatalities since modern bowmen began to hunt. The majority of the mortal wounds and accidents have been self-inflicted—the result of carelessness.

By the very nature of the sport of bowhunting, it's highly unlikely that one bowhunter would confuse a man with a game animal. The archer knows he must not only see his game clearly, but must also see it distinctly enough to aim for the chest cavity. While gunners should wear some red or bright-orange on their clothing, this is not necessary for bowhunters. Some local jurisdictions, however, require bright-colored clothes or a portion thereof to be worn by all hunters. Unfortunately, it's possible that there are greenhorns afield who are not aware of the fundamentals of bowhunting safety. They may not realize the elements of successful bowhunting and they may be prone to shoot at any object which resembles the quarry.

The first thing to bear in mind is that bowhunting tackle is deadly. If it's not deadly, it's worthless as hunting armament. The broadhead arrow is a threat even when it's not shot and should command the utmost respect. If the broadhead is not razor-sharp, it shouldn't be used. If it is razor-sharp, it's capable of causing serious injury when mishandled.

Here are the basics of safe bowhunting:

Be careful with your hands when mounting broadheads onto the arrow shaft and when sharpening them. A slip of your fingers or too much pressure in forcing the head onto the shaft may result in serious hemorrhage or injury to a hand.

While moving along a trail, *never follow too close behind*

Because of the safety hazard, bowhunters should not use bow quivers with exposed broadheads.

another hunter; you may trip or stumble and jab him with your arrow point.

Be sure your *quiver is designed for maximum safety.* Avoid a bow quiver which does not offer protection around the points of the broadheads.

Never shoot at an animal *if there's another human between you and the target,* even though he may be well off to one side of the line of flight.

Always be careful of jabbing yourself with one of your own broadheads.

This brings up the question of whether a bowhunter should move about with an arrow in drawing position on his bow. This is another subject on which not all archers agree. Some hold that a bowhunter with an unmounted arrow is the same as a rifleman stalking without a cartridge in his gun. Others claim that there's too great a bowhunting risk when the archer moves with an arrow on his bow.

The question must be answered judiciously. If a bowhunter is walking through slippery mud or across an icy slope or through an area where there are vines underfoot, he would be foolish to carry an arrow in shooting position. An unexpected tripping or loss of footing may result in serious injury. It may be argued that the shooter should be prepared to draw at all times, but the risk of injury, personal or otherwise, is too great to take a chance in certain types of terrain.

GUIDES AND HUNTING CAMPS

Many archers, both those who have arrowed some local game as well as those who have had no luck in their home states, are interested in arranging hunts in distant states. There are increasing numbers of hunting camps in the mountain states which make a specialty of catering to archers. As a rule, these outfits can be relied on; however, before deciding on which one to patronize, the bowhunter should ask for references and then follow them up with correspondence and phone calls.

Among those professional guides and hunting camps which advertise in the outdoor magazines, the majority are reliable. Many of them, though, are rifle-oriented and are not familiar with the special requirements of bowhunters. Prospective archer-customers must make a thorough investigation and check several references before booking a hunt. Some outfitters don't particularly want to handle bowmen because their work is more difficult with archers. Where a scope-equipped rifleman can shoot his trophy from a considerable distance, the bowhunter must be placed within less than 50 yards of the game.

WEATHER AND BOWHUNTING

Although it's not very pleasant to hunt during a steady rain, this may be a productive period. This is especially true for the stalker, because the leaves and brush are soft and not noisy, and the wind doesn't carry man's scent so readily. When a storm threatens, most types of wildlife react by being more active in their feeding. After a storm, too, their movements and feeding are more active.

The hunter is at an advantage when the ground is covered with snow. The dark shapes of the deer are more visible and their tracks reveal their presence and numbers. At this time, the savvy bowhunter wears a poncho made from an old bedsheet.

There have been no significant studies of the effects of solunar changes in bowhunting, but it is generally concluded that during a full moon the deer feed mostly at night. In fact, some hunters contend that when the moon is full, deer never feed during daylight. Some wildlife biologists disagree, saying that deer, like humans, become hungry at regular times and feed normally during the day. They concede, though, that the deer are somewhat less active during the day around the full of the moon.

In any case, the best hunting periods are the first two or three hours after dawn and the last two or three hours before sunset.

Special Bowhunting Equipment

BEGINNING WITH HIS clothing, the bowhunter requires some specialized articles that are not found in other types of archery nor in other kinds of hunting. Some of these are definite necessities; some are optional and depend on the individual's personal preferences.

Camouflage clothes are practically a must in almost all parts of the country. They are available in a number of different color patterns and garments—suits, parkas, coveralls, caps and gloves. While their function is to make the hunter resemble the natural foliage, they also serve another important purpose—providing the man with a silhouette which is mottled and broken in outline rather than an easily-spotted shape.

Bowhunters should avoid the stiff waterproof camouflage fabrics because they are noisy when the wearer moves. This is not important to a waterfowl gunner but it is vital to a hunting archer. On a windless day, the sound made by noisy garments may be detected by an animal from a surprising distance. Smart bowhunters replace their camouflage clothing when repeated washings cause the colors to fade and lose their deceptive pattern.

Camouflage headwear is available, too. The only possible disadvantage of a camouflage cap or hat is that the brim of the hat or the visor of the cap is rather stiff and may interfere with the bowstring when the archer comes to full-draw. For this reason, some bowhunters wear their caps backwards or with the visor turned to one side. Because of their shooting style, many bowmen have no problem on this score.

An otherwise perfectly camouflaged bowhunter can be detected on his deer stand or on a stalk if his face and hands are clearly visible. There are some bowhunters who ignore this and a good number of them get their share of game. Others use dark shades of grease paint to darken their faces. Camouflage head nets or face masks, made of transparent net material, accomplish the same thing and also offer some protection against insects. If the archer finds that the netting reduces his vision, he can cut eye holes in the cloth. Camouflage gloves also are made of the net material. They effectively disguise the light appearance of the bowman's hands. If his shooting glove is not too tight-fitting, he can slip it over the first three fingers of the thin net glove.

The bowhunter's drawing fingers must be kept warm at all times. While a gunner can shoot with a fairly cold trigger finger, the archer cannot afford to have cold string fingers. In cold climates or on very cold days in moderate climates, some archers use pocket handwarmers. When the shooting hand gets cold, they insert it in the jacket pocket to keep it warm. This is perfectly feasible for the

Some bowhunters use grease paint to darken their faces.

Others wear thin camouflage head nets or face masks.

This bowhunter, shooting at a squirrel, has a properly camouflaged bow.

archer who hunts from a stand because he usually has sufficient time to withdraw his hand before shooting. Another method of keeping the string fingers warm is by slipping an oversize glove or mitten over the right hand and the shooting glove. It must be very loose-fitting, so it can be slipped off in an instant.

To complete the camouflage, the bowhunter's weapon should not be shiny or light in color. Camouflage cloth sleeves which fit over the bow's lower limbs are popular. Or the bow can be wrapped with a special camouflage tape with an adhesive backing. It's possible also to spray the bow with several different shades of dark, flat paint.

Bowhunters are not in agreement over the color of their arrow shafts and fletching. Some insist on dark shafts and feathers because the whole camouflage effect is lost if light-hued arrows stand out in the woods. Others prefer light-colored shafts or fletching on the theory that in dim light the archer has a better chance of tracking his arrow in flight. He can tell whether he hits or misses. If he scores a hit, he can see which part of the deer's anatomy is struck. In the event of a missed shot, it's easier to find a light-colored arrow in the brush.

The bowstring should be darkened for hunting, so that its whiteness does not signal the game when the bow is raised. The string should be equipped with a pair of string silencers, which deaden the twang when the bow is shot. Without the silencers, the string's vibrations set up a sound that can sometimes cause a deer to make an evasive, reflexive leap before the arrow reaches him. This is known as "jumping the string" and can be partially controlled by the silencers. Brush buttons are another useful accessory for the bowhunter. These are small rubber balls which fit onto the bowstring and are placed near the bow's tips. They somewhat deaden the string's sound and also prevent twigs from becoming wedged into the space between the string and the bow at the two tips.

The bowhunter must remember that his is a short-range type of hunting. A number of hunting archers use some type of scent for this reason. Scents come in two general varieties, one of which is simply for disguising or covering the natural human odor. The other type, made from animal musk, is for attracting the male deer. The latter type is rather offensive and is put on the hunter's boots and the cuffs of his trousers. When the archer is hunting

Note how the light-colored arrow shafts stand out on the bow quiver. In the case of this particular archer, this is not a problem, since he's hunting pheasants. Note flu-flu arrows. Avoid bow quivers which do not have protective covers over the broadheads.

from a more or less permanent stand or blind, he can put a few drops of the musk on the bushes near his location. The first type of scent is not objectionable and can be applied anywhere on the bowman's clothing.

Some bowhunters claim success with the use of a deer call. Most, however, are reluctant to try this method of luring a deer, because if not used properly, the call will alarm more deer than it attracts.

An arrow-holder is a useful accessory, particularly when the weather is cold. A small device which attaches to the bow near the arrow rest, the holder is designed so that the arrow can be drawn a few inches and held by the accessory. This permits the hunter to relax his left index finger, which ordinarily holds the partly-drawn arrow under tension. When the arrow is fully drawn for a shot, the arrow holder frees the shaft and springs away from the bow.

The arrow-holder is not the only way to keep a partly-drawn arrow locked under tension. There's a simple way to accomplish the same thing. The archer dips the end of the arrow nock into hot water, being careful not to submerge the entire nock and thus risk loosening the cement. When the plastic nock-tips soften, they can be pinched together slightly. This makes the nock fit tightly on the bowstring and, when properly done, does not affect the arrow's flight.

Another practical aid in bowhunting is a folding stool. The best type is constructed of lightweight aluminum tubing, painted green with flat, non-reflective paint. The seat is made of camouflage cloth with a deep, zippered pocket to accommodate a number of accessories which might otherwise make the bowman's pockets too bulky. Less comfortable because it's lower to the ground, another folding seat is so compact that it can be carried on the hunter's belt or in his pocket.

Neither of these seats can be recommended for the stalker; but for the bowman who takes a stand or hunts from a blind, they are helpful. They enable the bowhunter to have a lower silhouette and an outline which does not resemble a human. Also, when seated, the hunter's movements are greatly reduced.

In addition to a light file for sharpening broadheads in the field, the rest of the bowhunter's equipment is the same as that of the firearms hunter—compass, light binoculars, well-broken in footwear and underwear to match the climate. In the cutlery department, he carries a knife for dressing his trophy, and he may also carry a hand ax, a machete or a folding pocket saw for blind building or for lopping off tree branches that may inhibit his shots.

Hunting Quivers

TO SOME ARCHERS, a quiver is merely something to hold the arrows. To a knowledgeable bowhunter, the choice of a quiver may mean the difference between success and failure in the hunting field. True, the quiver does hold the bowman's arrow supply but there's much more to it than that.

In the 1950's, most bowhunters wore shoulder quivers, which are now rejected by the majority of hunting archers. While they have a large arrow capacity, shoulder quivers have some disadvantages. Most of them hold the arrows loosely, so that the broadhead blades rub against one another, dulling their edges. The arrows may rattle in a shoulder quiver and when the wearer ducks under low branches, the arrows may hang up. A major objection is that the bowhunter, in withdrawing an arrow from a shoulder quiver, must go through some attention-getting arm movements.

Most bowhunters prefer either a bow quiver, a belt quiver or a center-back quiver. The first two types do not have the capacity of a shoulder quiver, but in most kinds of bowhunting it's not necessary to carry more than six or eight arrows on a day's outing.

Bow quivers are attached to the bow, the arrows parallel to the bow. They hold up to eight arrows and are less likely to interfere with brush than is the case with a shoulder quiver. The shafts are separated and held securely with clips. To reload his bow after a shot, the archer simply snaps an arrow out of the quiver. The bow does not need to be lowered and the bowman's right arm is moved unobtrusively when the arrow is withdrawn. Bow quivers are produced by a number of different manufacturers. For the sake of their own safety, archers should not use the type that leaves the broadheads exposed. The best bow quivers are those which have protective covers for the sharp points. Not only are they better from the safety angle, but they also protect the broadhead blades from contact with brush.

Some belt quivers also have clips separating the shafts. When the archer moves through thick cover, he can slide the belt quiver around to the rear, where it won't engage any brush.

The third kind of hunting quiver is held in place with straps similar to a pack harness and hangs down the middle of the bowman's back. It consists of an open framework with a ledge on the bottom and a covered top; it holds a dozen or more arrows separately and firmly. To remove an arrow, the archer simply

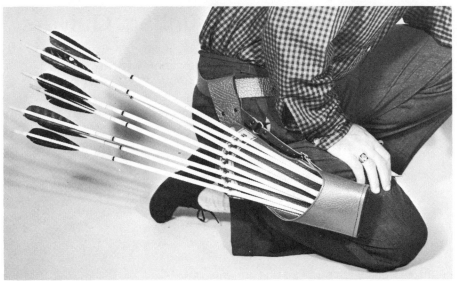

Many bowhunters use belt quivers which have clips holding the arrows.

moves his arm along his side to the rear and slips the shaft from the bottom of the quiver. There is a minimum of arm movement and little, if any, sound. Center-back quivers are adjustable to take arrows of different lengths and they are covered at the top to protect the fletching against the elements. A final important feature of the center-back quiver is that the arrows are shielded from sharp-eyed animals. Light-colored arrows stand out in the woods when carried in a bow quiver, giving a signal each time the hunter moves his bow. With the center-back quiver, this is not the case.

Hunting With A Bowsight

THERE ARE THREE aiming methods for bowhunters—the so-called instinctive method, gap-shooting and shooting with a bowsight. The truly instinctive shooter is comparatively rare, while the gap method is a perfected technique by many field archers who use it in the hunting field.

Shooting with a sight was once almost unheard of among bowhunters. The principle of a sight was considered impractical in hunting, because it involved setting the sight pin at a fixed distance. Upon seeing game, the archer estimates the range and adjusts his sight setting before taking a shot. That's hardly a satisfactory procedure on the hunting trail.

More recently, special hunting sights have been developed and these have changed the opinions of many archers. As a result, a considerable number of bowmen now do use sights for hunting, either a single-pin sight or a multi-pin sight.

In using a single-pin sight, the bowhunter zeroes in to hit the target at a sensible hunting distance—30 or 35 yards, for example. After being set, the sight pin is fixed in position. By means of steady practice, the archer learns how much to elevate or lower his bow for other distances.

The multi-pin sight has two, three, or more pins, beads or peepholes, permanently set for different yardages. The bowman sizes up the range and then puts the right sighting pin, bead or peephole on the target. If the game appears to be at an intermediate distance, the archer holds so that the animal is lined up be-;tween two of the pins.

To use single and multi-pin bowsights effectively, the archer must judge distances accurately. Some archers have no such ability, but the skill can be developed by much practice. This knack is much more important in stalking and still-hunting than it is when hunting from a blind. Before settling into his blind, a bowman can step off the distances to various, trees, rocks and other marks around his position.

The pins on some hunting bowsights consist of three or four different-size rings or transparent plastic rectangles with a dot in the center. When the movable pins are in proper adjustment, they also serve as rangefinders. On spotting a deer, the bowhunter raises his bow and aligns one of the sight's circles or rectangles on the deer's chest. If the deer's chest cavity does not fill the space in the circle or plastic rectangle, the bowman lowers or raises his bow arm until the animal's vital area conforms to the outline of the sight.

One variation is a hunting sight which has four sight pins and, directly above the pins, a rangefinder grid. The hunter lines up the appropriate grid section on the deer, then uses the corresponding yardage pin.

It's a mistake for every bowhunter to use a sight. Some archers are opposed to the idea as a matter of principle. But the shooting aid is undoubtedly beneficial for those who are dissatisfied with their shooting with a bare bow and for those who are uncertain about where to hold at all ranges.

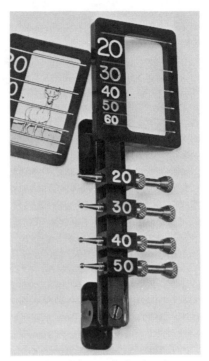

With this multi-pin hunting sight, the archer can tell where to hold by aligning the upper grid on the deer, as shown at upper left.

The Bowhunter's Kit

THE BOWHUNTER WITH the least equipment problem is the lucky archer who can step off his back porch, sit in a blind at the edge of his cornfield and wait for a deer to appear. All he requires is his bow and a handful of arrows. In fact, in most states, since he's hunting on his own property, he doesn't even need a license. If he shoots a deer he can drive his pickup to the cornfield and take the animal home in style. Few archers are able to hunt this way and few would want to, but it does eliminate all concern about how much gear to carry along on a hunt.

At the opposite extreme is the fellow who's going on a hunt in remote territory for the first time. He must make up for his lack of knowledge of the hunting area by including everything in his outfit that might possibly come in handy. When he's in doubt about taking something like insect repellent or a second set of insulated underwear, he throws them into his duffel anyway, reasoning that it's better to have too much than to be caught short.

If the hunt is a guided one, the guide should supply a list of suggested clothing and gear. But unless the guide is a bowhunter himself, he can't possibly think of all the paraphernalia needed to equip an archer properly for a hunt—things which a non-archer would never think of, such as bowstring wax, extra shooting glove, file, arrow-repair kit, pliers, waterproofing for feathers and a dozen more items of archery tackle.

The amount of gear a bowhunter takes on a hunt is roughly proportionate to the distance he travels from home and his past experience with the hunting area. In many parts of the country, an archer can drive from his home to good deer hunting in a few hours. All he needs is a day's supply of arrows and a few basic pieces of equipment. He can leave his lunch and even emergency articles in his car. On the other hand, the bowhunter traveling to a wilderness area must take, in addition to his tackle, enough stuff to keep him dry, warm and comfortable for the duration of his stay.

When the hunt is to be in a strange place, there are some things which are difficult to decide on beforehand. Take the number of arrows, for example. For deer hunting in most areas, a couple of dozen broadhead arrows is usually plenty because the bowman should be able to recover at least half of his missed shots. It all depends on the cover and the terrain. A hunt in a primitive area is a lot different from a trip to farming country where the deer are numerous. For a combined moose-caribou hunt in Alaska, an experienced bowhunting guide suggests a minimum of three dozen hunting arrows. Furthermore, since it's almost impossible to recover arrows in the tundra, the guide advises that five dozen are not too many for the average bowman on a 10-day hunt. Add to that another dozen blunts for small game and practice shots, and the archer's equipment looks like the archery department of a large sporting goods store.

Familiarity with the hunting area generally means a more efficient equipment list. A good example of this is the experience of an eastern bowman who went for three successive seasons to a hunting camp in Michigan. On the first trip, knowing little about the local conditions, he took everything he could think of that might have been useful. His outfit the following year was considerably different. It wasn't much smaller but it was altered as a result of what he'd learned about the country and the set-up in the hunting camp. He didn't include his sleeping bag because he found out the camp was heated and had an adequate supply of blankets. He didn't take along his machete either, since he found that the camp's proprietor supplied axes for blind building. He did take extra smoking supplies and some spare flashlight batteries, because the first year he had run low on cigarettes and pipe tobacco and he had used his flashlight more than he'd expected. On his third trip to the camp, his kit was exactly right—complete without being excessive.

The bowhunter who can drive to a distant hunting area with a companion has an advantage over the one who goes by air. With a station wagon or a luggage rack on a standard vehicle, the hunters can take more than enough equipment to see them through a two-week hunt. They can save time by driving non-stop, one sleeping while the other drives. And, if they both bag their game, they have plenty of room to bring back the trophies and meat.

Due to the mountain of tackle and equipment needed to shoot

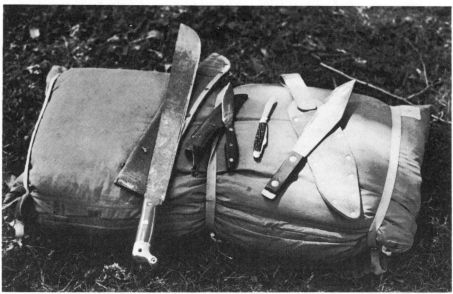

On a hunt far from home, should the bowhunter take his sleeping bag and machete? Which pieces of cutlery should he include? The answers depend on his knowledge of the hunting set-up.

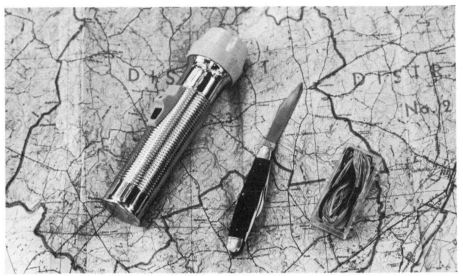

A flashlight, sturdy pocketknife and extra bowstring should be included in the bowhunter's kit. The topographic map (background) is often very useful.

big game with the bow and arrow, the traveling bowhunter may have serious problems if he makes his trip by commercial airline. Arrow boxes, quivers, a couple of bows, two pairs of boots, and plenty of clothing add up to considerable weight. If his gear exceeds the airline's weight limit for baggage, he's stuck with an extra charge, which can run rather high.

CLOTHING

After his shooting equipment the bowhunter's clothing is next in importance. What he takes depends on where he plans to hunt, but it's a wise bowhunter who makes allowances for a wide range of temperatures and climates. For obvious reasons the intelligent bowhunter won't take a snakebite kit to Newfoundland, although if he's been around he knows that cold-weather clothing may come in handy in some of the Deep South states during the winter. Fortunately, a down-filled jacket is light in weight and can be stowed into a small space in the duffel bag.

THE MASTER LIST

The bowhunter's master equipment list includes all the boots, socks, underwear, jackets, sweaters, foul-weather gear and other articles which are standard for most hunters. It also contains many necessities peculiar to bowhunters, plus an odd assortment of other items which often come in handy. It goes without saying that a bowhunter should take a spare bow on a hunt to some distant area. Likewise, he should have an extra glove, an armguard, and several bowstrings, well broken in. And, of course, he'll have a large heavy file for keeping his broadheads keen, as well as a simplified arrow-repair kit to replace broken nocks and beat-up points.

Where it's necessary to skin out animals before coming home, the bowman should have a stone for sharpening his hunting knife. Skinning a small whitetail may not take the edge off a knife, but with most of the larger animals, skinning and then fleshing the hide will dull a blade.

Boots, belts, knife sheaths and other leather articles may become stiff and develop squeaks, usually from drying out after a soaking rain. If there is sufficient room in the bowman's duffel, he should include a small can of neat'sfoot oil or some other preparation to soften leather articles and prevent them from creaking during a stalk.

The following is the advice of an expert bowhunter on the subject of his equipment.

"In addition to the bowhunter's major pieces of equipment, there are certain essentials which he should have in the pockets of his hunting jacket at all times. Though most hunters prefer a belt knife, a large clasp knife will take care of the field dressing job if it's sharp and big enough. A pocket first aid kit takes up little room and weighs only about an ounce. The extra bowstring is another small but important necessity. I usually carry half a dozen kitchen matches bound together with paraffin, which also waterproofs them. The matches are rolled up in a large pliofilm bag. It makes a neat container for taking a deer liver back to camp. For those who use shoulder quivers, the plastic bag can be placed around the tops of the arrows to keep the fletching dry during a rain. I also carry a length of rope, with a round wooden handle, for handling a big-game animal after the kill.

"The final item in my basic field kit is a police-type whistle, to be used only in case of emergency. The shrill, piercing blasts of the whistle carry much better than the human voice, particularly over the noise of a swift mountain stream or the roar of a strong wind blowing through the treetops. If a hunter carries a whistle, the other members of his party should be told about it so they'll know what to do if they hear it.

"Except when I'm hunting in open farmland, I add a compass to my pocket outfit, and, whenever possible, a topographic map of the country. Sometimes, depending on the circumstances, I take a small canteen and a flashlight. In much of the East, binoculars aren't necessary because of the dense growth; however, where the terrain is more open, they are often a big help. Other optional articles, which are sometimes very important, are a snakebite kit and a hand-warmer. Those of us who are dependent on eyeglasses should never be without an extra pair during a hunt. Sunglasses, too, are often a big help during the hunt."

In assembling his bowhunting kit, the archer should use plenty of ingenuity and adapt the various articles to his personal needs and the type of country he's hunting in. More than once a hunting trip that should have been enjoyable has turned into a miserable fiasco because of an inadequate outfit or because the hunter overlooked some small but vital article.

Where To Hit Big Game

SINCE IT'S IMPERATIVE for a bowhunter to pick an aiming spot instead of shooting for the whole animal, he should know where to try to hit a deer.

Almost every bowhunter knows he should aim for a deer's chest cavity, because that's where the animal's vital organs are—the heart and the large blood vessels that lead into it, the lungs and the liver. A hit there gives a razor-sharp broadhead the best chance to do its job. When the steel blades slice into any one of those organs, the hit will be fatal, although the deer may cover an amazing amount of ground before dropping.

When a broadhead hits an animal, there is no significant amount of shock such as is produced by a bullet fired from a high-powered rifle. The archer must depend on loss of blood, or hemorrhage, to kill a deer. The greater the hemorrhage and the quicker it happens, the better. To make a killing shot, the archer must have a knowledge of the animal's anatomy, he must shoot accurately and he must follow up his shot by tracking the quarry to the finish.

A deer's heart is lower in the chest than one may think. It's directly behind the place at which the upper foreleg joins the body.

From some angles, the hunter can see a shaded area or a fold of skin that pinpoints the heart's location. If the arrow hits there, the deer is as good as dead, although it may run for several hundred yards.

An arrow that barely misses the heart may sever one of the arteries that branch from the organ. When that happens, the blood trail is often heavier than it is when the heart itself is pierced. The deer may go some distance, but there's little difficulty in following the trail because of the massive hemorrhage.

A hit that is a bit high or a little to the rear will usually hit the lungs, another sure kill. A lung-shot deer, although practically dead on its feet, can cover some ground before going down. Lung shots are supposed to cause a good blood trail, but the bowhunter cannot always count on this.

A deer's liver is to the rear of the heart and more toward the center of its body, although it is in the forward half. Liver hits are usually effective but they can result in extended tracking, sometimes with almost no blood trail. If the liver's connecting blood vessels are cut, the blood loss is greater and the trail is easier to follow and usually shorter.

A broadside chance at a deer may seem like an ideal shot because the animal presents a large target. In a practical sense, however, much of the seemingly large target is useless; the arrow will not kill unless it hits a vital spot.

The quartering shot from the rear is by far the best. The silhouette is not so large, but more of what you see is vulnerable tissue. In fact, if you aim for the right spot and your arrow finds its mark, it's possible for a single broadhead to rip into three vital organs— liver, lungs and heart. Another very important thing about the quartering shot from behind is that the animal is less likely to spot the archer than he is when the deer is broadside. With a rear-quartering shot, the right aiming point is just ahead of the place where the hind leg joins the body in the lower third of the deer's body.

The front-quartering shot and the head-on shot are the least desirable. The deer is more likely to detect the bowhunter when he draws, and the deer's bones are greater obstacles from the front than they are from side and rear angles.

A shot at a deer's hind end, while certainly not the most desirable, can be surprisingly effective, especially with a comparatively heavy bow. It's not a shot bowhunters dream about, but it's better than a facing shot. There's very little chance that the deer will pick up the movement of your draw. The silhouette is small, but that's really a blessing. The archer aims dead-center for that rear end. If he misses, it's fairly certain that it will be a clean miss. If the arrow hits, it's highly likely that the broadhead will plow through to some of the vital organs up front.

There's no doubt that it's best to aim for the chest cavity, but if the arrow strikes elsewhere all is not lost. Several things may happen. The broadhead may cause a superficial flesh wound, or it may lodge in a bone. In such cases, the deer usually recovers. On the other hand, a hit outside the chest cavity may be fatal. If there's a fair blood trail and if the archer knows his tracking, he'll probably find the deer.

Even when an arrow goes wide of the vital organs, it often cuts an artery. The broadhead may not touch an artery on impact, but it can still be fatal. Because of the deer's running or because of protruding brush, the broadhead works back and forth, cutting additional tissue and perhaps an important blood vessel. This kind of hit is often better than a lung or liver hit, because it produces an unmistakable blood trail and a fairly quick kill.

When a broadhead penetrates a deer's brain or spine, it usually falls on the spot, though it may take another shot to finish the animal. Such shots are lucky accidents, since bowhunters rarely take deliberate aim at a deer's brain or spine.

While ground-based bowhunters don't usually aim at an animal's spine, the spine over the chest cavity is often the best choice for an archer in a tree stand. For instance, if the deer is directly under the archer, the spine is the logical target.

The thing to avoid is the gut shot. Even when fatal, an arrow in a deer's paunch may leave no blood trail. There may be a great amount of internal hemorrhage but little or no external bleeding.

Whether or not to wait after a hit is the subject of endless discussion among bowhunters. The consensus seems to be that the hunter should wait from a half-hour to an hour before following the deer if the arrow struck the liver area or the rear half of the deer. If he's true to form, the animal will bed down after an initial run. After following his trail, the archer should find him in a weak, stiffened condition.

If the hit is in a non-vital section forward of the midsection, it's often smart to keep pushing the animal. An embedded arrow will continue to cut. Even if the arrow passes through the deer or drops out, the deer should not be given an opportunity to lie down so that the severed blood vessels can clot.

If there's a definite hit in the chest cavity and plenty of blood, it doesn't matter whether the bowman waits or not, because the deer is undoubtedly finished. When the arrow misses the chest section but cuts a big artery, the archer will know it, because of the unbelievable quantity of blood at the scene and leading away from it. The bowhunter can then relax, because the dead deer will be waiting for him at the end of the bloody trail.

When something, perhaps rain or falling snow, may obliterate the blood trail, it's not practical for the bowman to wait after a shot. In certain sections of heavily-populated states, the woods are so full of hunters that the hunter is obliged to follow his deer almost immediately after a good hit. If he doesn't, someone else may claim the animal. The deer should also be followed at once if the light is failing. This holds true particularly on a warm fall evening, when the carcass may spoil during the night. During cold weather, the bowman can take up the trail the next morning. He should be leery of following a blood trail at night with a flashlight, since a suspicious game warden may charge him with jacklighting.

Another extremely important part of bowhunting ethics is to find the arrow after a shot. It's not always possible to see clearly whether the arrow hit or missed. Sometimes an arrow passes completely through a deer, and the animal shows very little reaction, which leads an inexperienced bowhunter to think he missed his target.

There have been cases where the archer thought he missed the animal. But upon recovering his arrow, he found blood on it. If he had not found his arrow, he would have been under the impression that his shot went wide.

By examining the arrow after it's found, an experienced bowhunter can tell roughly where the deer was hit. Green digestive matter on the shaft obviously indicates a gut shot. Dark red blood usually means the heart or an artery has been struck. Lung shots show up as bubbly blood along the arrow shaft, while a greasy, neutral-colored coating on the shaft and feathers means a superficial flesh wound, the arrow passing through the fatty tissues near the surface.

Practice For Bowhunting

WHEN THE HUNTING archer warms up for the deer season (and it should not be just a few days before the season opens) he should

For hunting practice, shoot at simulated deer target.

put on the same clothes he wears in the hunting field. He should use his hunting bow, which is equipped exactly as it would be on a hunt—string silencers, bow sock and a bow quiver if he uses one on a hunt.

The target should be a simulated deer, so that the archer will not become dependent on aiming at a bullseye. This way, he'll get into the habit of picking a particular point on the deer's anatomy. It's advisable to use a lifesize deer target, available from most good dealers and from the better mail order outfits.

Well before the hunting season starts, the bowman should use broadheads for his practice shooting. The hunting heads may weigh the same as his field points but they usually fly differently than field arrows. If the bowman has good archery form and exceptionally well-tuned tackle, his broadheads fly almost exactly the same as the field points.

It's best not to stand in one place and shoot arrow after arrow at the practice target. For the best hunting practice, the archer should shoot two or three arrows from one position, then move forward or backward, so that his practicing takes in a variety of ranges. Instead of taking all of his shots at a broadside target, he should shift from right to left and vice versa.

The most beneficial hunting practice is roving around fields and woods, taking random shots with broadheads from different distances. The targets may be clumps of grass, or a patch of leaves or any other object which stands out on the ground. If the archer has some blunts in his quiver, he can take some shots at stumps and logs. The important consideration here is to get some practice from different ranges and in natural hunting country. Again, his clothing, footwear and archery gear should be the same as he uses on an actual hunt.

If the bowman gets most of his shots at game from a standing position, he should practice accordingly. If he hunts mostly from a seat in a blind or if he sometimes sits on a log or a stump in the hunting field, he should do some practicing from a seated position. Those who prefer tree stands should do most of their preparatory shooting from a corresponding elevation, because shooting downward is tricky, particularly when the bowman must aim from different angles. He may get a shot at a deer directly below or at one that's at a 45-degree angle from his perch.

The practice shooting should include many shots from awkward, unusual positions, in order to prepare the archer for bowhunting situations. For example, suppose the bowman—either standing or seated—observes a deer on his right. Because of the noise factor, he can't shift his feet and assume a proper stance. So he must twist his upper torso and try to get off an accurate shot.

Since it's possible that an archer may get a shot at a deer while he's kneeling, he should do some practicing from that position. He should also try some practice shots with one foot on a higher level

Practice from a variety of different positions, including kneeling.

than the other. It's a good idea to shoot occasionally from behind a screen of brush and from behind a tree trunk with the body leaning to one side. That, too, helps to prepare the hunting archer for the realities of an actual hunt. Likewise, he should make a point of practicing at least a few times during a rain. Then he'll know how his tackle is affected by the rain and whether his shooting suffers from the discomfort.

During a hunt, there may be an occasion where the bowhunter must draw and release in one motion. To prepare himself for this, the archer should try a few snap-shots. While it's certainly not recommended as a shooting technique and it can result in picking up a bad habit, the ability to snap-shoot accurately may come in handy.

By the same token, the practicing bowhunter should try a few shots that are beyond the range of his accuracy. Although the average bowhunter should not take 60-yard shots, there's no harm in his trying a few arrows from that distance. If nothing else, it will impress on him the fact that he can't place his shots accurately beyond a certain range.

Every part of the practice sessions should be done with realism in mind, so the bowhunter will be accustomed in his shooting to the actual conditions of a hunt.

In practicing with broadheads, the archer must be especially careful. The path to the target must be free of obstructions which could cause an arrow to glance off to one side. The area behind the target must be a place where people or domestic animals do not wander around.

The target, itself—or rather the target backstop, is often a problem when shooting broadheads. Straw archery matts are not recommended, because broadheads are hard to remove and when withdrawn usually pull out a considerable amount of the straw, thus lessening the life-span of the matt. The same applies to bales of hay or straw, although they are effective arrow-stoppers. On most field archery courses where the bales are used for backstops, a series of bales are set up exclusively for broadheads and archers are not permitted to shoot hunting arrows at the regular bales on the course.

Mounds of sod are good arrow-stoppers; so are sandpiles. It's possible to obtain plastic materials for arrow backstops.

Needless to say, between the time a bowhunter concludes his pre-season practice shooting and the time he enters the hunting field, his broadheads must be thoroughly sharpened.

Where To Hunt
and Landowner Relations

WITHIN A GIVEN state, there may be year-to-year or decade-to-decade changes in the most favorable sections for arrowing a deer. To find out currently where a bowhunter has the best chance of collecting a trophy, the best avenue of approach is through the state game department. Since it's the responsibility of that agency to promote the maximum propagation of game animals and then to see that sportsmen utilize the game supply, in most states the wildlife departments are very cooperative.

On request, they can advise bowmen where their best chances will be, and they are generally most anxious that hunters find satisfactory sport. In return, it behooves the responsible sportsman to familiarize himself with the hunting laws and to obey them.

In the eastern part of the country—the typical habitat of the whitetail deer—the best bowhunting is usually in the farm-fringe areas. Mostly, these are acreages where the crops are good and nearby there are wood patches and forests where the animals can take refuge. In vast forests and timbered areas it's possible that the deer-per-square-mile ratio may be better, but deep woods are not necessarily synonymous with good bowhunting.

In some parts of the country—notably the Southwest—huge ranches are posted, the hunting rights leased to affluent syndicates of sportsmen. There are other sections where U.S.-owned public lands are leased to cattlemen, who assume the right to say who may hunt on the property.

When the archer plans to hunt in his own region, it should not be difficult for him to investigate the best possibilities. He should contact the state game authorities and the archery leaders in the locale. In this way he can learn the best deer areas in the state and the top bowhunting sections. He should also request a county-by-county breakdown of the deer kill by archers during the previous season. In quite a few states there's a problem of crop depredation as a result of increasing deer populations. The state game department can supply information on this also. The bowman, in turn, can be fairly certain that he will be welcomed by landowners in those areas.

The increasing trend toward the posting of privately-owned hunting lands presents an obstacle, although in most cases it's not an insurmountable one. There are two main reasons why farmers post their land. One is to realize some extra income from their property, which, they reason, supports a certain number of deer. Therefore, they feel they're entitled to be paid something by hunters, who reap some of the wildlife crop.

The other reason for posting land is that the landowners object to high-powered rifles being fired on their property. Added to this is the regrettable fact that too many hunters are so irresponsible and inconsiderate that they neglect to close gates, litter the fields and have no respect for valuable livestock and growing crops.

In many cases, archers can overcome this prejudice by approaching the landowner and explaining how they hunt. When the farmer is convinced that the archers are responsible sportsmen and that they don't disturb the wildlife and domestic stock, he may grant them permission to hunt.

A common practice is for groups of bowhunters or archery clubs, like gunners' organizations, to lease the hunting rights to a choice section of hunting land. The bowhunter would be wise to keep on good terms with the landowner during the off-season, whether or not he pays for hunting. Sending Christmas cards and bringing gifts for the farmer's wife and children, plus a box of cigars or some similar token of appreciation to the landowner, himself, are some ways for bowhunters to promote a cordial and lasting relationship with a property owner.

North American Big Game

WHILE THE FOREGOING bowhunting principles apply chiefly to deer—the bowman's most popular target—in a general way the same fundamentals are applicable to hunting other big-game animals. It's a fact that the archer who is skilled in deer hunting is qualified to go after other animals. Some of the latter, though perhaps larger and more glamorous, may seem like easy prey after deer hunting.

BEAR, MOOSE, ETC.

Of the other big-game animals, it's probable that more black bears are taken by bowhunters than any other species. Despite their

Aside from deer, the black bear is probably the bowhunter's favorite quarry. Note bow quiver with cover over the broadheads.

fierce reputation among non-hunters, black bears are not ordinarily dangerous creatures to hunt. Still, there's always the chance that a bruin may be a mean one or may have a toothache or could be suffering from a painful wound. If that's the case, he's unpredictable and may come for the hunter. A female with cubs can be aggressive, too, if she thinks anyone is after one of her offspring. So the element of danger lurks in the background of bear hunting and is an attraction for the more adventurous bowhunters. Some archers carry handguns on a bear hunt, but most experienced bowhunters after bear are armed only with their archery gear.

Another sporty aspect about hunting the black bear is that he is exceedingly wary and cunning. He's often thought of as a sluggish, clumsy animal, but with the right motivation he can move quickly and run fast. His senses of hearing and smell are at least as keen as those of a deer, but he does not have the deer's curiosity. So, all in all, the black bear is a formidable trophy for the bowman.

Some black bears are tracked by the hounds of hunting guides. When the bear is treed or cornered by the dogs, the archer moves in for a shot. However, the favored method of hunting blackies with archery tackle is to lure them to baits that are placed near a blind or a tree stand. It's also possible to get shooting at black bears at the garbage dumps of some northern villages and lumber camps. Black bears are more nocturnal than deer are, so the hunter sometimes has a long wait until a bear shows himself. They're tough animals but a well-directed broadhead with its blood-letting capability is lethal.

The big bears—grizzlies, Alaskan brown bears and Polar bears—are larger, tougher and fiercer. All three have been taken by archers, including several lady bowhunters. Grizzlies are hunted from tree stands and along the banks of streams where they gorge themselves on spawning salmon. Hunting brown bears involves an experienced guide, who usually backs up the bowman with a firearm. Hunting Polar bears is a highly specialized activity, since it takes place on the ice caps of the Arctic. It has been curtailed recently, because survival of the big white bear as a species of wildlife is believed to be endangered.

Fred Bear with his huge Alaska brownie, taken with one arrow.

Here's Fred Bear with a fine bull moose.

Caribous are big and unpredictable, make spectacular trophies.

Moose, caribou and elk, with their large racks, make spectacular trophies in an archer's den. They're big, challenging animals, and any bowhunter who takes one can be proud of his accomplishment. Of the three, the caribou is the least smart and also the least predictable. Moose and elk hunting is synonymous with stalking, but during the rutting season both species can be attracted by calling.

An archer must be in first-class physical condition to attempt hunting for Rocky Mountain goats, and for the three recognized species of wild sheep—Bighorns, Stone sheep and Dall sheep. Good lung power and a lot of climbing are required. Because they're in remote regions, a guide or outfitter is needed to pack the hunters into the high country.

The pronghorn antelope, due to its keen eyes and open habitat, is a difficult adversary for the archer's short-range weapons. For this reason, one of the most practical methods of bowhunting for pronghorns is by building a blind near a spot where the animals come to water.

Few jaguars have been taken by bowmen, mainly because of their limited range in the dense jungles of Latin America. It's a different story with the cougar, or mountain lion. Each year, a sizable number of the big cats have fallen to bowmen. Cougar hunting is done with a guide and a pack of hounds. It may seem like an easy matter for an archer to shoot down a treed mountain lion. But the feat is made difficult by the tension of the hunt, especially at the end of a long, grueling chase in rugged country.

OTHER BIG-GAME ANIMALS

The javelina is not a large animal and his range is limited to a few states in the Southwest and in Central America. Nevertheless, bowmen from many parts of the country travel to javelina country to hunt the little tuskers.

On Catalina Island, a herd of Spanish goats provides sporty shooting for bowhunters. They're tough animals and very wary, traveling in large bands for security. The old ones, with wide spreads on their horns, make fine trophies.

Some Texas ranches offer hunting for Corsican rams, or mouflon, on a fee basis. Although they look no wilder than domestic sheep when seen in a large pasture from a distance, mouflon are difficult for the archer to approach within range. Their natural evasiveness is aided by the fact they they stay

Although javelinas are not large, they're a challenge for bowhunters.

Wild Spanish goats, like this one taken on Catalina Island, are tough, wary animals.

Wild European boars are difficult to subdue, and are coveted trophies by many bowhunters.

together in large herds, always with at least one old ram as the sentry.

Wild European boars are coveted as trophies by many bowhunters. They're exceptionally difficult to subdue with any weapon, including archery tackle, and their curved white tusks make impressive mounted trophies. The customary hunting procedure is with a pack of hounds. The most popular hunting areas for wild boar are in the mountains of North Carolina and Tennessee.

HUNTING PRESERVES

In some parts of the country there are commercial hunting preserves, a few of which are exclusively for bowmen. A variety of game is offered, including wild boar, fallow deer, Spanish goats and wild sheep. The quality of the hunting depends on the management of the preserve and its size. On the larger spreads, a bowhunt is relatively close to hunting the same animals in the wild. On some of the smaller preserves, the fenced-in feature makes it a somewhat synthetic form of hunting. Veteran bowhunters frown on the preserve concept, saying that it lacks the element of chance and requires little or no hunting skills. However, up to a point, a bowhunt on a commercial preserve gives some encouragement to a novice bowhunter, who has the chance to see what his tackle can do.

SAFARIS

At one time, a bowhunt in Africa was considered the ultimate accomplishment among some hunting archers. For the present, African bowhunts are a thing of the past. It's possible that conditions there will stabilize and that bowmen will be welcome sometime in the future, but the current political unrest in Africa in general rules out any serious bowhunting safaris.

A few bowhunters have shot elephants and other African big game, but only one bowman, Bob Swinehart, has succeeded in taking the Big Five of Africa: elephant, lion, Cape buffalo, rhino and leopard.

This bowhunter is Bob Swinehart, the first archer to take the big five of African game—elephant, lion, rhino, buffalo and leopard.

ART YOUNG AWARDS

The National Field Archery Association provides recognition to those members who bag native North American big-game animals with the bow. Under this program, named for the great Arthur Young, the successful hunter receives an attractive pin in the shape of an arrowhead, plus a cloth patch. The pins for subsequent Art Young Big Game Awards are in the shape of arrows. The first three are golden arrow pins. If the bowman scores on additional trophies, his fifth, sixth and seventh awards are crossed-arrow pins. Upon completion of the series of awards over the years, the bowhunter may look forward to getting the Art Young Master Bowhunting Medal, but first he must meet similar requirements on small game (see later section on Bowhunting For Small Game; also Rules for Art Young Small Game Award, Part X).

The Pope and Young Club

IT'S NOT UNUSUAL now for bowhunters to pass up shots at legal big-game animals, although at one time it would have been unheard of. These are the selective bowhunters of today. If the animal is not of trophy size, the selective bowhunter prefers not to shoot. He'll continue to hunt, not satisfied until he can line up his broadhead on an above-average animal. During the final part of his hunt he may lower his standards and shoot an ordinary deer

Some of the trophies recorded by the Pope and Young Club.

Members of the Pope and Young Club are interested in taking outstanding specimens of North American big game.

or moose or whatever he's hunting, but only after he has exhausted the possibilities of taking one which will make the record book. In a two-deer area, he may shoot the first one that presents a shot, but the second deer must meet his standards.

This archer is a trophy bowhunter. In most cases he's not interested in simply hanging another mounted head on the wall of his den. He simply prefers to shoot a good specimen rather than an average or sub-average animal. He has taken enough game with the bow that he does not feel the need to prove his marksmanship and his hunting skills. Like the majority of bowhunters, he probably first became interested in the sport because of its challenge. Now, having met the challenge of taking numerous big-game animals with the bow, he wants an even more difficult challenge—downing a superior animal with his archery tackle. Fortunately for these hunting archers, there's an organization which encourages selective bowhunting by maintaining a list of the best trophies shot by archers.

The organization which supervises North American big-game records for bowhunters is the Pope and Young Club. Its name honors Dr. Saxton Pope, the father of modern bowhunting, and his friend, Art Young. In that way, the club resembles the Boone and

Crockett Club, the rifleman's organization which is named for two famous pioneers in the hunting field. There are other similarities.

When the Pope and Young Club was first organized it was recognized by the respected, already established Boone and Crockett Club. The latter club granted the bowmen permission to use the measuring system which had been carefully worked out over a number of years by a group of scientists and sportsmen. Thus, nationally, there's a standard method of scoring each of the various species of North American big-game animals. The scores are not based on weight or the number of antler points, or—in the case of bears and cougars—on overall length. Instead, there's a formula for each species, based on the dimensions of the skull, antlers or horns. So that unusual antler formations can be recorded, there are separate non-typical classifications for whitetails, mule deer and Coues deer.

Both the Pope and Young and the Boone and Crockett Clubs maintain permanent archives which contain the records of the best specimens taken throughout the continent. This serves the interests

A fine Canada moose and a Rocky Mountain goat are among the bowhunting trophies of the Pope and Young Club.

of scientists as well as sportsmen, in that we can ascertain whether the quality of the various animal species is improving or deteriorating. The archives also reveal which parts of North America harbor the best examples of the different species.

Like the Boone and Crockett Club, the bowhunters' organization promotes the concept of quality hunting, giving archer-sportsmen an incentive to seek the higher challenge of bagging exceptionally good specimens. When the measurements of an animal exceed certain minimum scores, the animal is officially declared a trophy of record and is entered on the books as such, along with the hunter's name and the date and location of the kill. Among the different species, the minimum scores of the Pope and Young Club are about 20 percent lower than those of the Boone and Crockett Club. If a bowhunter takes a particularly fine trophy, it may exceed both the Pope and Young and the Boone and Crockett minimum scores, in which case it will go on the record books of both organizations.

Below is the list of minimum scores for the species recognized by the Pope and Young Club. It should be noted that the minimum scores for some animals have been revised upward in recent years. These species are: whitetail deer, mule deer, Yellowstone elk, barren ground caribou, Alaska-Yukon moose, Rocky Mountain goat, grizzly bear, black bear, polar bear and jaguar.

Whitetail deer, typical	125
Whitetail deer, non-typical	150
Mule deer, typical	145
Mule deer, non-typical	160
Columbian blacktail deer	90
Coues deer, typical	68
Coues deer, non-typical	78
Yellowstone elk (wapiti)	240
Roosevelt elk (Olympic elk)	210
Woodland caribou	220
Mountain caribou	265
Barren ground caribou	300
Pronghorn (antelope)	57
Wyoming moose	115
Canada moose	135
Alaska-Yukon moose	170
Bighorn sheep	130
Dall or white sheep	120
Stone sheep	120
Desert bighorn sheep	115
Bison	80
Rocky Mountain goat	40

Alaska brown bear	20
Grizzly bear	19
Black bear	18
*Polar bear	20
*Jaguar	14
Cougar	13

*No entries will be accepted in these categories until further notice.

After several years of working out the organizational details, the Pope and Young Club in 1963 was formally incorporated as a scientific, non-profit organization. The sportsman who steered the fledgling group through its first stages was Glenn St. Charles, a well-known bowhunter from the State of Washington.

The club's membership consists of a maximum of 100 members, more than 500 associate members, and an elite group of over 30 senior members. In order to become a regular member, a bowhunter must have bagged at least three different species of North American big game, at least one of which meets the minimum score in its species. Senior members must have been regular members for five years and must have taken four big-game species, three of which meet or exceed the minimum scores. Due to the stiff requirements of these two classes of membership, the Pope and Young Club is one of the most exclusive hunting groups in the country.

Associate members of the Pope and Young Club are those bowhunters who support the records program and the conservation concepts of the organization. Some of them are eligible for regular membership and are placed on a waiting list pending a vacancy in the limited roster of regular members.

The honor of having a trophy listed in the bowhunting records is open to any archer, with or without any affiliation with any archery organization. All that's needed to have your trophy recorded in the Pope and Young Club books is to have it checked and approved by an official measurer. Needless to say, the trophy must have been shot with the bow and arrow during the legal hunting season, and in conformity with the recognized rules of fair chase. Under those rules, game animals taken under the following conditions are not eligible:

1. Helpless in or because of deep snow
2. Helpless in water, on ice, or in a trap
3. While confined behind fences as on game farms or preserves
4. In defiance of game laws, after legal hours, or out of season
5. By jacklighting or shining at night

6. From any power vehicle or power boat

7. By the use of any aircraft for herding, driving, landing alongside any animal or herd, or using an aircraft to communicate with or direct a hunter on the ground

8. By any other method considered by the board of directors of the Pope and Young Club as unsportsmanlike.

HOW TO HAVE YOUR TROPHY CHECKED

Let's say a bowman bags a deer with a rack that he thinks is of trophy rank. The first step is to request an official measuring form from the Pope and Young Club records chairman, Scott M. Showalter, Box 1001, Garden City, Kansas 67846.

The form shows the step-by-step procedure for scoring the trophy. It may seem a bit complicated at first, but it's not too difficult to get the hang of it enough to make a preliminary measurement. The archer checks it out and finds that, indeed, the rack tops the minimum figure. His next move is to take or send the trophy to the nearest official measurer, whose name and address he has obtained from the club's records chairman. Scattered through key points in the U.S., Pope and Young Club measurers are volunteers and make no charge for the measuring service.

Before transporting the antlers, preferably unmounted, to the measurer, the bowhunter should contact him and find out when it would be convenient for the measurer to score the trophy. The measurer scores the rack or skull officially and returns it, notifying the hunter of the results. If it qualifies for trophy status the trophy owner sends the completed form to the records chairman, together with his check for $20. The bowman will then be informed that the trophy has made the record books and he will receive a citation.

Until 1970 there was no charge to the archer, except for the expense of shipping the trophy to the measurer. Because of mounting costs it became necessary to set a $20 fee for the listing and a citation award suitable for framing.

A bowhunter may be in for additional honors if the trophy is a truly outstanding example of its species. While the odds are against it, the head may set a new record. Even though the rack is not sufficiently sizable to move into first place on the record books, there is a chance that it will rank high in the biannual recording periods of the Pope and Young Club.

When a bowman bags a fine trophy which looks as if it could be a winner in the Pope and Young competition or a potential new record, he should defer having it mounted. Before a trophy can be declared a new record or a biannual winner, it must be checked by a panel of expert measurers. This requires the owner to ship the trophy to a designated place. Shipping problems are lessened when an unmounted rack or skull is sent. Also, before a final confirmation as a winner or a new record, a mounted trophy must be subjected to some minor surgery to determine that the antlers or horns or skull have not been tampered with. Bears, cougars and jaguars are scored on the basis of the combined length and width dimensions of the skull. Obviously, it is impossible to take these measurements accurately if the head is mounted and covered with fur.

Not all bowhunters listed in the record book are deliberate trophy hunters. Many of them are average hunting bowmen who shoot at the first legal animal to come into range. Luckily, sometimes that animal turns out to be an award-winner and the hunter is appropriately honored. He could even be a complete neophyte in bowhunting. One whitetail buck shattered the existing first-place record score and remained in first place for several years. It was shot by a greenhorn archer who was on his first hunt.

It's not necessary for the trophy to have been bagged currently. If a bowman shot a trophy-class animal a decade ago but has just learned of the Pope and Young Club, he is eligible to enter the trophy in the current two-year recording period.

Bowhunting
With Tranquilizers

A RATHER CONTROVERSIAL bowhunting technique has come up in recent years—hunting with drug-tipped arrows. The first shot by this method was taken in 1960 during an experimental hunt organized by wildlife biologists. They were assisted by a veteran bowhunter who used a special arrowhead tipped with a hypodermic needle, which was loaded with a then-new drug called succinylcholine chloride.

This drug was at first available only to qualified professionals. Medical men—mostly psychiatrists—have used it as a tranquilizer for some of their patients. Veterinarians find it useful as an anaesthetic and also to put animals to sleep permanently. Wildlife scientists had been using it in their studies, propelling a hypodermic dart by means of a CO_2 dart gun. The quick-acting drug can be varied so as to immobilize and relax a deer or, in a stronger dose, to dispatch the animal in a few seconds.

The purpose of that experimental bow-hunt was not to establish drug arrows as hunting equipment for archers, in general, but to determine whether the hypo-drug combination is practical with archery tackle. If so, the scientists themselves were interested in using it in their work, since drug arrows offer certain advantages over the dart gun. The special arrow tips are less costly than the hypo darts, and the bow makes less noise than the gun, which often scatters deer herds when the biologist wants to take several specimens from a single deer herd.

When the news of the tranquilizer arrow was released, it was met with mixed reactions. Many bowhunters were horrified at the prospect of drug arrows becoming widely used, while some believed the new development to be a boon to the sport. The veteran hunting archers disliked the idea on moral grounds as well as on the basis of sportsmanship. They also disapproved of it because it tends to eliminate the need for accurate shooting in the hunting field, thus reducing the high standards called for by successful bowhunters. There were some who applauded the principle because it would reduce the number of cripples and unrecovered deer. The proficient, concerned bowhunters countered by charging that unrecovered game is part of any form of hunting and that it's the result, not of the weapon which is used, but of a lack of shooting and hunting skill on the part of the hunter, regardless of whether he uses a bow or a gun.

Since that time, succinylcholine chloride has been made available to more of the public. In the late Sixties, it was accepted for legal bowhunting in the State of Mississippi by most bowhunters as well as the director of the State's game and fish commission.

The thing which really spread the concept of hunting with chemicals in Mississippi was the development of the "pod," a rubber-and-plastic device which contains the drug in powder form and which fits on a hunting arrow immediately behind the broadhead. It weighs only about one grain—not enough to affect the arrow's flight. The hypo, by contrast, is heavier and awkward to shoot.

When the broadhead penetrates, the contact of the animal tissue peels back the soft rubber on the shaft, releasing the deadly drug into the bloodstream. If for some reason the drug does not take ef-

A broadhead and a drug-filled pod. On contact, the rubber covering of the pod peels back and the powdered drug is released.

fect or the pod doesn't work properly, there's still a chance that the broadhead will do the job itself by severing important blood vessels.

It's possible to make a simplified version of the pod by snipping off the neck of a small balloon, which is stretched over the arrow shaft and then filled with succinylcholine chloride powder. The more refined pod consists of a cylindrical sleeve which fits snugly over the shaft. The plastic sleeve is covered with the balloon neck and the drug is inserted between the rubber and the plastic. The front end of the rubber, while tight, is free enough to peel back; the rear end is secured with a small rubber washer.

While sportsmen in Mississippi are favorable toward the drug form of bowhunting, the situation in most of the other states is quite different. For years there has been a stipulation in the bowhunting laws of most states that "poison-tipped" arrows are illegal. Is a lethal dose of a tranquilizer—enough to cause death in a matter of minutes or less—a poison? This may be a question for the courts to decide, but at least one state has added to its bowhunting laws a provision that poison-tipped "or chemical-laden" arrowheads are illegal.

There's no question about the destructive power and the effectiveness of arrows equipped with succinylcholine chloride. A deer hit practically anywhere but on the lower legs and antlers will die within seconds after the chemical enters the blood stream. The animal's locomotor system fails, followed by a collapse of the respiratory system. Finally, the last vital organ, the heart, stops pumping. Traces of the drug generally disappear in about an hour. Succinylcholine chloride is non-toxic and does not affect the

215

edibility of the meat. Some people believe that the drug will not work on members of the hog family, due to their tough hide, layers of fat, and body chemistry, although wildlife scientists do not agree.

Its effect on humans is lethal also. The massive overdose used by some Mississippi bowhunters would finish a man quickly, though he could be revived if artificial respiration were applied promptly. When physicians use the drug, it is dripped slowly into the patient and survival equipment is nearby.

Another objection to the use of drugs in archery-hunting is that some game officials believe it to be an ideal weapon for poachers. State and city police departments also dislike the introduction of a new murder weapon which could not be traced through an autopsy and which makes no report when it is shot.

The final objection to bowhunters using drug-tipped arrows comes from the serious bowhunters themselves. A trophy animal killed in this way would not be recognized in the record books of the Pope and Young Club, whose rules declare it a violation of the rules of fair chase.

Bowhunting For Small Game

IN THIS CONTEXT, the term "small game" is used loosely, because it includes predators and vermin, along with game animals.

The N.F.A.A.'s program for the Art Young Small Game Award is similar to the Big Game Award in that the first award is a silver arrowhead pin. Subsequent awards are in the shape of silver arrows, until three have been earned. After that, the next three awards are crossed arrows. After he completes the series of seven small-game awards, the bowman will have finished half of the requirements for the Art Young Master Bowhunting Medal. The other half is the series of seven big-game awards.

The small-game award is more interesting than the big-game award, and in one sense, it's more challenging. First, because of the variety of eligible animals, it permits and encourages the archer to hunt the year round. Second, with a few exceptions, it requires that the hunter take a variety of small game. Otherwise, if an archer kills any one of these— wolf, coyote, bobcat, lynx, javelina and wild turkey— he may also earn the award. The smaller animals are rated on a point system, the archer earning an award when he has accumulated 30 points. The more challenging species earn more points than do those that are considered easier to shoot. Thus, a bow-killed fox is good for 10 points, while a prairie dog scores three points. Stressing variety, the program requires that archers take at least three small-game species to earn each award. (For the N.F.A.A. rules for the Art Young Small Game Award, see Part X.)

Thanks to the N.F.A.A. small-game award program, archers have an incentive to hunt over a 12-month span. Though it doesn't get the attention that many bowhunters think it deserves, the small-game program is one of the most commendable activities of the N.F.A.A. With the list of game covered by the program, it's possible for an archer to hunt some kind of small game every day of the year. The more he uses his tackle during the winter, spring and summer, the better prepared he'll be for the deer season in the fall and the better all-around bowhunter he'll become.

The best example of this is the woodchuck. A bowhunter who can shoot several woodchucks during the summer months has given proof of his qualifications to hunt deer. To a great extent, the same requirements are present in hunting groundhogs and deer: scouting the hunting area to find the best place to hunt, stealth, the ability

A bowhunter who can hunt woodchucks successfully has the qualifications for deer hunting.

Bowhunting for chucks calls for many of the techniques of deer hunting.

to keep movements to a minimum, patience and marksmanship. In fact, the last-named requirement is possibly more necessary in chuck hunting than in deer hunting, because the chuck is a much smaller target. Also, he's a tough little critter and the broadhead, in order to be effective, must strike a vital zone.

Then too, the N.F.A.A. small-game program encompasses predators, such as foxes and crows, and objectionable reptiles, like rattlesnakes and Gila monsters, plus carp, gars, sharks and stingrays.

Hunting Seasons and Regulations

BOWHUNTING LAWS

In many states, archers have the most liberal rules and regulations of all sportsmen. In general, the deer seasons are satisfyingly long and in some states it's possible to take two deer per year.

As far as equipment is concerned, few bowhunters have any reasonable complaints. When bowhunting was first recognized by state wildlife departments, the game managers had very little knowledge about the newly-revived sport. In some cases, they sought advice from the archery leaders in their states, who assisted the authorities in establishing sensible regulations.

Today, there are not many restrictions on the specifications of bows and arrows in hunting. Bowmen must use steel broadheads, of course, and they must be a minimum of 7/8-inch in width in most states. Poison-tipped and explosive-tipped arrows are prohibited in the majority of states.

As for the draw weight of a legal hunting bow, there is not much uniformity in the laws of the various states. At least one state places no restriction on bow weight in the belief that a bowhunter is intelligent enough and a good enough sportsman to use an efficient weapon. Some states specify that the bow must pull a minimum of 30 pounds at 28 inches. A few states require that the hunting bow must be capable of propelling a hunting arrow at least 125 yards. That regulation is practically unenforcable in the field, since in typical deer country it's not often possible to find a level, cleared area of 125 yards.

In the average state there's a spirit of cooperation between the game authorities and the archers. In fact, a sizable number of game department personnel are enthusiastic bowhunters themselves. There are some state and federal areas which have been opened for bowhunting only. These include certain military bases, game refuges and state parks, all of which have an overabundant deer herd but are not suitable for gunning.

Because there are sometimes changes from year to year in the archery-hunting seasons of the various states, it would not be practicable to list the current seasons here. In order to ascertain the latest bowhunting regulations and seasons, sportsmen can write to the appropriate agency in each state. For a complete listing of the addresses of the game departments in all 50 states, and the Canadian provinces as well, see Part X.

Part VII

Targets In
The Water
—Bowfishing

FISHING WITH THE bow and arrow goes back thousands of years. It's a pastime of modern American archers as well as primitive peoples living in remote parts of the world.

Bowfishing is not like bait fishing or casting to likely looking spots for bass. It's more like the delicate approach of a fly fisherman as he tries to outwit a rising trout. It also has something in common with bonefishing, in which the angler must unobtrusively locate his quarry first and then make a faultless cast.

Bowfishing For Carp

BOWANGLERS SHOOT AT suckers, eels, gar, sharks, rays, bullfrogs, snapping turtles and their favorite aquatic target, the carp. Carp are most popular because they're the fish most often available to bowmen. To the average rod-and-reel angler the carp is sluggish, but to the bowfisherman it is a target that will disappear in a split-second swirl of muddy water if approached carelessly. When a fish arrow catches a carp amidships, a quiet cove may be churned to a froth by the thrashing fish.

The carp is the bowfisherman's favorite target.

FINDING AND STALKING CARP

First, one must locate the fish. This means that it is necessary to do some checking of possible carp waters or to know of someone who has seen the fish. In other words, successful bowfishing for carp usually calls for reconnaissance.

Along the marshy fringes of many Midwestern lakes carp will often be found swimming or wallowing in the very shallow receding overflow waters caused by heavy thunderstorms or rain showers. Such conditions bring forth the local carp spearmen as well as others so the bowfisherman frequently has competition. Under

The spring spawning period is the best time to bowfish for carp.

223

these circumstances the bowfisherman will do well to double-check whatever shallows he fishes to insure no hazard to others also searching for carp in the vicinity with other equipment. Then, too, there is a good possibility that other bowfishermen will be out, hence it is well to keep safety in mind.

The time to fish such areas, of course, is while the water is high—as soon as possible after the rains and sometimes even before the rain has stopped, for such waters recede rapidly. What may be excellent carp fishing possibilities under such conditions one day can easily be gone the next.

Apart from rain gear, about the only special equipment necessary for bowfishing under such conditions consists of hip boots or waders.

There are bodies of water that harbor carp throughout the year. However, spring and early summer are the best times for carp shooting, because that's when the rough fish carry on their spawning activities. It's on the shallow flats, where they come for their spawning rites, that you can find the most carp activity. When the bowman strikes it right, it's not unusual to come upon a whole school of spawning carp wallowing and splashing on a muddy flat. They're so involved in their business that it's possible to wade among them and shoot at will. They may be so thick that some of them will actually bump against the bowman's legs. That's when some bowfishermen use ordinary field arrows. With a field point on the end of the arrow instead of a fish point, the shooter can simply flip one or two carp up on the bank rather than going to the trouble of disengaging the barb of a fish arrow after each shot. Spawning is the only time when bowfishing for carp is that easy though, and it's a fairly short period.

Usually it's necessary to stalk carp, and bowfishermen sometimes use binoculars. After glassing a marsh or a mudflat to be sure carp are there, the archer plans his stalk. He must take into consideration any shadows cast by the sun. Although the water is usually cloudy, it's also shallow and the carp are so close to the surface that they can detect movements and shadows from some distance away. The experienced bowfisherman knows he must move slowly and take advantage of trees and other cover.

After taking a shot, and regardless of whether his arrow hits or misses, the archer normally has to wait a while or move on to another spot. As soon as the arrow slaps the water, one sees the wakes of fleeing carp. If the arrow spears a fish, the water disturbance will cause all the other carp in the vicinity to beeline for

Carp are found in both large and small bodies of water.

safety. By remaining motionless, the shooter may be able to wait until the fish return. If they're badly spooked, however, they probably won't come back for quite a while. If the carp don't return after about 15 minutes, it's best to try another place.

If the water is a rather small stream, it's possible for an archer to get some action by working quietly and slowly along the banks. In larger bodies of water, such as broad rivers and lakes, wading or shooting from a boat is better. Some archers make a specialty of hunting carp from boats and use specially-built craft. Usually, two men work together, one handling the boat or paddling and the other shooting. They alternate positions at intervals.

Carp shooting from a boat at night is sometimes productive. With a two-man arrangement, a bright lantern is mounted on the boat's bow. After arriving at the fishing area, the stern man paddles the craft while the archer up forward has his bow half-drawn for a quick shot at any carp that may show itself in the glare of the light. A team of three archers can operate the same way. One man takes care of the power and steering, another uses a hand-held, battery-operated light to spot the fish, and the third man does the shooting. Some very large carp have been taken this way, for instance, from the Susquehanna and other rivers.

For variety, some archers try a float trip in a canoe or an auto-top boat. If the season and the place are right, it's possible to get shots at both carp and woodchucks. Chucks often build dens along the banks of streams. Since they anticipate danger only from the inland side of the den, they don't usually become alarmed when the hunter approaches silently by boat. If the wind doesn't betray the bowman, it's possible to move quite close.

A flat-bottomed boat is more practical for bowfishing or hunting than a canoe or V-bottomed boat. The archer should stand up so that he'll have a better view and better shooting angles. Marksmanship may be affected if he must be concerned with keeping his balance.

When carp stay deep in a lake or river, they sometimes can be lured to the surface by throwing out bits of bread or corn kernels. This works best where the carp are so numerous that they must compete for food. If they begin to rise, quick shooting is called for. The bowman can't expect more than one or two shots at each school.

HOW TO AIM

Whether the bowfishing is done from bank or from a boat, the water refraction may present a problem, although experienced bowmen have a fairly good idea of where to aim. Actually, refraction is serious only when the fish are deeper than about six inches, and most fish are arrowed in rather shallow water. The archer can get the feel of water refraction by holding a bit lower than usual. The range, the angle of the shaft, and depth of the fish are the three variables which determine the correct point of aim.

It may be difficult to practice shooting at aquatic targets by shooting at inanimate objects. One can't put an empty can in the water for a target, because that would be littering. Likewise, a submerged rock can't be used as a target, because of the possible damage to the fish point. Some archers practice on rolled-up newspapers placed at different depths. But refraction isn't really too much of a problem. The main thing to bear in mind is to hold somewhat lower when the fish are deeper than six inches.

Although some degree of marksmanship is required in bowfishing, pinpoint accuracy is not essential, nor is it necessary to hit a vital spot. A hit almost anywhere on a fish is sufficient to hang up the barb of a fish point. Then the line is hauled in and the fish is in the bag.

Precision shooting is not necessary in bowfishing. This gar was arrowed in back.

After shooting some carp there's the question of what to do with them. While they are edible and nourishing when properly cleaned and cooked, not many bowfishermen eat them. Whatever he does with his carp, the bowman should not leave the fish on the bank to rot. They should either be given to some family who will appreciate them, or used for fertilizer, or placed deep in the woods where raccoons and opossums can have a feast.

TACKLE

Since bowfishing does not require sharpshooting, it's an excellent form of sport for young archers and beginners. The tackle used by most bowanglers is simple and inexpensive. Though a bow reel and fish arrows are easy to make in the home workshop, commercial products do a better job. A bow reel is merely a cylindrical or drum-like object from which the line uncoils in the same way that line pays out from a spinning reel. A crude fish arrow can be made from a cedar field arrow by driving a long nail through the shaft

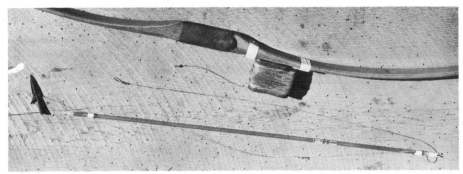

A simple bow reel is easy to make, but a commercial model does a better job.

just behind the metal head. The hole should be drilled first at an angle with an undersize bit. Then the nail is forced through the hole with the point angled to the rear.

Bow reels cost between $3 and $5, sometimes more. They're made of aluminum and are taped or clipped to the bow below the

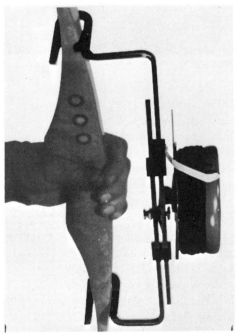

A bow reel is a drum-shaped attachment which is taped or clipped to the bow.

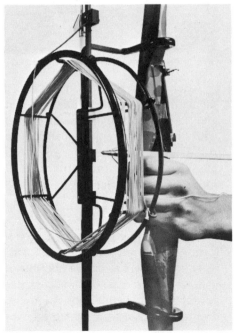

With some bow reels, the archer shoots his arrow through the hollow center of the reel.

handle. Factory-made fish arrows cost about $2 each. They're made of solid fiberglass and are considerably heavier than cedar shafts or tubular-glass arrows. The extra weight is a big help in penetrating water, though most bowfishermen don't expect to do much damage in water deeper than a few feet. Another advantage of a solid-glass shaft is that it's practically unbreakable. A fish may roll on it, but won't snap it.

Factory-made fish arrows have one or two barbs, and most of them have rubber fletching. Experienced bowfishermen usually remove the fletching, because it's not needed for such short-range shooting.

There are many different fish points to choose from, costing from fifty cents to $3.50. It's doubtful that many fish are lost because of a single-barb point, but the double barb makes for added security and does not increase the cost much. Almost all fish points have barbs that are retractable in one way or another to simplify the removal of the arrow from the fish. After a hit, the point is forced completely through the fish. Then the barb, or barbs, are retracted and the shaft is withdrawn.

The fish point should have a hole drilled in it, so the line can be attached at that point. Then, if the fish should somehow break the arrow shaft, the line will still be connected to both the point and

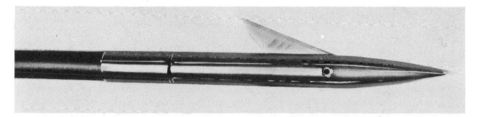

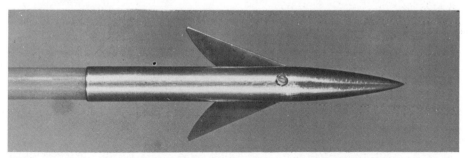

Fish arrows have either one or two barbs. These are streamlined models; on both of them, the barbs can be pressed down into grooves, making it easy to withdraw the arrow from a fish.

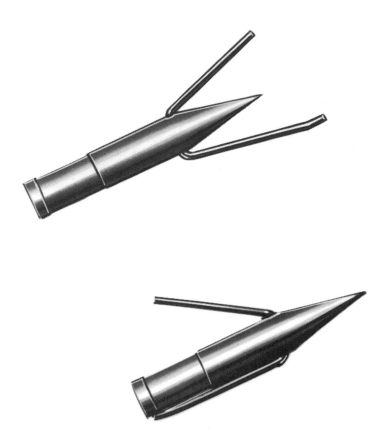

Lower view shows point in shooting position. After it strikes a fish, the point is forced completely through the flesh and the barbs are flipped forward for easy withdrawal.

the impaled fish. The line should run from the point along the length of the shaft, and should be secured to the nock-end, from which it goes to the bow reel.

The line used in freshwater bowfishing is usually about 80-lb. test braided nylon, but not because the archer will likely tangle with heavy fish. The strong line is necessary to yank arrows out of deep mud and streamside brush and grass.

Saltwater Bowfishing

IN SALTWATER BOWFISHING, heavier line—at least 100-lb. test—is needed. The quarry here is predatory fish, like sharks and stingrays. Because these fish are bigger and stronger, there's an added thrill in saltwater bowfishing. To add to the spice, there's an element of danger. Almost all sharks are potential man-eaters, regardless of size; but the bowman is generally free of danger if he's careful. Stingrays have a whip-like tail with a serrated barb. Though there's no poison in the barb, it is usually so encrusted with filth that it's capable of causing infection if it lacerates a human.

Many saltwater bowfishermen don't use bow reels. Instead, the line is coiled on the deck of the boat or on a seat, while the free end is tied to a large float. When a hit is made, the fish makes its run and the float is heaved overboard. The float slows the fish's progress and also shows its course. The helmsman steers the boat after the float so that the archer eventually can pick it up and work his trophy toward the boat. If the fish is a battler, it may be necessary to put one or two more arrows into it. With several lines to haul on, the fish can be maneuvered more easily when it's being pulled toward the craft. For this reason, it's wise to have more than one arrow and line rigged and ready.

It's possible for a bowfisherman to have some extra sport in saltwater shooting. Instead of using a float on his line, he can secure the line's free end to a deep-sea rod and reel. After sinking his arrow in a fish, he can have the fun of playing it with the rod. This often calls for a delicate touch. The archer-angler can't horse the fish in, because the barbed arrowpoint may pull out of a soft-fleshed fish.

Law and Regulations

IT'S WISE TO check beforehand about the legality of the type of bowfishing you intend to do. Fishing licenses are required for bowfishing in some states. There are local regulations which protect certain species—bullfrogs or snapping turtles, for example—while in an adjoining state it may be perfectly lawful to shoot the same creatures with a bow.

Bowfishing is constructive, since in most cases it rids the waters of undesirable inhabitants. It's inexpensive and it does not require great shooting skill. Finally, it gives the archer an outlet at a time of year when hunting land-based game is usually out of season.

Part VIII

Archery Careers

Archery As A Career

THERE HAVE BEEN cases where expert bowmen have been in branches of the military service and have been sent at government expense to tournaments in various parts of the world. There have been cases, too, where industries, recognizing the public relations value of an employee who is a national archery contender, have supported him in terms of time off from work and travel expenses. While those individuals don't depend on the sport for a livelihood, archery has been a big help in their careers.

It's possible to make a living from one's expertise in shooting or one's technical knowledge of how bows and arrows work although at present it's not a recommended profession for a person who has other options.

There are several ways for an exceptionally good archer to turn his ability into dollars and cents. Assuming that he has approached the top echelon in tournaments and that he has no desire to maintain his amateur standing, he should consider joining the Professional Archers Association.

TOURNAMENTS AND OPPORTUNITIES FOR THE PROFESSIONAL

The P.A.A. promotes the sport of archery in general and has established a strict set of standards for certifying qualified archery coaches. To become a member of the P.A.A., an archer must serve

The P.A.A. outdoor round is designed so the spectators can see both the archers and the targets.

a one-year apprenticeship. During this probationary period, his qualifications are examined by the group's membership. Upon successfully meeting the strict P.A.A. criteria, the archer becomes a full-fledged member.

The national headquarters of the P.A.A. are at 1500 N. Chatsworth Street, St. Paul, Minnesota 55117.

The standard outdoor P.A.A. round is shot on a course designed for spectators. In shape, the layout is similar to a wheel. The audience is in the center close to the archers, and the shooting lanes spread outward like spokes. The distances are comparatively short (16 to 65 yards), while the targets have large bullseyes. The black-and-white target faces are 14, 22 and 30 inches in diameter. The targets have three scoring zones. Five points are counted for a hit in the innermost ring, four for the next ring and three for the outermost ring. The P.A.A. round consists of two ten-target units; three arrows are shot at each target. That means a total of 60 arrows are shot, so that a perfect score is 300. The participants are so skilled that perfect scores are frequently made, sometimes resulting in a thrilling shoot-off.

The P.A.A. has a three-year contract for its national championships. The plan calls for a five-day shoot each September, in which the purses escalate: $15,000 in 1971, $20,000 in 1972 and $25,000 in 1973. Michigan is the permanent site of the championship match, which is open only to P.A.A. members.

Cash purses amounting to thousands of dollars are an attraction to hundreds of professional archers. This is a large indoor tournament in Detroit.

In many parts of the country, there are other tournaments with cash prizes, some of them amounting to thousands of dollars. The two most prominent ones are held in Detroit and Las Vegas. In addition, there are regional matches with smaller purses. Attendance at these money shoots is not limited to members of the P.A.A. So far, there are not enough cash-purse tournaments to enable an archer to make his living from them, in the sense that a top-notch pro golfer can earn a lucrative income on the tournament circuit. In the unlikely event that one bowman or lady pro could win every tournament in the country, he or she could receive a good income. But, in practical terms, the cash purses in archery tourneys should be considered only as supplementary income.

OTHER FORMS OF INCOME FROM ARCHERY

Some bowmen who have made a name for themselves in tournaments are employed by archery manufacturers as sales agents

As more people require archery instruction, there's a growing demand in the archery coaching field.

With some financial backing, a knowledgeable bowman may have a good future in an indoor archery range.

Large firms dominate the arrow business, but a skilled individual arrowsmith can make it on his own if he has a personal following in an area where archery interest is high.

and goodwill ambassadors. There's a growing future in the archery coaching field—in clubs, indoor ranges, camps and Y.M.C.A. programs. As competition in schools and colleges continues to expand, there will be a greater demand for coaches who have the ability to develop young athletes into good archers.

There's also a future for the enterprising bowman to open an archery shop or a commercial indoor shooting range. To be successful in such a venture, the location must be in an area where there is a large amount of archery interest.

While the large manufacturers dominate the field, there are a few archers who turn out their own line of bows, some of them very fine products. In some instances, these are part-time operations, but some are full-time businesses. The picture is largely the same in the arrow business. The large firms offer tough competition but a skilled arrowsmith with a personal following can earn a living if he's a good businessman. One young man started his own arrow business while still in high school. He was so successful that he was able to put himself through college.

Part IX

◎◎◎◎◎◎◎◎◎◎◎◎◎◎◎◎◎◎◎◎◎◎◎◎

The Future Of Archery

The Future of Archery

CRYSTAL BALLS AND similar methods of prediction went out generations ago, although there is currently a renewed interest among some segments of the population in the effect of the zodiac and the stars on human behavior patterns. Interestingly enough, one of the zodiacial signs is Sagittarius, or the Archer.

Is archery headed for a zenith of popularity and participation? That's anybody's guess. There are, however, certain indications that the ancient sport may in the future assume greater importance than it now enjoys.

On the national level, the bow and arrow and bow-shooting have never attracted masses of people, when compared to a sport like golf, as an example. Public golf courses abound, as do affluent country clubs where golf is the principal activity. Big business deals have been consummated on the fairways and a profusion of celebrities are golfing fans. All of this contributes to golf as an "in" sport.

By contrast, few well-known newsmakers and public figures are involved in archery. No presidents, no movie stars and practically no television luminaries are devotees of the bow and arrow. That, of course, is one reason why the sport has not had wider acceptance. There's also the fact that competitive archery leaves a lot to be desired as a spectator sport. On the contrary, it's strictly a participant sport, because it's dull to watch, even for an archery fan. In an age where viewing sports events attracts more people

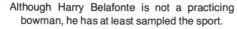

| Although Harry Belafonte is not a practicing bowman, he has at least sampled the sport. | Television's Efrem Zimbalist (left) is among the few luminaries in the entertainment field who have had archery experience. Another is Johnny Carson. |

than does participation, it seems doubtful that archery will become a sport that's accepted by more than the few who have actually tried it.

On the other hand, the growth of archery competition on the international level is spreading the gospel of the bow and arrow. It's possible that archery in the Olympic Games will awaken people to the advantages of the sport. Compared to some other Olympic events—equitation, for example, archery is inexpensive. In contrast to skiing and sailing, it's a sport that can be practiced in any region and at any time of year.

In the U.S., thanks to the enthusiasm and dedication on the part of some archery leaders, the sport is advancing in the hunting field as well as in the competitive area—among the general public and in schools and colleges. In that context, archery was at one time limited to a few vestal institutions where young ladies shot arrows only to absolve a physical-education requirement in their college curriculum. Today, intercollegiate archery competition—among both men and women—is coming into its own. At any rate, bows and arrows are being shot on more campuses now than at any time in the history of the bow.

Each year, there's an impressive national intercollegiate archery tournament. Also, there's an Intercollegiate All-American Archery Team. It's certainly possible that the future will see national

Although there's a large gathering of spectators viewing this tournament, archery is not noted for being a spectator sport.

Some Special Forces troops, like those shown here, have had training in archery.

divisions in archery competition, just as in football there are the Big Ten and the Ivy League divisions.

In this respect the sport has much going for it. Unlike football and baseball, there's an insignificant amount of professional aspiration among college archers, plus the fact that it's a sport that can be pursued over a lifetime.

As hunting lands diminish with the spread of populations, cities, highways and vast suburban shopping centers, there's every reason to believe that the concept of bowhunting will spread. Relatively few deer are taken when hunters use bows and arrows, so the game populations are not endangered. It's a safe method of hunting and it does not mean any objectionable noise to disturb the populace. It provides a substantial number of recreation man-hours, yet without taxing the wildlife.

All forms of warfare are horrible. It would be less than realistic to hope that modern armies would revert to spears, sabers and bows. Yet such a prospect would certainly be preferable to mortars, land mines and nuclear weapons. But—one never knows.

Commandos are reported to have used bows during World War II. Some Special Forces troops have been trained in archery warfare and no doubt used their expertise in Vietnam, along with native Montagnards who had their own crude crossbows.

While the bow and arrow originated as a means of providing food and to protect man against his enemies, in the contemporary context, archery means sports competition, exercise and healthy recreation. As more and more people—in the U.S. and throughout the world—are exposed to the fun and challenge of shooting the bow, the sport may once again have an important place in society.

Part X

References
For Archers

Glossary

American Archery Council   A promotional and regulatory body, composed of some of the leaders in all branches of archery.

American Indoor Archery Association   A promotional and standardizing organization concerned with indoor shooting.

Archery Lane Owners Association   An organization for the improvement and promotion of commercial indoor archery establishments.

American Round   A type of competition in target archery.

Archery Manufacturers Organization   The A.M.O. establishes certain standards in the industry.

Anchor   The point at which the archer's bow hand comes to rest when the arrow is fully drawn.

Animal Round   A type of field archery competition in which the targets are pictures of animals.

Armguard   A leather or plastic pad to protect the arm from the slap of the bowstring.

Arrow Rest   A ledge, or shelf, across which the arrow is drawn. On some target bows, the arrow rest is adjustable.

Arrowsmith   One who is skilled at making arrows.

Arthur Young   Hunting companion of Dr. Saxton Pope, the father of modern bowhunting.

Art Young Awards   Offered by the N.F.A.A. for bowhunters who bag big and small game.

Back   The front, or outer, surface of the bow; the surface facing the target.

Backing   A reinforcing material bonded to the front surface of the bow. Its purpose is to strengthen the bow and to improve its cast.

Barebow   An archer who uses no sighting aid on his weapon.

Belly   The inner, or concave, surface of the bow.

Blind   A bowhunter's place of concealment.

Blunt   A flat-faced arrow point used for hunting some types of small game.

Bolt   The short arrow used in a crossbow.

Bow Quiver   Attached to the hunting bow, it holds the arrows in a vertical position, where they can be easily snapped out when needed.

Bow Reel   A drum-like device which is attached to the bow and on which the bowfisherman's line is coiled.

Bowsight   An aiming aid attached to the bow; it can be adjusted for various shooting distances.

Bow Sling   A strap, chain or cord, loosely holding the bow to the archer's bow hand. Its purpose is to enable the shooter to grip the bow lightly.

Bow Sock   A camouflage-cloth sleeve which fits over the limbs of a hunting bow.

Bowstringer   A device which aids the archer in bracing his bow.

Bow Weight   The number of pounds of energy required to pull a 28-inch arrow in a given bow.

Bowyer   One who makes bows.

Brace   A strung bow is braced. To brace a bow is to string it.

Brace Height   Also called string height; this is the space between the braced bowstring and the handle of the bow.

Broadhead   A sharpened steel arrow point with one or more blades, used in bowhunting.

Brush Buttons   Two globular rubber objects which bowhunters attach to the bowstring near its ends; they prevent twigs from lodging between the bow and the string at its ends.

Butt   The backstop, usually straw or excelsior to which the target is attached.

Cast   A bow's cast is its capacity to propel an arrow; the better the cast, the faster the arrow and the flatter its trajectory.

Center-shot   The cut-out section in the bow's upper limb just above the grip. In a full center-shot bow, the drawn arrow points straight ahead, instead of being angled to one side.

Chicago Round   A form of indoor archery competition.

Clout   A long-range competitive event in which the bullseye is laid out on the ground and is marked by a flag.

Cock Feather   The feather (on a three-feather arrow) which is at right-angles to the bowstring. It is usually a different color than the other feathers.

Columbia Round   A form of ladies' competition in target archery.

Composite   A composite bow is one which is made of two or more layers of different materials.

Compound Bow   The most recent development in bow design, incorporating several pulleys. Its draw weight is adjustable and for a given weight it is easier for the archer to hold than is a regular bow.

Course   A field archery layout.

Creeping   A fault in shooting form in which the archer permits the arrow to move forward slightly just before releasing.

Cresting   The painted bands on the arrow shaft, just forward of the fletching.

Crossbow   A bow mounted horizontally on a stock similar to a gunstock.

Deflex   A deflex bow, when unbraced, is bent toward the string.

Draw   The act of pulling the bow.

Draw Weight   The same as bow weight.

Duoflex   A bow design which incorporates both deflex and reflex bends.

End   A certain number of shots in competitive archery. In most target archery matches, there are six arrows per end; in a field round, four arrows constitute an end.

Face   The surface of the bow facing the archer.

Field Anchor   The point at which most field archers and bowhunters hold the drawing fingers at full draw, usually on the cheek or the corner of the mouth.

Field Archery   A form of competition in which archers shoot at targets of assorted sizes and from different, standardized yardages.

Fifteen-pin   An award given to a field archer who shoots three out of four perfect arrows at one target in a registered tournament.

Fistmele   An ancient term for brace height. To check on the height of his string, the bowman placed his hand against the grip of the bow and made a fist with his thumb extended toward the string.

FITA   The acronym for the Fédération Internationale de Tir à l'Arc, or the International Archery Federation.

FITA Round   The standard unit of competition in international tourneys; also referred to as the International round.

Fletching   The feathers on an arrow, also the feathered section of the arrow.

Flight Shooting   Shooting for distance. Competitive flight shooters use highly specialized tackle.

Flu-flu   An arrow with oversized feathers, usually used in bird hunting and shooting at aerial targets. The full fletching prevents the arrow from traveling a great distance.

Freestyle   A field archery division in which the shooters use bowsights.

Freezing   A psychological shooting problem, very common among experienced archers, in which the archer is unable to aim properly.

Gap Shooting   An aiming technique.

Glove   An archer's glove, or shooting glove, is a three-fingered covering—usually leather, but in some cases plastic—worn on the string fingers as protection against the bowstring.

Gold   The yellow center of the multi-colored bullseye in target archery.

Grain   The unit of weighing an arrow. An avoirdupois ounce contains 437.5 grains.

Hunter Round   A competitive unit in field archery in which the faintly-outlined scoring rings are not visible from the shooting position.

Handle Riser   The thick portion of the bow from which the limbs extend.

Index   A slightly raised ridge on the arrow nock. Since the nock index is in line with the cock feather, the archer can feel it and thus position his arrow correctly on the string without looking at it.

Instinctive   A method of aiming in archery.

International Archery Federation   The English translation of Fédération Internationale de Tir à l'Arc.

International Round   Another name for the FITA round.

Ishi   The Indian who was a strong influence in the archery interest of Dr. Saxton Pope.

Junior Olympic Archery Development Program   Also known as JOAD, an N.A.A. program for interesting young people in archery and to encourage the development of potential Olympic archers.

Jumping the String   When an animal hears the twang of the bowstring, he often makes a quick, instinctive move, sometimes evading the arrow. This is known as "jumping the string."

Kisser   A raised lump or small disc on the bowstring which comes into contact with the target archer's lips at full draw.

Laminations   The layers of different materials in a bow.

Limbs   The upper and lower parts of the bow, above and below the handle riser.

Longbow   Generically and legally, any bow which is not a crossbow.

Loose   The release, or the act of letting the string slip from the drawing fingers.

Matt   A circular disc of woven straw which holds the target and stops the arrows.

National Archery Association   The target archer's organization; affiliated with FITA, the N.A.A. is the U.S. link with the Olympic Games.

National Field Archery Association   A federation of field archery groups; the N.F.A.A. is the regulatory body of its branch of the sport.

Nock   The grooved plastic portion on the arrow's rear end; to nock an arrow is to place it on the bowstring. Also, on a bow, the grooves on both ends, into which the bowstring loops are placed.

Nocking Point   The location on the bowstring at which the arrow's nock is placed.

Paradox   Archer's paradox is the apparent tendency of an arrow to fly straight ahead, although it is pointed to one side on the bow. This is accomplished by a series of diminishing bends of the shaft, which ultimately straightens out in flight. Archer's paradox is not an important consideration with modern, center-shot bows.

Pod   A rubber and plastic device, loaded with an overdose of powdered tranquilizing drug. The pod is fitted onto the arrow shaft directly behind the broadhead. Upon contact with an animal, the pod opens and the drug enters the blood stream.

Point of Aim   A spot on which an archer aligns his arrow point in order to hit the target from a specified distance.

Pope   Dr. Saxton Pope, the founder of modern bowhunting.

Pope and Young Club   The bowhunters' organization for keeping permanent records of North American big-game trophies.

Professional Archers Association   An organization of instructors and archers who shoot for cash prizes.

Professional Bowhunters' Society   An organization of advanced bowhunters.

Quiver   The container of an archer's arrows.

Range   A field archery layout; also the designation for the shooting distance.

Recurve   A bow with curved tips.

Reflex   A reflex bow, when unbraced is curved away from the bowstring.

Release   Same as the loose.

Round   A shooting unit in archery competition.

Serving   A wrapping of thread, used to protect the bowstring at the major points of wear—the end loops and the center, where the arrow nock is placed.

Shooting Glove   A leather or plastic accessory to protect the archer's fingers from the string and to provide a smooth release.

Sight-shooter   An archer who uses a bowsight.

Six-Gold   A target archery achievement in which all six arrows in an end strike the bullseye. A Six-Gold pin is awarded the archer for shooting a perfect end in a properly registered match.

Snap-shooting   A fault in which the archer releases prematurely or before he holds and aims carefully.

Spine   The relative stiffness of an arrow shaft.

Spine Tester   A device for measuring the stiffness of arrow shafts.

Stabilizer   A metal rod (sometimes two) extending from the front of the bow, to absorb its vibrations and make possible a steadier shot.

Stacked   A stacked bow is one which requires a disproportionate amount of drawing energy in the final inches of the draw.

Stance   An element of archery form; the way an archer stands.

String Height   The same as brace height.

String Silencers   Small rubber attachments to the bowstring for reducing the noise from the bowstring's twang.

String-walking   A shooting technique in which the archer varies the location of his nocking point with different shooting distances.

Tab   A flat pad which serves the same purpose as the shooting glove.

Tackle   The archer's equipment.

Target Archery   A form of archery competition in which the contestants shoot at large targets, from known distances and on cleared, level terrain.

Three Fingers Under   An unorthodox drawing and aiming technique in which the shooter places the three string fingers under the arrow nock.

Three Hundred Round   A competitive round in which a score of 300 is a perfect round.

Tillering   A step in bow manufacturing in which the desired curvature of the limbs is accomplished.

Tip   The extreme ends of the bow or the forward extremity of an arrow.

Toxophilite   One who is an archer or an archery fan, from the Greek.

Toxophilus   The name of a book by Roger Ascham. Written in the Sixteenth Century, it was the first written explanation of the archer's correct form.

Tuning   Adjusting the bowstring, the nocking point and the arrow rest for maximum efficiency for an individual archer's shooting style.

Twenty Pin   An award given by the N.F.A.A. to members who shoot a perfect target in a registered match.

Wand   A wand shoot is a competitive round for target archers in which the target is a long, narrow slat made of soft wood. The emphasis in a wand shoot is on horizontal accuracy.

York Round   A competitive round for target archers.

Publications, Organizations and Suppliers

ADDITIONAL INFORMATION ON archery is available from other sources, which include organizations, publications, manufacturers and a few of the mail order firms which specialize in archery equipment. The firms listed here offer catalogues which cover practically everything that may be useful to archers, as well as worthwhile information on shooting technique.

ORGANIZATIONS

Archery Manufacturers Organization
R.D. 1, Box 119
Bechtelsville, Penna. 19505

ARCHERY ORGANIZATIONS

American Archery Council, 200 Castlewood Road, North Palm Beach, Florida 33408

Archery Lane Operators' Association, 1500 North Chatsworth Street, St. Paul, Minnesota 55117

Archery Manufacturers Organization, 200 Castlewood Road, North Palm Beach, Florida 33408

Bowhunters Who Care, Box 476, Columbus, Nebraska 68601

Fred Bear Sports Club, Rural Route 4, Gainesville, Florida 32601

National Archery Association, 1750 East Boulder Street, Colorado Springs, Colorado 80909

National Field Archery Association, Route 2, Box 514, Redlands, California 92373

Pope and Young Club, Route 1, Box 147, Salmon, Idaho 83467

Professional Archers Association, c/o Mrs. Joyce Otter, 4711 Brennan Road, Hemlock, Michigan 48621

Professional Bowhunters Society, Box 13, New Concord, Ohio 43726

ARCHERY MANUFACTURERS AND DEALERS

(Because of the high turnover in the archery business, it's possible to list only some of the best-known firms in the industry.)

Allen Archery, 201 Washington Street, Billings, Missouri 65610

American Archery Company, Box 100, Oconto Falls, Wisconsin 54154

Anderson Archery Corporation, Grand Ledge, Michigan 48837

Baker Manufacturing Company, Box 1003, Valdosta, Georgia 31601

Bear Archery Company, Rural Route 4, Gainesville, Florida 32601

Bingham Projects, Box 3013, Ogden, Utah 84409

Browning, Morgan, Utah 84050

Doug Kittredge Bow Hut, Box 598, Mammoth Lakes, California 93546

Easton Aluminum, 7800 Haskell Avenue, Van Nuys, California 91406

Gordon Plastics, Vista, California 92083

Herter's, Inc., Waseca, Minnesota 56093

Howard Hill Archery, Route 1, Box 1397, Hamilton, Montana 59840

Hoyt Archery Company, 11510 Natural Bridge, Bridgeton, Missouri 63044

Jeffrey Enterprises, Inc., 821 Pepper Street, Columbia, South Carolina 29209

Jennings Compound Bow, Inc., 28756 North Castaic Canyon Road, Valencia, California 91355

Kwikee Quiver Company, 7292 Peaceful Valley Road, Acme, Michigan 49610

L. C. Whiffen Company, Inc., 923 South 16th Street, Milwaukee, Wisconsin 53204

Martin Archery, Inc., Route 5, Box 127, Walla Walla, Washington 99362

Precision Shooting Equipment, Inc., Mahomet, Illinois 61853

Saunders Archery Company, Columbus, Nebraska 68601

Savora Archery, Inc., Box 594, Kirkland, Washington 98033

Sweetland Products, 1010 Arrowsmith Street, Eugene, Oregon 97402

The Old Master Crafters, 130 Lebaron Street, Waukegan, Illinois 60085

Trueflight Manufacturing Company, Inc., Manitowish Waters, Wisconsin 54545

Yamaha International, 6600 Orangethorpe Avenue, Buena Park, California 90620

York Archery, Box 110, Independence, Missouri 64051

ARCHERY PUBLICATIONS

Archery World, 225 East Michigan, Milwaukee, Wisconsin 53202

Bow and Arrow, 34249 Camino Capistrano, Box 88, Capistrano Beach, California 92624

Bowhunter, 3808 South Calhoun Street, Fort Wayne, Indiana 46807

EXCERPTS—The Archer's Handbook (NAA)

ABOUT THE NATIONAL ARCHERY ASSOCIATION

OBJECTIVES

Much could be written about the purpose of the N.A.A.; however the most important objective of the Association is to promote archery. This promotion includes *all* forms of archery. The benefits and services of the N.A.A. are available to *all* archers whether they are target archers, field archers, or bowhunters; whether they are instinctive or free style shooters.

All N.A.A. Championship Tournaments have two divisions, professional and amateur. The National Champion may be a free style or instinctive shooter. The only requirement for winning the National Championship is that the archer shoot the highest score in the specified Championship Rounds. Both an Amateur and Professional N.A.A. Champion are named.

The N.A.A. is a nonprofit organization incorporated under the laws of the state of Illinois. The names of the past officers and members of the board of governors of the N.A.A. read like a Who's Who of Archery.

Today the N.A.A. promotes participation in Olympic Games and World Field and Target Archery Championship Tournaments.

SERVICES

Services provided members of the N.A.A. of the United States are many and varied. The association:

1. Keeps records of the Six-Golds Club and awards Six-Golds Pins, Range Buttons, 54 Pins, 450 Pins, and 500 Pins.
2. Provides a classification system for archers of different levels of proficiency.
3. Publishes annually a list of the top ranking archers of the United States compiled from their performance in N.A.A. Registered Tournaments and International Tournaments.
4. Compiles lists of and publishes dates of affiliated major regional, state, and club tournaments.
5. Maintains the Wing Club records and furnishes membership cards and pins for superior flight records.
6. Furnishes a twelve month subscription to *Archery World* to all members. This magazine carries reports of N.A.A. activities each month, gives the scores made in tournaments all over the United States, and presents a wealth of other articles of interest to all archers.
7. Publishes tournament and safety rules.
8. Keeps all official Six-Golds Tournament and N.A.A. Championship Tournament records and publishes them in the annual report issued to members.
9. Issues Certificates of Merit to champions and record holders in the various classifications.
10. Sends out literature and pamphlets in answer to inquiries from all over the world regarding formation of clubs, tournament rules, and ways of increasing interest in club activities, etc.
11. Standardizes tournament rules, procedures, and rounds so that a comparison of scores from different tournaments is possible, no matter in what part of the United States they are held.
12. Provides cards attesting to the Classification and Amateur Standing of the archer.
13. Provides a Tournament Handbook for clubs or associations interested in sponsoring the National Championship Tournament.

253

PROGRAMS

The N.A.A. conducts a varied program which includes:
1. The annual National Championship Tournaments open to members only.
2. The Indoor Winter League Tournament.
3. An Intercollegiate Mail Match.
4. An Interscholastic Meet.
5. A Nationwide Flight Shoot.
6. The United States Team Tryouts which select a Ladies' and a Gentlemen's Team to represent the United States in International and Olympic Competition.
7. A Junior Olympic Archery Development Program.
8. The North American Team Championship Tournament.
9. An N.A.A. Certified Instructors Program.
10. Sanctions an All American Collegiate Archery Team— for men and women.
11. Sponsors the U.S. Intercollegiate Championship Tournament.

With the exceptions of the National Championship Tournament and the International Tournaments, all matches are shot on the home ranges of the competing clubs, and scores are sent in by mail. Medals, trophies, and certificates are awarded for all mail matches as well as for the Annual National Championship Tournament. Your club will profit by entering all the events for which it has qualified members.

MEMBERSHIP

Membership in the N.A.A. is available on an individual basis for $5.00 per year, or on a family basis (husband and wife) for $6.00 per year. Junior memberships are available with family memberships for $1.00 per year for each dependent under 18 years of age. Junior membership other than with a family membership is $3.50.

Club memberships are available for $8.50 per year. A special reduced membership rate plan is offered for six or more individuals who join at the time their club becomes affiliated with the N.A.A.

ORGANIZING A TOURNAMENT

Many beginning archers ask, "Why have tournaments?" The answers are obvious. Tournaments give the archer a chance to demonstrate the skills that he has developed in shooting the bow. True, he can demonstrate this to himself on the practice field, but shooting in competition with other archers is the final proof of achievement. Also, it is fun to meet and shoot with out-of-town archers and to observe the shooting techniques of known top shooters. Of course, the fact that tournaments very definitely help promote the sport is important to archery enthusiasts also.

Shooting in competition is really the best way of practicing. One top archer said that a one-day tournament did him more good than a week of practicing alone. There seems to be something about shooting in competition that just cannot be duplicated on the practice range. This same well-known archer said that the difference between the "chump" and the "champ" was that each could shoot a 700 American Round in practice, but in the tournament, the "chump" would shoot 650 and the "champ" would shoot 750. This difference in scores does not indicate a lack of intestinal fortitude on the part of the so-called chump. It is just that when one gets on the tournament line it is very difficult to maintain the necessary concentration and bear down and "shoot every arrow". Maybe it is that little extra shot of adrenalin that makes it more difficult to hold steady and concentrate.

The deer hunter, whether he is a gun hunter or a bow hunter, is quite familiar with the proverbial "buck fever". It seems to attack many hunters when they first go out in the bush. Just as the hunter who has been hunting for many years is unlikely to become afflicted with "buck fever", so is the archer who has shot in many tournaments less likely to be affected by "tournament jitters".

Shooting the bow and arrow is not complicated but it requires complete concentration. The more you compete and the tougher the competition, the better you will shoot.

One might say that there is a natural sequence of tournaments: First are local Club Tournaments, then Regional, National, and International Championships. The ultimate goal of an archer interested in tournament competition is participation in an Olympic Championship.

A suggestion for clubs is to hold three tournaments a year: Spring, Mid-Summer, and Club Championships. All of the club tournaments should be "open shoots"; that is, open to all kinds of archers— amateurs, professionals, sight shooters, and bare bow archers. The club championship awards, of course, must be restricted to club members. However, in a Championship Shoot it is customary to have first, second, and third place awards for non-club members.

Tournaments are not held extemporaneously. Plans should be made three or four months before the spring tournament. A Range Master, a Publicity Chairman, and also an Awards Chairman should be appointed. The club, of course, should be affiliated with the N.A.A. and should register their shoots with the national organization as Six-Golds Shoots. (Even when the local club is affiliated with the N.A.A., only individual N.A.A. members are eligible to receive the beautiful Six-Golds Pin from the National Organization. This pin is awarded to any member archer who shoots a perfect end; that is to say, six arrows into the gold at any official distance.)

PUBLICITY

The Publicity Chairman is greatly responsible for the success of any given tournament. The home club supplies the proper range and targets, but without archers the tournament will not be a success. Let all archers in your area know about your coming tournament. All archery clubs keep a permanent mailing list of known archers throughout the immediate area and of any other area from which they can draw archers. The Publicity Chairman can contact the secretary of his local state archery association and ask for a list of state-affiliated archery clubs. An announcement about your tournament can be sent to each of these clubs. Maybe you can obtain a working agreement with other clubs to exchange mailing lists of members. If so, send an announcement to individual club members.

A complete announcement is very important in drawing people to your tournament. This announcement should be received by the tentative participant about two weeks before the actual shooting date. If you mail it earlier than that he might forget the shoot. If you send it later than the two week period, the archer may have plans for that particular day. The announcement should give the date, the starting time of the shoot (Standard or Daylight Saving Time), and the location of your range. There should be a drawing included which will show the routes or streets that lead to the range. The announcement should state clearly what Rounds are going to be shot, what the shooting fees will be, and what type of awards will be given: ribbons, medals, or trophies. Emphasize that the shoot is a Six-Golds Tournament.

The Publicity Chairman should also contact all the local news media and ask them to help publicize the coming tournament. Posters can be made for display in the local sporting goods stores. Dealers are more than willing to cooperate in this kind of publicity for the local archery club.

More clubs try to have one big tournament a year. The other two are usually on a much smaller scale. The big tournament should be staged as early in the year as is possible. Most tournament archers wish to get in as much tournament experience as possible before the state, regional, and national championships.

CLASSIFICATION

The N.A.A. realizes that there is more enjoyment on the part of the archer when he competes with other archers of similar ability. Therefore the N.A.A. has established a classification system. The American Round is the Classification Round and only Six-Golds Tournaments are accepted for establishing classification. The American Round consists of 30 arrows at 60 yards, 30 arrows at 50 yards, and 30 arrows at 40 yards.

Upon registering at a Six-Golds Tournament your membership card should be submitted to the tournament director so that proper entry can be made. In determining your class in a tournament, the most recent single American and the highest single American shot during the 12 month period prior to the tournament in which you desire to compete are added together. If the last score is the highest, your last two scores are added together. In the case of an individual who has not shot two American Rounds for Classification, this individual is automatically classed AA for the tournament.

It is the responsibility of the member to have his/her classification transferred from expired membership card to the new membership card. This information shall be transferred by a Club or Tournament Secretary.

MEN	CLASS	WOMEN
1400 and Up	AA	1300 and Up
1250 to 1399	A	1150 to 1299
1000 to 1249	B	950 to 1149
Below 1000	C	Below 950

The breakdown on archers, according to age, is as follows: Senior Men and Women, 18 years or over; Intermediate Boys and Girls, 15 to 18 years old; Junior Boys and Girls, 12 to 15 years old; and Cadet Boys and Girls, under 12 years old. Sometimes Cadet Boys and Girls are classified as Beginners.

An archer may, by choice, before shooting starts, compete in a higher class than that one in which he is normally classified, but he may not shoot in a lower class. Women and girls can compete against men or boys in a higher class, but men or boys cannot compete in girls' or women's classes.

AWARDS

In a sizable tournament where all classes and divisions are represented, it is necessary to have quite a few awards. There should be first, second, and third place awards for both men and women in all four classes: AA, A, B, and C, Junior Boys and Junior Girls. It may be necessary to provide awards for both sight and bare bow shooters. In tournaments at local club level, amateurs and professionals may compete for the same awards as long as no money is involved. Awards are of three types: ribbons, medals and trophies. Ribbons are the least expensive; and they can be ordered from several sources. If ribbons are used, it is Gold for first place, Red for second place, and Blue for third place. These colors are the three highest scoring colors on the target face. Medals and trophies can be purchased through regular retail or wholesale channels.

Some clubs have been quite successful in making very attractive trophies for their featured Invitational Shoot. For example, the Maumee Valley Bowmen of Toledo, Ohio has held their big Invitational Tournament on Mother's Day for the last 35 years. For practically all of these tournaments the club has made its own trophies. By making these trophies the club not only saves money, but can give the archers something unique that is highly prized by the fortunate winners.

SCORECARDS

Ample supply of score cards must be on hand for the tournament. Score cards may be purchased or may be printed or mimeographed by the individual club.

TOURNAMENT REGISTRATION

Efficiency in registration is important. If registration is handled promptly, the archers are well pleased, and they can get on the practice line and shoot a few arrows before official practice starts. It is suggested that there should be two registration desks. Card tables or park benches serve the purpose very nicely. Women and girls should register at one desk, men and boys at the other. In small tournaments one registration desk can do double duty. The registrars must be sure that the correct name and address of the archer are written on the score card and that the card is marked to show the particular class in which the archer is shooting and his professional or amateur status. Each archer is issued two cards, an original and a duplicate, because scoring in tournaments is always done in duplicate. There are several ways of assigning archers to their respective targets. The simplest is to assign the first four men to register to #1 Target, the next four to #2 Target and so on; the same procedure can be used for women. Sometimes a group of out-of-town archers will request that they be assigned to the same targets. The host club usually grants this courtesy. Some clubs assign a home club archer to each target with three guest archers. Some clubs will also group free style archers together and bare bow shooters together. Sometimes archers may be grouped according to their classification. It is more fun for the archers to have AA and A archers shoot together than to have, for example: three AA class archers and one C class archer on the same target.

If the announcement of the tournament stated that registration would start at 9:00 A.M., the registrars should be ready to accept registration no later than 9:00 A.M. and preferably ten to fifteen minutes before that time. An out-of-town archer has to get up quite early and drive a considerable distance to attend your tournament. If he arrives at 9:00 A.M. and finds that the targets are not on the line or that the range master is just beginning to place the targets and that the registrars are not ready, he is, to say the least, a little bit perturbed.

FIELD CAPTAIN

The duties of the most important official have purposely been left to the last. This official is the Field Captain who is appointed by the host club. The duties of the Field Captain are precisely defined in Section 7.1 to 7.5 of the Official Tournament Rules. He is responsible for conducting the tournament according to these rules.

The Field Captain should be a person with as much tournament experience as possible. Local clubs should have different club members act as Field Captain for their small shoots. This practice gives several individuals experience in running tournaments. The most important consideration for the Field Captain is stated in the Primary Tournament Rules under Section A: "Every precaution taken to insure the highest possible safety standards has precedence over all other considerations or rules. Any practices, attitudes, equipment, or conditions either mentioned herein, or not mentioned herein, which are in the least degree unsafe, are prohibited."

Not only is it incumbent upon the Field Captain to have a clear knowledge of the shooting rules, but it is equally incumbent upon the individual archer to understand these rules and conduct himself accordingly.

SUMMARY OF TOURNAMENT OFFICIALS' DUTIES

The following will sum up the duties of the various officials and committees. We have mentioned the duties before the shoot, the following summary will reiterate those duties and also specify the duties after the shoot.

DUTIES OF SECRETARY

Before the shoot

See that the tournament is registered as a N.A.A. Six-Golds Tournament.

See that announcements are mailed out to as many prospective guests as possible.

After the shoot:

See that the names and duplicate score cards of any Six-Golds Pin winners or archers setting new tournament records are mailed immediately to N.A.A. Headquarters.

See that results of the Tournament are mailed to all archers who competed.

DUTIES OF PUBLICITY CHAIRMAN

Before the shoot:

Contact all possible news media and advise them about the coming tournament.

After the shoot:

Contact news media again and give the results of the tournament. In reporting the results it is usually customary to give the name of only the major winners along with any special details such as the establishment of new records. These results should be given immediately. (It is not news to tell them about something that happened a week ago. That's history!)

DUTIES OF AWARDS COMMITTEE

Before the shoot:

See that a sufficient quantity of different class awards will be available for the shoot. These awards should be on display well back of the line, normally at the registrar's desks, during the day of the tournament.

After the shoot:

Assist in the presentation of the awards after the tournament.

DUTIES OF RANGE MASTER

Before the shoot:

See that the range is in good order and that all portable targets are tied down. This practice prevents the targets being blown over by gusty winds.

Have suitable wind flags back of the targets.

After the shoot:

See that the portable targets are properly stored.

See that the range is well policed and left in a clean and orderly manner.

DUTIES OF REGISTRATION COMMITTEE CHAIRMAN

Before the shoot:

See that score cards are provided.

Assign each committee member a specific task to be carried out during registration.

If Amateur and Professional divisions are provided be certain that each archer is aware of the qualifications before he registers.

DUTIES OF FIELD CAPTAIN

Before the shoot:

Arrive at the range well before the start of the tournament.

Assure himself that the targets are mounted correctly and well tied down, that distances are correct and that the range is in good condition.

At the end of the tournament, it is customary to ask if any members of out-of-town clubs would like to make announcements on their coming tournaments. These clubs are as interested in having successful tournaments as your club is. If your club members patronize the tournaments of other clubs, their archers, in turn, will patronize your tournaments.

The duties of the various tournament officials have been roughly covered above. The rules that the tournament officials must observe are covered in the Official Tournament Rules.

PARTICIPANTS

Rules for the individual archer participating in a tournament are also covered in the Tournament Rules. However, very little is said about the duties of the individual archer.

The archer should arrive at the tournament in time to complete his registration so he will be able to get on the shooting line at the announced start of the tournament. He should be equipped with extra arrows so that if he is unable to find an arrow that misses the target, he can return to the line and shoot his extra arrows. (During the noon hour or after the tournament he can hunt for the lost arrows.) He should have an extra bow string.

When it is his turn to shoot, he should be on the line promptly. He should not waste time down at the targets before or after scoring; he should score promptly and get back to the shooting line. He should be quiet when his shooting mates are shooting. Archery is a game of concentration. Unnecessary conversation immediately behind the line can be distracting to other archers. (The archer should never have friends or relatives sitting and talking with him in the tackle or bench area. Between ends, and when the archer is not on the shooting line, he can walk back to the spectators area and greet and talk with these friends.) No archer should ever handle another archer's equipment without first asking permission. He should never converse with his target mates or other archers when either he or they are on the firing line.

The most important consideration both on the part of the individual archer and on the part of the tournament official is *promptness.* Don't waste time, score promptly, get back on the line, and be ready to shoot. Take all the needed time for good shooting but *do not* waste time unnecessarily.

The reason for promptness is simply that everyone wants to get the shoot over at a reasonable hour so that they can have their awards, enjoy a little casual conversation, and return home. Realize that if, in a Double American Round, which consists of 30 ends, *four* minutes are wasted on each end, there is a total of *two hours* wasted during the day. A tournament that should be over at five o'clock would not end until seven o'clock!! Many archers say that they do not patronize certain club tournaments because the shoots never start promptly and so much time is wasted during the shoot that the archer never gets away from the range until after dark. When it becomes known that your club runs its tournaments in an efficient manner, you will have many out-of-town archers participating.

ARCHERY ROUNDS

Details of all Championship Rounds will be found in Section 9 of the Official Tournament Rules in Chapter 11. These details give the number of arrows shot at the various distances of all Championship and Non-Championship Rounds.

The word "Round" designates the number of arrows and the distances at which they are shot. For instance an American Round consists of 90 arrows: 30 arrows at 60 yards, 30 at 50 yards and 30 at 40 yards. For a Double American Round two such Rounds are shot. Rounds are broken up into ends. This terminology is very similar to other sports that have "Innings", "Frames", "Chukkers", "Periods", etc. After each end the archers go to the target, score their hits, and retrieve their arrows. All target ends consist of six arrows with the exception of the International Round (FITA) 50 and 30 meter distances. At these short distances the end consists of three arrows.

N.A.A. ROUNDS

The Rounds shot in an N.A.A. Championship Tournament are: for Men, the FITA Round, the American Round and the 900 Round; for Women, the FITA Round, the American Round and the 900 Round. This combination of Rounds is a good one for a National Tournament because the archers have to shoot at various distances. During the tournament, the men shoot from 90 meters, 70 meters, 60 yards, 50 meters, 50 yards, 40 yards and 30 meters. Women shoot at 70 meters, 60 meters, 60 yards, 50 meters, 50 yards, 40 yards and 30 meters.

For club tournaments, the Double American Round for all Senior contestants and a Double Junior American Round for Juniors is satisfactory. However, many top shooters are not interested in tournaments that do not feature a York Round or a FITA Round; they desire the competitive practice at the longer, more difficult distances. A very popular one day club Invitational Tournament consists of a Double American for Women, a Double Junior American for Juniors, and the choice of a York Round and a Single American Round or a Double American Round for Men.

Many clubs are now using the FITA Round for their local shoots. This is really an ideal round for any type of competition. There is a great variance in the distances, and it tests the skill of the archer probably more thoroughly than any other round. When the FITA Round is shot in a club tournament, it is customary to assign four archers to a target and have them shoot two at a time. In national and international competition only three archers are assigned to each target, and the archers shoot one at a time. This practice allows the archer to concentrate upon his shooting. Shooting two at a time is like having two putters putting at the same time on the green. Local clubs should adopt this system of having only one archer at a time on the line at each target.

INDOOR ROUNDS

With the development of automated archery ranges, indoor shooting, particularly in the winter time, has become very popular. One of the oldest Indoor Rounds is the Chicago Round. It consists of 96 arrows (16 ends) shot at 20 yards on a 16 inch target face. This face is one-third the size of the 48 inch outdoor target face; it has the same colors: gold, red, blue, black and white; the same scoring: 9, 7, 5, 3, and 1.

The Duryee Round is also a good Indoor Round. The Duryee Round consists of 90 arrows at 30 yards on a 48 inch target. A good archer does not find it too difficult to shoot a perfect score, 810, in this round.

Both the indoor P.A.A. Round and the 300 Round consist of 60 arrows at 20 yards. Twelve ends are shot with five arrows to the end. The P.A.A. Round uses a 16 inch black face target with a white center spot. A 300 Round is shot on a 16 inch multicolored face. The target face is divided into five scoring areas. However, the arrows score: 5, 4, 3, 2 and 1 instead of 9, 7, 5, 3 and 1. Thus a perfect end is 25 and a perfect round 300.

Indoor shooting can be lots of fun, particularly in parts of the country where weather conditions practically prohibit outdoor shooting for part of the year. Clubs that do not have access to an automated or public range may set up their own indoor range. This does not take a great deal of space. A distance of 20 yards is sufficient for shooting; naturally, additional space must be left to accommodate the archers behind the shooting line. Some clubs set up a bank of straw bales at one end of the range. Others set up 48 inch portable targets. Each one of these 48 inch targets will accommodate four 16 inch indoor target faces. Members of the clubs usually form teams and compete in a regular winter session. Generally each team shoots once a week. Handicaps are arranged for the individual archers and for each team. The same system that is used to handicap bowlers is satisfactory in handicapping archers for indoor shooting.

One important aspect of indoor shooting should be mentioned. It is very easy for the archer to become careless in his shooting since, at short distances, little errors do not make a great deal of difference. However, these same errors committed at 60, 80 or at 100 yards will throw the arrow completely off the target.

ANNUAL MEETING

1. The N.A.A. shall hold its annual meeting in connection with the annual tournament, at a time and place designated by the Board of Governors.

2. The members present at the annual meeting shall constitute a quorum for the transaction of such business as may come before the meeting. There shall be no voting by proxy.

AMATEUR AND PROFESSIONAL DIVISION

The N.A.A. shall recognize and provide for an Amateur and a Professional Division of its activities. The Board of Governors shall be empowered to make such rules and regulations governing each division as may be desirable or required to qualify for acceptance and participation in the Olympics or other National or International Competition in archery. The Board of Governors shall have authority to make such changes in the rules as they may deem advisable.

MEMBERSHIP DUES

1. The annual dues for Active and Junior membership shall be $5.00 for one year, or $12.50 for three years, and the annual dues for Family membership shall be $6.00 for one year, or $15.00 for three years, for husband and wife plus $1.00 per year for each dependent under 18 years of age, except when membership is under the Club Plan.

2. The annual dues for Sustaining membership shall be such an amount as may be offered but not less than $25.00 per annum. Sustaining membership shall be non-voting.

3. Upon payment of the annual dues, except under the Club Plan, membership shall be granted for one year from the first day of the month in which the dues were paid.

4. Any member who is more than one month in arrears in the payment of dues shall be dropped from the rolls and may be reinstated again only as a new member.

ANNUAL TOURNAMENT: DATE, PLACE AND MANAGEMENT

1. An Annual Tournament, to determine the N.A.A. archery championships of the United States and for other appropriate competition in archery, shall be held between July 15th and September 1st.

2. The Annual Tournament shall be held in one of the three geographical regions, the Atlantic region, the Pacific region, or the Central region, observing a yearly rotation, if possible.

3. The Board of Governors shall decide where the Annual Tournament shall be held and the place for the next tournament shall be announced at the annual business meeting if possible.

4. The Tournament Committee, appointed by the Tournament Director, shall, subject to the guidance and approval of the Board of Governors, arrange and manage all details of the annual tournament.

5. The Annual Tournament shall, in general, follow the rules and regulations as approved by the Board of Governors for the preceding tournament. The same rounds, events, and archery activities shall be held, and any change in the regular program shall have received the prior approval of the Board of Governors.

6. Out of the Tournament fees collected from each registration, the Tournament Committee shall pay a sum, set by the Board of Governors, to the N.A.A.

7. Only members of the N.A.A. who have paid their dues, and who are not obligated to the N.A.A. in any way, may participate in any activities of the N.A.A.

TOURNAMENT RULES

1. All tournament competition shall be in accordance with official N.A.A. Tournament Rules.

2. The Tournament Rules may be changed or amended at any time by the Board of Governors.

3. Those members of the Board of Governors present at the tournament may act on any matters requiring an immediate decision, and may interpret, but not change, any Tournament Rule, except when acting in accordance with Article V, Section 5 of the Constitution.

4. The Tournament Rules may be changed or amended by the membership of the N.A.A. in the same manner as that provided for a change in the By-Laws.

ANNUAL TOURNAMENT: PRIZES AND TROPHIES

1. The Executive Secretary, assisted by the Trophy Committee, shall be the custodian of all prizes and trophies of the N.A.A. and shall keep a record of them, including the names of donors, the conditions of competition governing their award and the names and scores of those who win them.

2. Archers awarded the temporary custody of prizes and trophies, shall give a written receipt for them and shall be responsible for their return, in good order, to the local awards chairman of the sponsoring organization for the coming tournament, at least four weeks before the tournament.

3. The Cyrus E. Dallin medal, usually called the Dallin medal, shall be the championship medal of the N.A.A. It shall be awarded only to those in the Amateur division. In gold, it shall be awarded, as a gift of the N.A.A., to the man and woman champions and to no one else. In silver, it may be given to the intermediate boy and girl champions and to the winners of the second places in the championship standings for men and women. In bronze, it may be given to the winners of second places for intermediate boys and girls and of third places for men and women. No Dallin medals shall be given or awarded other than as above.

4. Except as set forth in Section 3 of this Article, the Board of Governors may authorize or provide for such trophies or other awards as they may deem proper for all divisions of the N.A.A., or they may change or retire at any time any awards which they feel should be discontinued.

CHAMPIONSHIPS AND TITLES

1. All titles shall be recorded and dated as of the year in which they are won, but they shall be held until the next annual tournament, even though that be more than one year later.

2. The champion archers shall be decided on the highest combined scores of all regular target rounds in the respective divisions. Where there is a division of both Amateurs and Professionals, then there shall be a Champion Amateur and a Champion Professional.

3. The Champion Archer of the U.S. shall be the winner in the men's division.

The Champion Woman Archer of the U.S. shall be the winner in the women's division.

The Champion Intermediate Boy Archer of the U.S. shall be the winner in the intermediate boy's division.

The Champion Intermediate Girl Archer of the U.S. shall be the winner in the intermediate girl's division.

The Champion Junior Boy Archer of the U.S. shall be the winner in the junior boy's division.

The Champion Junior Girl Archer of the U.S. shall be the winner in the junior girl's division.

The Champion Beginner Boy Archer of the U.S. shall be the winner in the beginner boy's division.

The Champion Beginner Girl Archer of the U.S. shall be the winner in the beginner girl's division.

The Champion Flight Archer of the U.S. shall be the one who made the longest shot, regular style, regardless of class.

The Champion Woman Flight Archer of the U.S. shall be the woman or girl who shot farther, in regular style, than any one else of her sex.

AFFILIATED CLUBS AND ASSOCIATES

1. Any regular organized archery club whose members live geographically near each other so that they meet together reasonably often for practice, may apply to the Executive Secretary of the N.A.A. for affiliation and may be accepted by approval of the Executive Secretary of the N.A.A. for affiliation and may be accepted by approval of the Executive Secretary and the Chairman of the Board of Governors on payment of annual dues of $8.50.

2. Membership in an affiliated club does not convey individual membership in the N.A.A. However, any member of such a club whose current club dues are paid may secure individual N.A.A. membership under the Club Plan.

3. Members of affiliated clubs may secure "Family Membership" in the N.A.A. to include husband and wife and their dependents under 18 years of age under the Club Plan.

4. Any State, Sectional, or Regional Association may affiliate with the N.A.A. upon approval of the Executive Secretary and the Chairman of the Board of Governors, provided its membership is representative of the archers of the territory over which it has jurisdiction, upon payment of annual dues of $8.50.

5. To qualify for N.A.A. awards for tournament shooting, tournaments of affiliated Associations and Clubs must be conducted strictly in accord with N.A.A. Tournament Rules and, if required, satisfactory evidence to this effect must be furnished to the Executive Secretary of the N.A.A.

CLUB PLAN

1. Individual and family dues under the Club Plan shall be available to members of clubs affiliated with the N.A.A., having six or more N.A.A. members, and complying with the Club Plan rules, as follows:

Active N.A.A. Membership .... $4.00 per year
Family membership (husband and wife) .... $5.00 per year
Children under 18 years of age registered under a Family Plan shall increase family dues by $1.00 for each child registered.

2. Regulations and requirements to be followed by the Clubs and their secretaries, including collection and remittance of N.A.A. dues, notices and distribution of material from the N.A.A. office to N.A.A. members of the clubs, and other matters in connection with the Club Plan purpose, shall be in accordance with rules as set forth by the Board of Governors and may be changed by them.

CLASSIFICATION SYSTEM

The Classification System of the N.A.A. shall be established by the Board of Governors, and may be changed by them. It may also be changed or amended by the membership of the N.A.A. in the same manner as that provided for a change in the By-Laws.

OFFICIAL N.A.A.
TOURNAMENT RULES

FOREWORD

The rules contained herein govern conduct and competition in the National Archery Association Annual Tournament and all six-golds tournaments, officially recognized by the National Archery Association.

Because local conditions may prevent elaborate field arrangements, properties, or personnel usage, MINIMUM RULES are stated, and allowable tolerances are indicated. In the interests of uniformity, local clubs and associations are urged to adopt these rules to govern local archery competition.

Such local clubs or associations may adopt special regulations, or additional rules, providing that such additions do not conflict with, nor in any way alter, one or more of the rules contained herein.

Decisions not regulated by the Official Tournament Rules of the National Archery Association, or by specific regulations of local clubs and associations, shall fall under the authority of the tournament officials involved.

PRIMARY RULES

SAFETY AND COURTESY

A. Every precaution must be taken to insure the highest possible safety standards has precedence over all other considerations or rules. Any practices, attitudes, equipment, or conditions, either mentioned herein, or not mentioned herein, which are in the least degree unsafe, are prohibited. Repetition, after one warning by a tournament official, shall require the offending participant, or participants, to be expelled from the tournament without refund. It shall be the responsibility of every N.A.A. member to insist upon strict maintenance of safety standards at all times.
B. To insure a fair enjoyment of archery competition by all contestants, a high standard of personal courtesy and sportsmanship is enjoined upon all. Discourteous unsportsmanlike conduct is an unwarranted offense against other archers and an affront to the heritage of dignity and tradition which is an integral part of the sport of archery. Per-

sistence in discourteous or unsportsmanlike conduct shall, after one warning by a tournament official, be considered grounds for expulsion from the tournament, without refund, of the offending participants.

1.0 THE ARCHERY RANGE

1.1 The target field shall be laid out so that shooting is from South to North. A maximum deviation of 45% is allowed for N.A.A. Annual Tournaments. Local tournament deviation from this rule is allowed, if required by terrain available.

1.2 The targets shall be equally spaced 5, plus or minus 1, yards (4 to 6 yards) apart, measured from the center of the gold to the center of the gold of the adjacent target.

1.3 Range distances shall be accurately measured from a point on the ground perpendicular to the center of the gold on the target face to the shooting point.

1.4 Target lines and shooting lines, or range lines shall be plainly and accurately marked on the ground, and shall be not more than 6 inches in width. Target lines or shooting lines may be arranged to require the shooters to move forward from the longest range to lesser distances while the targets remain stationary, or to require the targets to be brought forward from longer to lesser distances while the shooters use a stationary line.

1.5 Individual target lanes shall be suitably and plainly marked either by center lines, or by lines designating the side boundaries of each lane. Pegs, chalk lines, trenches, or mowed strips are suitable markings. Local tournaments may deviate from this rule.

1.6 There shall be a minimum of 20 yards clear space behind the targets, which may be reduced by a suitable bunker or backstop. Spectators, participants or pedestrians shall not be allowed behind the targets while shooting is in progress, or even beyond 20 yards if there is the slightest possibility of being struck by the wildest arrow.

1.7 There shall be a clear area of at least 20 yards on each side of the field as a safety lane.

1.8 Bow racks, tackle boxes, or other objects which protrude above the ground shall not be allowed within six feet of the shooting line.

1.9 At least every third target should have a small wind flag, of a size and color easily visible from the 100 yard line, mounted at least two feet above the top of the target. Local tournaments may deviate from this rule.

1.10 Staggered shooting lines, wherein one group of archers shoot from a position forward of another group, are considered unsafe. In emergency, they may be used provided an unused lateral safety lane of at least 20 yards is maintained as a buffer.

2.0 TARGET BUTTS AND BASTS

2.1 The target backstop shall be of any suitable material that will not damage arrows nor allow them to pass through or bounce out frequently.

2.2 The target backstop shall be not less than 50 inches in diameter.

2.3 Target backstops shall be securely anchored to the ground to prevent accidental toppling.

2.4 Target identification shall be by means of numerals at least 8 inches high, on soft cardboard or other suitable material, so as to be easily visible at 100 yards and should be mounted near the base of the target.

3.0 THE TARGET FACE

3.1 The Official Target Face of the N.A.A. must be used for the N.A.A. Annual Tournament and all official 6-golds shoots.

3.2 The target face may be of any suitable material that will not damage arrows and that will retain stability of size, shape, and color under adverse weather conditions.

3.3 The scoring area of the target face shall be forty-eight (48) inches in diameter. The target face is divided into 5 concentric color zones arranged from the center outwards as follows: — Gold (yellow), Red, Blue, Black and White.

Each color zone is in turn divided by a thin line, not more than 1/10 inch in width, into two zones of equal width, thus making in all ten (10) scoring zones of equal width measured from the center of the gold. Such dividing lines, and any dividing lines which may be used between colors shall be entirely within the higher scoring zone.

3.4 Target face colors should be reasonably "dull" and "non-glaring" and conform as closely as possible to the following color code, as specified in the Munsell Color Charts. Colors are listed from the center out.

Color	Hue	Value	Chroma	Notation
Gold (Yellow)	6.5Y	8.1	10.7	5.OY-8.0-12.0
Red	8.5R	4.9	12.6	5.OR-4.0-14.0
Blue	5.0B	6.5	8.0	5.OB-7.0-6.0
Black	1.5RP	2.9	0.3	None-2.0-0.0
White	0.5GY	8.94	0.6	None-9.0-0.0

3.5 The center of the gold on the target face shall be mounted 51 inches from the ground. Schools and camps may omit this requirement. The target face shall be inclined away from the shooting line at an angle of from 12 to 18 degrees from the vertical.

4.0 DEFINITIONS

4.1 SHOOTING AREA — an area starting at the shooting line and extending 6 feet to the rear, and which runs parallel to and adjacent to the shooting line.

4.2 TACKLE AND BENCH AREA — an area starting at the rear limit of the Shooting Area and extending 6 feet to the rear, and which runs parallel to and adjacent to the shooting area.

4.3 SPECTATOR'S AREA — the area behind the Tackle and Bench Area.

4.4 AN END — Consists of six arrows shot in two groups of three.

4.5 COMPLETED END — a field official shall signal the finish of each end. Unless this signal is immediately challenged by those archers who have not released 6 arrows, the end shall be considered complete, and the archer shall have no recourse to shooting additional arrows.

4.6 PERFECT END — Six consecutive arrows in the gold in one end shall constitute a perfect end.

5.0 ARCHERY TACKLE

5.1 Any kind of bow may be used, providing it is shot by holding it in one hand and the string in the other, without mechanical assistance or support which in the opinion of the tournament officials would give undue advantage over other competitors.

5.2 Any kind of arrow may be used provided that it does not, in the opinion of the tournament officials, damage the targets unreasonably.

5.3 Any type of sight or aiming device attached to the bow may be used. Any type of point-of-aim may be used which does not protrude more than six inches above the ground and does not interfere with shooting or scoring.

5.4 Any type of releasing aid, such as gloves, tabs, straps, flippers, ledges and other developments of traditional release aids is permitted, except that mechanical releases consisting of two or more working parts are not permitted. Unusual release aids should be submitted to the tournament officials for eligibility before shooting.

5.5 Binoculars or any other visual aids may be used on the shooting line by a contestant between shots.

5.6 Foot markers may be left on the shooting line during the round provided they are embedded in the turf and do not extend more than (½) inch above the ground.

5.7 Ground quivers may be placed on the shooting line while the archer is in the process of shooting but must be removed to the tackle area while others are shooting and during the scoring interval.

6.0 ELIGIBILITY AND CLASSIFICATION

6.1 Archers shall be classed in the following groups:
   a. Men . . . . 18 years old or over
   b. Women . . . . 18 years old or over
   c. Intermediate Boys . . . . 15 to 18 years old
   d. Intermediate Girls . . . . 15 to 18 years old
   e. Junior Boys . . . . 12 to 15 years old
   f. Junior Girls . . . . 12 to 15 years old
   g. Cadet Boys* . . . . less than 12 years old
   h. Cadet Girls* . . . . less than 12 years old
   *May also be called Beginners.

6.2 An archer must shoot in the highest class if the official start of the tournament shall be on or after the birthday which places him in the higher class. However; an archer whose birthday occurs after March 31st in the year of his/her 12th, 15th, 18th birthday shall be permitted to compete in the lower age group until October 1st of the same year.

6.3 An archer may, by election before shooting starts, compete in a higher class than normally classed, but may not shoot in a lower class. This includes the right of women or girls to compete against men or boys in higher classes, but does not permit men or boys to compete against girls' or women's classes.

6.4 No archer shall be barred from a tournament because of a physical handicap unless his or her shooting requires mechanical aids which, in the judgment of the Field Officials, would give him or her undue advantage over the other archers.

7.0 FIELD OFFICIALS

7.1 Field Officials shall be appointed by the tournament officials and shall rank in authority as follows: Field Captain, Lady Paramount, Assistants to Field Captain, Assistants to Lady Paramount.

7.2 The Field Officials shall have the responsibility and authority to organize, supervise and regulate all practice, shooting and competition in accordance with regulations and customs; to interpret and to decide questions of rules; TO MAINTAIN SAFETY CONDITIONS; to enforce sportsmanlike behavior; to score doubtful arrows; to signify the start, interruptions, delays, postponements and finish of competition.

7.3 Repeated rules infractions or discourteous or unsportsmanlike conduct, not sufficiently grave as to require expulsion, shall be penalized by the Field Officials after an appropriate warning, as follows: For the first repetition after warning the loss of the highest arrow of that end; for the second repetition, the loss of the end; for the third repetition, expulsion from the tournament without refund.

7.4 Decisions of the lesser field officials shall be final unless immediately appealed to the Field Captain.

7.5 Decisions of the Field Captain shall be final unless immediate verbal notice of intent to protest is given the Field Captain, and unless this is followed by the submission of a written protest to the Tournament Chairman within 3 hours of the completion of the tournament. Written protests will be reviewed by the Governing Board as soon as it can conveniently convene.

8.0 SHOOTING, SCORING, AND CONDUCT OF PARTICIPANTS

8.1 Initial target assignments may be made according to any system designated by the tournament officials. There shall not be less than three nor more than five archers assigned to each target in use, and four is customary.

8.2 Archers shall be re-assigned targets after each round on the basis of their total score for rounds completed.

8.3 There shall be at least three uninterrupted practice ends, at the longest distance, followed without interruption by the beginning of scoring for the round.

8.4 There shall be no practice permitted after a postponement or delay unless such postponement or delay exceeds thirty (30) minutes. In such cases the amount of practice shall be according to the following schedule.

1. Thirty (30) to sixty (60) minute delay — one practice end.

2. Sixty (60) minutes or more delay, unless interrupted by a scheduled lunch period or night fall — two practice ends.

8.5 A blast of the whistle shall be the signal to commence or cease shooting for each end. Two or more blasts signals an immediate interruption for all shooting.

8.6 An archer shall stand so that he has one foot on each side of the shooting line. He shall also stand 18″ from the center of the target lane or 18″ from the boundaries.

8.7 If an archer shoots less than six arrows in one end, he may shoot the remaining arrows if the omission is discovered before the end is officially completed, otherwise they shall score as misses. (See 4.5)

8.8 If an archer shoots more than six arrows in one end, only the lowest six shall score.

8.9 Archers may not make up lost rounds, ends, or arrows except as specified.

8.10 If a target falls before an end is scored, that end shall be shot over by all archers on that target.

8.11 Equipment failures, mishaps or other occurrences not specifically covered in other rules shall not entitle an archer to repeat a shot unless the mis-shot arrow can be reached by the bow from the archer's position on the shooting line.

8.12 Arrows in the standard target face shall be evaluated as follows: Gold — 9, Red — 7, Blue — 5, Black — 3, White — 1. Each color zone is in turn divided by a thin line into two zones of equal width, thus making in all ten (10) scoring zones of equal width. The zones are scored from the center outward — 10, 9, 8, 7, 6, 5, 4, 3, 2 and 1.

8.13 If an arrow in the target touches two scoring areas, breaking the outside edge of the black scoring line, the higher score shall count. Doubtful arrows must be determined for each end before the arrows or target face have been touched, otherwise the lower value must be taken.

8.14 An arrow that has passed through the scoring face so that it is not visible from the front shall count 7 at 60 yards or less, and 5 for ranges beyond 60 yards. Arrows passing completely through the target, if witnessed, are scored in same manner.

8.15 An arrow which rebounds from the scoring face, if witnessed, shall score the same as a pass through.

8.16 An arrow embedded in another arrow on the scoring face shall score the same as the arrow in which it is embedded.

8.17 If an arrow should hang from the target face, shooting shall be interrupted and a Field Official shall immediately reinsert the arrow in its proper place in the scoring face.

8.18 Hits on the wrong target shall score as misses.

8.19 The archer chosen to pull the arrows from the target, normally the first in the order of assignment, shall be the Target Captain and shall rule all questions on his target, subject to appeal to the Field Officials.

8.20 The target captain shall call the value of each arrow as he pulls it from the target and it shall then be recorded independently by two contestants acting as scorers, normally the next two assigned to the target. Scorers should check results after each end to avoid errors.

8.21 Each archer is individually responsible for seeing that his arrows are called correctly and properly entered on the score cards, and that his score cards are turned in to the proper officials.

8.22 Any archer should call to the attention of the Field Officials any rule infractions, unsportsmanlike or unseemly conduct, or ANY SAFETY HAZARDS. The Field Officials are empowered to take such steps as their judgment indicates to correct the situation including warning, scoring penalties, and even expulsion from the tournament in severe cases. (See 7.2)

8.23 Any archer may retire from the shooting line to avoid proximity to tackle or a shooting practice that he considers unsafe, and may resume shooting when safe conditions prevail.

8.24 Archers may not shoot at varying distances from different shooting lines, nor engage in unauthorized practice, unless separated laterally by the width of at least four target lanes.

8.25 In all officials 6-golds shoots ends shall be shot "three and three" Half (or the closest possible number to half) of the archers assigned to each target shall take position and shoot three arrows each. They shall then retire and the remaining archers assigned shall shoot three arrows. Then the first group shall shoot their remaining arrows. Finally the second group on each target shall shoot their remaining three arrows. The Field Captain may require shooting six arrows at a time only in an emergency where the time saved is necessary to complete the schedule.

8.26 Tie scores shall be resolved in favor of the archer shooting the highest score at the longest distance, then the next longest distances, in descending order. If still tied through all distances, then ties shall be resolved in favor of the archer with the greatest total number of Golds, then Reds, then Blues, then Blacks. If still tied, the tie shall be resolved in favor of the archer with the greatest total number of perfect ends. If still tied, it shall be so recorded.

8.27 Coaching an archer on the shooting line by means of inaudible and inconspicuous signs or symbols is permitted, providing that such coaching is not distracting to other contestants. If a contestant on the same target or adjacent targets complains that such activity is personally distracting, such coaching must be terminated immediately. Audible coaching of archers on the shooting line is not permitted.

9.0 CHAMPIONSHIP AND NON-CHAMPIONSHIP ROUNDS

9.1a. The Men's F.I.T.A. Round
    36 arrows at 90 meters (98.4 yards) 122 cm
        10 ring target face
    36 arrows at 70 meters (76.6 yards) 122 cm
        10 ring target face
    36 arrows at 50 meters (54.7 yards) 80 cm
        10 ring target face
    36 arrows at 30 meters (32.8 yards) 80 cm
        10 ring target face

9.2b. The Ladies' F.I.T.A. Round**
    36 arrows at 70 meters (76.6 yards) 122 cm
        10 ring target face
    36 arrows at 60 meters (65.6 yards) 122 cm
        10 ring target face
    36 arrows at 50 meters (54.7 yards) 80 cm
        10 ring target face
    36 arrows at 30 meters (32.8 yards) 80 cm
        10 ring target face
        Total 144 arrows

*International Archery Federation, Target Archery Rules apply.

*c. 900 Round (Men, Women, Intermediate Boys and Girls) Standard target face scored as follows: 10, 9, 8, 7, 6, 5, 4, 3, 2 and 1)
    30 Arrows at 60 yards
    30 Arrows at 50 yards
    30 Arrows at 40 yards

d. The American Round (Men, Women, Intermediate Boys and Girls) (Standard Target Face)
    30 arrows at 60 yards
    30 arrows at 50 yards
    30 arrows at 40 yards (Total 90 arrows)

e. The Junior Boys, Junior Girls, Jr. American Round (Standard Target Face)
    30 arrows at 50 yards
    30 arrows at 40 yards
    30 arrows at 30 yards (Total 90 arrows)
f. The Junior Columbia Round (Standard Target Face) (for all Beginners Boys or Girls under 12)
    24 arrows at 40 yards
    24 arrows at 30 yards
    24 arrows at 20 yards (Total 72 arrows)
g. The Team Rounds—96 Arrows (Standard Target Face)
    at 60 yards—Men and Intermediate Boys
    at 50 yards—Women and Intermediate Girls
    *at 40 yards—Junior Boys and Girls
    *at 30 yards—Cadet Boys
    *at 20 yards—Cadet Girls
h. The Clout Rounds—36 arrows (See Sec. 10.0)
    at 180 yards—Men
    at 140 yards—Women and Intermediate Boys
    at 120 yards—Women, Junior Boys, and Intermediate Girls
    *at 80 yards—Junior Boys and Girls, Cadet Boys and Girls
*i. The York Round (Men) (Standard Target Face)
    72 arrows at 100 yards
    48 arrows at 80 yards
    24 arrows at 60 yards (Total 144 arrows)
*j. The National Round (Women and Intermediate Girls) (Standard Target Face)
    48 arrows at 60 yards
    24 arrows at 50 yards (Total 72 arrows)
*k. The Columbia Round (Women, Intermediate Girls, Junior Girls) (Standard Target Face)
    24 arrows at 50 yards
    24 arrows at 40 yards
    24 arrows at 30 yards (Total 72 arrows)
*l. The Hereford Round (Women and Intermediate Boys) (Standard Target Face)
    72 arrows at 80 yards
    48 arrows at 60 yards
    24 arrows at 50 yards (Total 144 arrows)
*m. The Metropolitan Rounds: (Standard Target Face)

MEN	WOMEN, JR. BOYS & GIRLS	JR. MET. YOUNG BOYS & GIRLS
30 at 100 yards	30 to 60 yards	
30 at 80 yards	30 at 50 yards	30 at 40 yards
30 at 60 yards	30 at 40 yards	30 at 30 yards
30 at 50 yards	30 at 30 yards	30 at 20 yards
30 at 40 yards		
Total 150 arrows	Total 120 arrows	Total 90 arrows

*n. The Duryee Round (Men and Women) (Standard Target Face) 90 arrows at 30 yards
*o. The Chicago Round (Men and Women) (16 inch target face) 96 arrows at 20 yards
*p. 300 Indoor Round (16 inch black and white target face divided into 5 zones of equal width and scored from the center outward as follows: 5, 4, 3, 2 and 1) 60 arrows at 20 yards.
*q. The Junior Boys Hereford Round (Standard Target Face)
    72 arrows at 50 yards
    48 arrows at 40 yards
    24 arrows at 30 yards (Total 144 arrows)

*r. The Wand Rounds—36 arrows (See Sec. 12.0)
    at 100 yards—Men
    at 80 yards—Intermediate Boys
    at 60 yards—Women, Intermediate Girls
   *at 50 yards—Junior Boys
   *at 40 yards—Junior Girls, Cadet Boys
   *at 30 yards—Cadet Girls

*s. Cadet Girls National Round (Standard Target Face)
    48 arrows at 30 yards
    24 arrows at 20 yards (Total 72 arrows)

*t. Cadet Girls Columbia Round (Standard Target Face)
    24 arrows at 30 yards
    24 arrows at 20 yards (Total 48 arrows)

*u. The Junior Girls National Round (Standard Target Face)
    48 arrows at 40 yards
    24 arrows at 30 yards (Total 72 arrows)

*v. Cadet Boys Hereford Round (Standard Target Face)
    36 arrows at 40 yards
    24 arrows at 30 yards
    12 arrows at 20 yards (Total 72 arrows)

*w. Cadet American—Boys or Girls (Standard Target Face)
    15 arrows at 30 yards
    15 arrows at 20 yards (Total 30 arrows)
    *Non-championship rounds

10.0 THE CLOUT SHOOT

10.1 The Clout Target shall be laid out on the ground by means of white lines, approximately 2 inches wide, of a material non-injurious to arrows, in a ratio of 12 to 1 to the standard face. Local six gold shoots may dispense with the requirement for lines.

10.2 The center of the clout shall be indicated by a white marker not more than 36 inches square or less than 30 inches square, mounted on soft wooden slats perpendicular to, and with the bottom against, the ground. A solid color disc, not more than 9.6 inches in diameter, may be centered on this marker.

10.3 The rules and scoring applicable to target archery shall apply, except that rebounds shall be scored from the place at which the point of the arrow comes to final rest.

10.4 The Field Captain and Lady Paramount shall appoint a sufficient number of archers to pull and sort the arrows—(Usually one for each ring of the clout). Only those appointed shall enter the rings until all arrows have been pulled, sorted, and ready for scoring.

10.5 A wire or steel tape or chain, accurately marked for the appropriate rings of the clout, shall be rotated around a stake in the center of the clout, to indicate the exact value of all doubtful arrows, as determined by the point where the arrow emerges from the ground. Values of arrows that fail to stick in the ground shall be determined by the point of the arrow.

10.6 The Double scoring system shall be used, and the Field Captain and Lady Paramount shall appoint a set of scorers for approximately every 10 archers who are competing.

10.7 When all arrows are pulled and sorted and laid in the clout ring from which they were pulled, the scorers and archers will enter the clout area and each archer will call the values of his arrows beginning with golds.

11.0 THE TEAM SHOOT

11.1 *An official team shall consist of 4 archers who are active fellow members of at least one month's standing of an Archery Club affiliated with the N.A.A. If less than 4 archers wish to compete as a team, their score must count as a complete team.

* An official team must be so located geographically that members may meet reasonably often for practice.

11.2 Team Shoot entries, including names must be registered with the N.A.A. Secretary or his designate, on the day prior to the team shoot.

11.3 Groups of 4 archers who cannot qualify as an official team may register as above but shall not be eligible for the Winners Team Award.

11.4 The official Team making the highest aggregate score shall be the winner of the team award, and the highest scoring archer, whether on an official team or unofficial team, shall be the individual winner.

11.5 Shooting and scoring and all rules shall be in accordance with the rules for regular target rounds, except that one of the two scorers for each target shall be from an adjacent target.

12.0 THE WAND SHOOT

12.1 The wand shall be a slat of soft wood or other suitable material that will best hold arrows and minimize rebounds. (Balsa wood is best). It shall be two (2) inches wide. It shall be set in the ground and project up six feet.

The following option may be used: The wand may be three (3) inches wide, and if dark in color will have a two inch wide light colored stripe down the middle. If light in color it will have a two inch wide dark stripe down the middle.

12.2 Six ends (36 arrows) shall be shot in the competition. The rules of conduct applicable to target shooting shall apply.

12.3 Only those arrows shall be counted as hits which are actually embedded in the wand, or which are witnessed rebounds. A witness for each wand shall be stationed behind the shooting line to witness rebounds. An arrow embedded in the wand with the pile totally beneath the surface of the ground shall score as a miss.

13.0 CROSSBOWS

13.1 Crossbowmen do not compete with longbowmen. They compete with and against each other for awards within their own division.

13.2 TARGETS are (½) the size specified for longbows for the same round except for the Clout Round, where the same size target is used and in the King's Round which has no counterpart in the Longbow Division.

13.3 RULES are the same as for longbowmen except where in conflict with the rules given in this section.

13.4 THE CROSSBOW FIELD CAPTAIN is specifically appointed to supervise the crossbowmen. His duties and authority correspond to that of the Field Captain for longbowmen, his decisions being final unless appealed to the Board. (See 7.4)

13.5 The Crossbow and parts may be made of any material.

13.6 DRAWING; Crossbows shall be drawn by hand. No mechanical aids for drawing shall be permitted.

13.7 SHOOTING: Crossbowmen stand to shoot and shall shoot "offhand". No rests of any description shall be permitted.

13.8 ASSIGNMENT TO TARGETS: Two crossbowmen shall be assigned per target, until all targets are filled. Should the last (highest numbered), target have less than two archers assigned to it, then three archers may be assigned to this target.

13.9 ARROWS OR BOLTS may be made of any material and length but must not be of such design that they will unreasonably damage the target face or bast. They shall be plainly crested for ease of scoring.

13.10 SPOTTING AIDS: Binoculars or a spotting scope may be used AT ANY TIME to locate hits. Spotting scopes must be set up in the Bench and Tackle Area.

13.11 SIGHTS: Telescopic or magnifying sight shall not be permitted.

13.12 BOW WEIGHT: In flight shooting, or in other events where the weight of the bow is a governing factor in the competition, the various classifications set up shall be figured in direct proportion to the longbow for that class at twenty seven inches draw, using the inch-pound method to determine the class in which a bow may fall.

13.13 TARGET FACE: Target faces shall be (½) the size of the faces used by the longbowmen for the round shot, but similar in all other respects except the gold may be WHITE for better visibility. (See 13.2).

13.14 TARGET BACKSTOPS shall be round basts of woven or compressed straw or grass, of the greatest degree of firmness obtainable, and shall be 53 inches, plus or minus 3 inches, in diameter. (Rectangular bales of straw or other materials are not considered suitable for crossbows.)

13.15 SAFETY: Crossbowmen will keep their weapons when drawn, whether loaded or not, pointed in the direction of the target. All safety rules specified for archers also pertain to crossbowmen.

13.16 INFRACTIONS OF RULES: The Crossbow Field Captain may, at his discretion, penalize or even bar from further competition a shooter who exhibits carelessness in handling his weapon. The Field Captain may also bar from competition a crossbow he considers dangerous to other shooters or to spectators.

13.17 ROUNDS: The National Championship for both men and women shall be determined by the highest total scores shot, by each sex, in the Quadruple American Round. The Tournament officials may, at their discretion, add such other events as it considers desirable, such as Clout, King's Round, novelty rounds, etc., but the scores made in such events shall not count toward determining the Championships.

a. American Round (see 9.1b)

b. KING'S ROUND

1. PARTICIPANTS: Only three crossbowmen shooting the highest individual American Round Scores, while participating in the Championship Quadruple American Round Contest may shoot the King's round.

2. TARGET FACE: The target will be a special 48" face, that shall remain in the custody of the Secretary of the N.A.A. It shall contain (6) standard (4¾") Golds, clocked on an eighteen inch (18") radius at 12, 2, 4, 6 and 8 o'clock, respectively. Within each of the said Golds there is to be centered a Black (1") bullseye.

3. DISTANCE: The contest for the King's Round shall be staged at 40 yards.

4. SCORING: Bolts must cut the Gold to score. Each hit in the gold counts 9 points, while a hit in the black counts (10).

5. SHOOTING: One contestant shall shoot at a time, shooting one bolt and then stepping back from the shooting line. The person having the highest individual score in the Quadruple American Round Contest shall shoot first, the next highest second, etc. All shall shoot in turn, first at the 12 o'clock gold, then at 2 o'clock, etc. Each contestant shall shoot one end only of six bolts.

6. AWARDS: The contestant having the highest score shall be known as the King, (or Queen), and shall be awarded the Stevens King's Round Dagger, which may be held for the tournament year. The two runnersup shall be known as the King's Men. The National Crossbowmen will award symbolic crowns to the contestants annually, a gold crown to the King, and silver crowns to the two King's Men. The contestants may also place on their persons small crowns of either yellow or white as may be appropriate, to denote their participation and standing in a National King's Round Contest.

13.18 AWARDS:

a. MEN: First, second and third place medals for permanent possession. The Schaeffer Memorial Trophy for Men's National Crossbow Champion.

b. WOMEN: First, second and third place medals for permanent possession. The Bailey Trophy for Women's National Crossbow Champion.

c. HERALDRY: In addition to the foregoing awards, the National Crossbowmen have made rules governing the decoration of pennons or gonfalons which may be displayed. These rules may be obtained from the National Crossbowmen thru the Captain of the National Crossbowmen.

14.0 FLIGHT SHOOTING

14.1 FLIGHT OFFICIALS

a. FLIGHT CONTEST BOARD: shall consist of not less than three members, and shall be selected by the N.A.A. Flight Committee together with the Host Organization. The Board shall be made up of the Flight Captain, Assistant Flight Captain and such other assistants as may be necessary. (A Board member may be a contestant, but may not qualify his own tackle or judge his own arrows.)

b. FLIGHT CAPTAIN shall act as final arbiter of all matters concerning the contest.

c. ASSISTANT FLIGHT CAPTAINS shall aid the Flight Captain and act in his place at the Base Line or in the Field when required to do so.

d. Other members of the Contest Board shall serve as directed by the Flight Captain.

14.2 FLIGHT SHOOTING AREA

a. BASE LINE OR SHOOTING LINE: Defined as the line from which arrows are cast and from which measurements are made. It shall be at least 20 yards long. Contestants only may occupy base line while arrows are being cast.

b. FOUL LINE: Defined as one yard ahead of base line and parallel to it.

c. CONTEST SPACE: Defined as the area behind the base line at least 10 yards in depth, roped off to provide protection to contestants and their equipment. Only contestants, their assistants (one to each shooter) and officials will be allowed in this area.

d. FAIRWAY: Defined as the ground between base line and landing area, approximately 200 yards or more in length, as free as possible of view obstructing elements.

e. LANDING AREA: Defined as any ground on which arrows are expected to land in all classes being contested, 500 yards or more in length, and 200 yards or more in width. It shall be free of obstructions and hazards such as trees, buildings, fences, ditches, etc. It should provide turf or other ground favorable for arrows to land.

f. DISTANCE MEASUREMENTS: The Klopsteg or Rheingans Grid are approved by N.A.A. and the type of plats suitable for calculating an arrow's position in the field. Central Line calculations may be used in place of the stated Grids if the Contest Board so decides.

g. BOUNDARIES: shall be clearly designated by flags or other markers, showing the area restricted for contest purposes.

h. SPECIAL PROVISIONS: The shooting line may be advanced toward the Landing Area for the purpose of contesting events for women and juniors. In foot bow contests, the shooting line may be moved back of the base line to afford greater landing distance.

14.3 FLIGHT BOWS

a. FLIGHT BOWS shall be designated as hand bows, and foot bows, according to the manner in which they are employed.

b. WEIGHT CLASSES: The established weight limit classes shall be as follows:

Men—50 #—65 #—80 #—Unlimited—Foot Bow

Women—35 #—50 #—Unlimited—Foot Bow

Juniors—35 #—50 #—Unlimited—Foot Bow

(13.12 for crossbow weights)

c. BOW WEIGHING SCALES: Bows shall be weighed on scales tested within thirty days by Sealer of Weights or equal authority and must carry stamp of this test or certification of accuracy by qualified agency.

d. WEIGHING-IN REQUIREMENTS shall be as follows:

    1. Bows in all weight limit classes shall be qualified in advance of shooting, but not more than 24 hours prior to contest in which used. In event of postponement, bows previously qualified may be used if so ordered by the Contest Board.

    2. Weight of bow, length of arrow to be shot in the bow and the class for which

this combination is eligible, shall be recorded on a label affixed to the face of the bow.

3. Bows eligible for weight limit class may be used in a higher weight class without reweighing, provided longer arrows are not used.
4. Terms defined:
   FULL DRAW is draw required to bring point of arrow on the arrow track coincident with back of bow.
   ARROW TRACK is surface supporting arrow during draw and release.
   OVERDRAW is draw in track in excess of 1½ inches from back of bow. Any excess is considered a portion of arrow's length for bow weighting purposes.
5. No bow in excess of two pounds over the limit will be qualified under any circumstances. Conditions for any allowance will be temperature below 80°F. as follows: 70 to 79 degrees F.—one pound; 60 to 69 degrees F.—two pounds.

e. BOW QUALIFICATIONS FOR COMPETITION: One or more bows may be qualified for the same weight class by the same archer.

Open weight bows and foot bows need only qualify the arrows. After the stamp is affixed certifying qualification, the contestant must present the bow to the shooting line in the same condition in which it was first accepted.

In the event a bow is broken or damaged during the drawing, another bow may be qualified without loss of the shot. Breakage to string, or bow, after the arrow has been fairly cast, will not entitle the contestant to a replacement arrow.

14.4 FLIGHT ARROWS

a. Six arrows shall constitute an end.
b. Arrows must bear the following identifications:
   1. Name of contestant, affixed by contestant.
   2. Distinctive number, affixed by contestant.
   3. Stamp indicating class in which used; affixed by officials.
c. The length of an arrow shall be determined by measurement from the floor of the nock to the extremity of the point of the arrow.
d. Arrows in the field will be identified by officials according to name, number and bow class stamp and shall be so recorded on score cards.
e. An arrow's position in the field will be determined by location on Klopsteg or Rheingans Grids, or by right angle intersection of the Central Lines.
f. An arrow that comes to rest in other than the usual position shall be determined from the tip of the arrow, if visible, or from the point at which it enters any object other than the ground.
g. Arrows should not be pulled from field without consent of officials, or until event is declared completed.
h. Position of arrows in the field shall be marked by suitable means and the distance determinations should be made before the next event is shot, is possible. If distances are to be measured only at the conclusion of the day's events, the suitable markers, clearly visible, may be placed at the arrow's position with all pertinent data recorded thereon.
i. Any lost arrow must be reported to the officials, and full record made as to identity of this arrow before next event is shot. If found during subsequent events, and showing no evidence of having been moved or molested, the arrows may be judged for place in event for which marked, provided that no such arrow shall be eligible after all events have been declared closed by the Flight Captain.

14.5 FLIGHT-DRAW AND RELEASE METHODS

a. Mechanical drawing and release aids are prohibited in all N.A.A. tournaments and N.A.A. sponsored events.
   1. The term "Mechanical" shall be taken to mean any method that embodies a plurality of interacting parts, whether such are individual pieces or spring conjoined parts, capable of cooperatively acting to effect bow string release by a separating motion of at least one such part relative to another part.
b. The above rule does not apply to crossbows participating in flight events.

15.0 NAA SIX-GOLDS CLUB RULES
    1. To be eligible for membership in the Six Golds Club, an archer must shoot a perfect end in a tournament which is duly registered, prior to the date of the tournament, with the Office of the Secretary of the National Archery Association, as a "Six-Golds Shoot". Only affiliated Clubs and Associations, whose dues are paid in advance, are privileged to register, and hold, recognized Six-Golds Shoots, of which four per year are permitted. Each day's shooting is counted as a separate Six-Golds Shoot. Additional Six-Golds Shoots may be registered by paying a fee of $3.00 to the National Archery Association.
    2. Only bona-fide individual and family members of the National Archery Association are eligible for membership in the Six-Golds Club.
    3. The Six-Golds or perfect end, shall be shot in the following rounds only, (unless specifically excepted below).
    MEN: York, American, Team (60 yards), Metropolitan, St. George, Jersey, Potomac (no special range button to be awarded for the 70 yard distance), Clout Round (180 yards). F.I.T.A., 900.
    LADIES: All those included for men and: National, Metropolitan, Team (50 yards), Columbia, Hereford, Clout Round (140 and 120 yards).
    JUNIORS: All those included for men and women and: Junior American, Junior Columbia, Junior Metropolitan. F.I.T.A., 900.
    4. Should any Club or Association affiliated with the N.A.A., wish some round recognized other than those cited above, they may petition the Board of Governors through the Chairman. If any such round is recognized, the Chairman shall have it included in the "Operating Bulletin".
    5. All perfect ends made must be properly witnessed, dated and signed by the Field Captain or Lady Paramount, or their duly authorized assistants.
    6. The Secretary of the Club or Association must send to the N.A.A. Office the complete duplicate recorded score card, with the proper information entered on the Tournament Report Sheet, within five days after the meet. Tournament Report Sheets will be provided by the N.A.A. and must accompany the score card.
    7. All new members of the Six-Golds may purchase a range button from the N.A.A. Secretary, indicating the distance at which the Six-Golds was attained, and shall receive without cost, a Six-Golds pin with the Golden Arrow. Members of the Crossbow Division shall receive a Six-Golds pin with a Silver Arrow, without cost and in addition will receive a Range Bar, indicating the distance, to be appended to the Six-Golds Pin, from the National Company of Crossbowmen if the individual is a member of that organization. A new member is any N.A.A. archer shooting a perfect end for the first time in a tournament as described above. For successive perfect ends (shot at the same distance) the N.A.A. Secretary will enter the current facts in the permanent Six-Golds Membership file. No additional pins are issued at any time, but if a Six-Golds is attained at a new distance, that archer may purchase a button indicating the new range. Any archer having shot a Six-Golds previous to August, 1953, may purchase range buttons for $1.25 each, if he can substantiate his claim of having shot the Six-Golds in a regular Six-Golds tournament. Old Six-Golds Club members can purchase range buttons for the proper distances, and/or by attaining a Six-Golds at a distance never attained prior to August, 1953.
    8. Should a Six-Golds Club member lose his pin, he may apply for a replacement by paying the sum of $3.00 to cover the cost.
    9. When tournaments are registered as six-golds shoots, they must be shot on official N.A.A. target faces and under official N.A.A. tournament rules.
16.0 N.A.A. 54 PIN RULES
    1. A 54 pin is presented to members shooting one end of 6 arrows into the center scoring ring of a 16 inch multicolored N.A.A. Official target face while competing in the Chicago Round.
    2. The event must be registered in advance with the N.A.A. office.

3. Available to members only upon payment of $1.50.

4. The first request is registered and only one pin is presented each member.

17.0 N.A.A. 450 AND 500 PIN RULE

1. A 450 pin is available to any member scoring at least 450 points in a field of 28 targets under the rules as presented by the INTERNATIONAL ARCHERY FEDERATION for BARE BOW.

2. A 500 pin is available to any member scoring at least 500 points in a field of 28 targets under the rules as presented by the INTERNATIONAL ARCHERY FEDERATION for FREE STYLE.

3. The event must be registered in advance with the N.A.A. office.

4. A fee of $1.75 is charged for each pin. The pin is presented only once to each member. Mail fee with application requesting pin.

NATIONAL ARCHERY ASSOCIATION OF THE UNITED STATES REGULATIONS GOVERNING ALL AMATEUR ARCHERY COMPETITION

1. PRIZES— The amateur archer shall not compete for cash. Awards shall not exceed the cost of $70.00 for first place, $40.00 for second place, and $30.00 for third place. Challenge trophies and other similar prizes may be authorized by the Eligibility Committee and approved by the National Archery Association Board of Governors.

2. EXHIBITIONS— The amateur archer shall not exhibit his skill as an archer for personal monetary gain.

3. INSTRUCTION— The amateur archer shall not accept pay for coaching. A school or college teacher (including physical education teachers) and other individuals such as camp counselors and those working for community organizations, recreation associations or councils, or religious, eleemosynary organizations, or other non-profit entities whose work is solely educational and who are paid for coaching for competition shall be eligible as amateurs.

4. ENDORSEMENT— The amateur shall not permit his name or picture to be used in print, over television, radio, or other public communication system, in an advertisement or in the endorsement of any company or product. The use of an archer's photograph in news media or the participation in radio broadcast or telecast is not prohibited, provided the archer receives no compensation of any kind, directly or indirectly, in connection with the use of such photograph or such participation provided permission is granted by the Eligibility Committee.

5. EXPENSES— The maximum expenses which an amateur archer may request, receive, or accept in connection with his competition or participation in any event, exhibition, or tournament, shall not exceed (a) his actual expenditures for travel up to the cost of first class public transportation fare, including the cost of such transportation to and from airport or railroad terminal; and (b) his actual expenditures for maintenance, including lodging, and meals, up to a total of twenty ($20) dollars per day for each day during the time occupied between going to and returning from the event, exclusive of necessary travel time. The period for which expenses may be allowed shall not exceed one (1) day after the event unless for good reason a longer period is expressly approved by the National Archery Association Board of Governors; (c) vouchers or receipts evidencing payment of actual expenditures for transportation and lodging shall be furnished by the archer and attached to the expense statement to be submitted to the National Archery Association Board of Governors. If in any case an archer has been unable to obtain reasonably suitable hotel accommodations and/or meals at a cost within the amount allowable above, and if in any one or more days he has been required to spend more than such allowable amount, the sponsoring organization and the archer may jointly apply to the National Archery Association

Board of Governors for permission to pay and accept respectively a supplemental allowance for expenses equal to the excess amount the archer has been required to spend in any such day or days, but which supplemental allowance shall in no event exceed five ($5) dollars for any one day.

6. EMPLOYMENT BY A FIRM— The amateur archer shall not accept money from a firm or individual engaged in some phase of archery promotion without regularly being on the payroll and work at a specific job in that organization. If he is employed by an archery manufacturer or sales firm, he shall not receive paid time off during the normal work week (35 hours) for the practice of archery and shall not have his expenses paid in any way by the firm in which he is employed. The above shall not preclude attending a tournament during the normal two-week paid vacation period available to most people.

7. SELF-EMPLOYMENT— The amateur archer if self-employed in the manufacture of archery tackle must not use his shooting prowess or his name or photograph as a basis for selling his wares.

8. AMATEUR COMPETITION WITH A PROFESSIONAL— The amateur may participate for awards or prizes in open competition with the professional in competitive events below the State level where the prizes or awards do not violate rule #1 of these amateur regulations. The professional may participate with the amateur in State, Regional, National or International events but shall not compete for the same titles, prizes, or awards as the amateur. Open events or tournaments, exhibitions or clinics shall be registered and sanctioned by the National Archery Association in advance of such events.

9. REINSTATEMENT TO ELIGIBILITY TO COMPETE AS AN AMATEUR— Any archer professionalized under these regulations, regardless of age, may apply for reinstatement to amateur status, and if such application is approved, be eligible to participate in amateur competition after one year from the date of last acts of professionalism. An archer shall be reinstated only upon recommendation of the Eligibility Committee and approval of the National Archery Association Board of Governors. An archer so reinstated shall not be eligible to compete in any State Championships, Districts (2 or more States) Championship, National Championship, International competition or Olympic Games.

10. EFFECTIVE DATE— The effective date of these regulations in September 1, 1965.

FITA Field Archery Rules

FIELD ARCHERY

RULES OF SHOOTING

TERMS

(a) Some of the Terms as used in Field Archery

UNIT — A 14 target course including all official shots.

ROUND — Two Units, or twice around one Unit — 28 targets.

FACE — Target face.

SPOT — The aiming center of the face.

BUTT — Any object upon which a face is fixed.

POST — Shooting position.

SHOT— Used in connection with the post number, i.e. 1st, 2nd, 3rd or 4th shot, etc.

(b) Two 28 target Standard Rounds are recognized:

(i) The Field Round

(ii) The Hunters Round

with 112 arrows in each Round.

277

THE FIELD ROUND

The Standard Field Round Unit consists of 14 shots —
   4 arrows at each distance.

15, 20, 25 and 30 meters at a 30 cm. face —	total 16 arrows.
35, 40 and 45 meters at a 45 cm. face —	total 12 arrows.
50, 55 and 60 meters at a 60 cm. face —	total 12 arrows.

And the following four posts — each arrow to be shot from a different post or at a different face:

35 meters at a 45 cm. face, all four arrows from the same distance (the fan shot) —	total 4 arrows.
6, 8, 10 and 12 meters at a 15 cm. face —	total 4 arrows.
30, 35, 40 and 45 meters at a 45 cm. face —	total 4 arrows.
45, 50, 55 and 60 meters at a 60 cm. face —	total 4 arrows.
Total number of arrows in the Field Round Unit —	56 arrows.

All 14 shots shall be mixed to give maximum variety.

Conversion	Yards	Feet	Inches
1 Centimeter (CM)			0.3937
15 Centimeter			5.90
30 Centimeter			11.80
45 Centimeter		1.	5.70
60 Centimeter		1.	11.60
1 Meter		3.	3.37
6 Meters	6.	1.	7.0
8 Meters	8.	2.	2.0
10 Meters	10.	2.	7.0
12 Meters	13.		.4
15 Meters	16.	1.	2.0
20 Meters	21.	2.	7.4
25 Meters	27.	1.	.029
30 Meters	32.	2.	5.1
35 Meters	38.		9.9
40 Meters	43.	2.	2.68
45 Meters	49.		7.68
50 Meters	54.	2.	.50
55 Meters	60.		.529
60 Meters	65.	1.	10.20
65 Meters	71.		2.97
75 Meters	82.		.68

THE FIELD ROUND FACES

(a) There are four standard circular faces:
   (i)   60 cm. diameter
   (ii)   45 cm. diameter
   (iii) 30 cm. diameter
   (iv)   15 cm. diameter

All four faces to consist of an outside ring, which shall be black, an inner ring, which shall be white, and a center circular spot, which shall be black.
The white ring shall have a diameter half the diameter of the outer black ring, i.e.
   (i) 30 cm.   (ii) 22.5 cm.   (iii) 15 cm.   (iv) 7.5 cm.

The black circular spot shall have a diameter one sixth the diameter of the outer black ring, i.e.
   (i) 10.0 cm.   (ii) 7.5 cm.   (iii) 5.0 cm.   (iv) 2.5 cm.

(b) Animal pictures bearing the Field Round faces may also be used. Such faces need only be outlined but all lines shall be entirely within the scoring area outlined (the higher scoring area). The spot to be a contrasting color and to be plainly visible.

(c) The scoring values are:

the inner ring including the center spot —   5 points
the outside black ring —   3 points

THE HUNTERS ROUND

The Standard Hunters Round Unit consists of 14 shots with:
one arrow from each of four different posts for each target:
TWO TARGETS with a 15 cm. face placed between 5 and 15 meters. The total distance for the 8 arrows shall be 80 meters.
FOUR TARGETS with a 30 cm. face placed between 10 and 30 meters. The total distance for the 16 arrows shall be 320 meters.
FIVE TARGETS with a 45 cm. face placed between 20 and 40 meters. The total distance for the 20 arrows shall be 600 meters.
THREE TARGETS with a 60 cm. face placed between 30 and 50 meters. The total distance for the 12 arrows shall be 480 meters.
Total number of arrows in the Hunters Round Unit — 56 arrows.
Total length of a Unit — 1480 meters.

THE HUNTERS ROUND FACES

(a)   There shall be four standard faces with exactly the same dimensions as for the Field Round (Art. 802) but the faces shall be black with a white spot. The lines to be invisible from the posts but an exception may be made for the 15 cm. face as the distance is so short.
(b)   Animal pictures bearing the Hunters Round faces may also be used.
The inner ring shall be inside the animal figure.
The spot shall be a contrasting color to be plainly visible.
(c)   The scoring values are:

The inner ring including the center spot — 5 points
The outside ring — 3 points.

FIELD COURSE LAYOUT

(a)   Two or more posts at any or all one position shots may be used provided that the posts are equidistant from the target.
(b)   All posts shall be numbered together with the number of arrows to be shot.
(c)   The distances *may* be stated.

Note: Organizers of Field Shoots may themselves decide whether the distances shall be marked or not marked in either Round.

(d)   All butts must be placed so that the full face is exposed to the archer.
(e)   Faces shall not be placed over any larger face, nor shall there be any marks on the butt or foreground that could be used as points of aim.
(f)   In the Field Round a 5 percent variation in distances is permitted where necessary because of terrain, but any variations must be made up on another target in the same group.
(g)   Direction arrows indicating the way round the Field Course should be placed as necessary to ensure safety.

FIELD COURSE CONTROL AND SAFETY

(a)   A Field Captain shall be appointed to be in control of the Field Shoot.
(b)   The duties of the Field Captain shall be:
(i)   To satisfy himself that safety precautions have been observed in the layout of the Field Course.

(ii)   To arrange with the Organizers for any additional safety precautions he may find advisable before shooting commences.

(iii)   To address the competitors and officials on the safety precautions and any other matter concerning the shooting that he may judge to be necessary.

(iv)   To see that a Target Captain and two scorers are appointed for each group.

(v)   To designate the order in which groups are to shoot *or* assign the posts at which each group is to start shooting.

(vi)   To ensure that one group does not hold up the following group. Search for lost arrows must not delay groups, such arrows to be sought *after* shooting has finished.

(vii)   To resolve disputes and queries that may arise in connection with the Rules or the conduct of shooting.

SEPARATE CLASSES

(a)   There shall be two classes for both ladies and gentlemen:
      (i)   Instinctive or Bare-bow
      (ii)   Free style

(b)   Instinctive and Free style archers shall shoot in separate classes.

(c)   Ladies may compete against gentlemen but gentlemen may not compete in ladies events.

EQUIPMENT

A. Instinctive or Bare-bow Class

1. The following equipment *may* be used:

(i)   Bows of any type, except cross bows.

(ii)   The bow must be bare and free from any sights, protrusions, marks or blemishes which could be used for aiming.

The inside of the upper limb shall be without any trade marks. Draw check indicators are not to be attached. The ends or edges of laminated pieces must not be specially constructed to provide some graduation which could be used for aiming.

(iii)   The bowstring shall be of one color. The serving may be of a different single color. There shall be no hanging threads nor more than one nocking point.

(iv)   Arrows of any type, except broadheads, or arrows which may cause damage to faces and butts. All arrows shall be marked with the competitor's name or insignia.

(v)   Finger tabs, gloves, armguards, bracers and quivers.

2. The following equipment may *not* be used:

(i)   Field glasses or other visual aids.

(ii)   Any draw device, apart from tabs or gloves, or any device that helps in the release.

(iii)   Any aid for estimating distances.

(iv)   Any memoranda that assist in improving scores.

B. Free style Class

1. The following equipment *may* be used:

(i)   Bows of any type except cross bows.

(ii)   Simple bowsights or bow marks.

(iii)   Draw check indicators.

(iv)   One attachment on the string, not exceeding a diameter of 1 cm. in any direction.

(v)   Finger tabs, gloves, armguards, bracers and quivers.

(vi)   Stabilizers on the bow provided they do not exceed the length of the archer's own arrows measured from a center line on the bow, and further that they do not serve as a string guide or touch anything but the bow and do not cause an obstacle to other archers either at their shooting place or visibility to the target.

(vii)   Arrows of any type, except broadheads, or arrows that may cause damage to faces and butts. All arrows shall be marked with the competitor's name or insignia.

2. The following equipment may *not* be used:

(i)   Field glasses or other visual aids.

(ii)   Any draw device, apart from gloves or tabs, or any device that helps in the release.

(iii)   Any aid for estimating distances.

(iv)   Any memoranda that assist in improving scores.

(v)   Any sights embodying a prism, lens, or any other magnifying device.

(vi)   Levelling devices.

SHOOTING

(a)   Archers shall shoot in groups of four if possible, but never less than three nor more than five.

(b)   The archers shall be numbered in each group — A, B, C, and D — prefixed with 1, 2, 3, etc. indicating the number of each group (1A, 1B, 1C, 1D — 2A, 2B, 2C, 2D).

(c)   The shooting shall take place in rotating order:

(i)   Preferably two archers shall shoot together, one from each side of the post —

A/B : C/D
C/D : A/B
A/B : C/D, etc.

At the 15 cm. face archers may shoot one at a time.

(ii)   Rotation of four archers shooting one at a time:

A — B — C — D
D — A — B — C
C — D — A — B
B — C — D — A
A — B — C — D, etc.

(iii)   If there are three archers in a Group:

A/B — C
C/A — B
B/C — A
A/B — C, etc.

and similarly for five archers in a group.

(d)   The order of shooting may be changed temporarily for the purpose of changing a string or making other minor adjustments to equipment.

(e)   A broken bow may be replaced by a borrowed bow.

(f)   (i)   Archers shall stand with both feet behind the shooting line which is an imaginary line parallel to the target.

(ii)   Archers waiting their turn to shoot shall stand well back behind the archers on the shooting line.

(iii)   No archer shall approach the target until all have finished shooting except as permitted under Art. 810 (b) when shooting at the 30 cm. and 15 cm. faces.

(g)   An arrow shall not be deemed to have been shot if the archer can touch it with his bow without moving his feet from their position in relation to the shooting line.

(h)   Under no other circumstances may an arrow be reshot.

SCORING

(a)   Two scorers shall be appointed in each group (Art. 806) (b) (iv).

(b)   Scoring shall take place after all archers in the group have shot their arrows, except on the 30 cm. face where scoring may take place after two archers have shot and after each archer has shot on the 15 cm. face.

(c) Scorers shall record the scores made on the score card alongside the correct number of the post. Where groups are assigned to start at different posts they will complete the round up to and including the numbered post previous to the one at which they commenced.

(d) Scorers shall enter the value of each arrow on the score card as called out by the archer to whom the arrows belong. Other archers in the group shall check the value of each arrow so called.

Scorers to compare their scores before any arrows are drawn.

(e) Neither the arrows nor the face shall be touched until all arrows on that target have been recorded and scores checked.

(f) An arrow shall be scored according to the position of the shaft on the face.

(g) Should the shaft of an arrow touch two colors, or any dividing line between scoring zones, that arrow shall score the higher value of the zones affected.

(h) Arrows passing through the face, but still in the butt, may be pushed back and scored according to the position of the shaft in the face.

(i) Another arrow in the nock and remaining embedded therein shall score according to the value of the arrow struck.

(j) Skids or glances into the face shall not score.

(k) Witnessed bouncers or arrows passing through the butt may be scored as 3 points except at Championships.

(l) In the case of a tie in scores, the result shall be determined as follows:

(i) The archer, of those tying, with the greatest number of hit targets.

(ii) If this is also a tie, then the archer with greatest number of scoring arrows (hits).

(iii) If this is also a tie, the result shall be determined by shooting off on a sufficient number of targets, starting with shot No. 1.

(m) The target captain shall be the final judge of disputed arrows except at Tournaments.

TOURNAMENT RULES

(a) International Tournaments are the responsibility of the Member Associations. If organized by a Club, Region or similar Body, the Tournament must be recognized by the National Archery Association and this must be indicated on all Tournament notices, advertisements and invitations.

(b) International Tournaments shall be conducted in accordance with F.I.T.A. Field Archery Rules.

(c) Tournament Organizers shall announce in advance and shall state in all notices etc., which Round(s) are to be shot and whether distances will be indicated or not.

(d) Practice must not take place on the Field Course laid out for the Tournament. Special practice targets shall be made available elsewhere the day before the Tournament.

(e) A Technical Commission (T.C.) shall be appointed with the Field Captain as Chairman. The duties of the T.C. shall be:

(i) To check competitor's equipment before the Tournament is due to start (time to be stated on the Tournament program) and at any time thereafter during the Tournament.

(ii) To settle any query concerning the value of an arrow. Their ruling shall be final.

(iii) To check the conduct of the shooting and to resolve any disputes or appeals that may arise.

(iv) To consider requests from Target Captains regarding Field equipment and, where applicable, to take suitable action.

(f) Questions concerning the conduct of the shooting or the conduct of a competitor shall be lodged with the T.C. without any undue delay and in any event must be lodged before the prize giving. The ruling of the T.C. shall be final.

CHAMPIONSHIP REGULATIONS

(a) World and Continental/Regional Championships shall be decided on two consecutive days' shooting. On the first day, the Hunters Round, where distances must *not* be indicated. On the second day, the Field Round, where distances shall be indicated.

(b) The Standard Field Round and Hunters Round faces are to be used.

(c) The Field Captain shall assign the post from which each group will commence shooting.

(d) All arrow holes to be suitably marked.

(e) Bouncers or arrows passing through the face, to be scored according to their point of impact on the face and provided that an unmarked hole or indentation can be identified.

(f) A Technical Commission (T.C.) shall be appointed consisting of five or more members with the Field Captain as Chairman. The Chairman shall be appointed by the Organizing Committee but the members shall be appointed by the Team Captains, in meeting, on the day before the Tournament. The duties of the T.C. shall be:

    (i) To inspect the Field Course layout.

    (ii) To satisfy themselves that safety precautions have been observed in the layout.

    (iii) To check the competitors' equipment one hour before the Tournament is due to start and at any time thereafter during the Tournament.

    (iv) To settle any query concerning the value of an arrow. Their ruling shall be final.

    (v) To check the conduct of the shooting and to resolve any disputes or appeals that may arise.

    (vi) To consider requests from Team Captains and Target Captains regarding Field equipment and, where applicable, to take suitable action.

C. Dress Regulations for F.I.T.A. Target Archery Championships

    (i) The World Championship Tournament as well as the Continental Championships are majestic occasions honored by the attendance of many dignitaries. It is therefore with respect and propriety that all Archers, Team Captains, Officials, etc. participating in the Opening and Closing Ceremonies, should be properly and fully dressed in the uniform dress of their respective Associations.

    (ii) During the Tournament, Ladies are required to wear dresses or skirts and suitable blouses or tops and Gentlemen full length slacks and long or short sleeved shirts. Sweaters/Cardigans may be worn. In adverse weather suitable protective clothing may be worn.

    (iii) Footwear must be worn by all competitors at all times during the Tournament.

    (iv) Slacks or shorts for Ladies and sleeveless singlets, underwear vests or shorts for Gentlemen, as well as track suits, will not be allowed at any time.

    (v) No advertising of any kind whatsoever shall appear on clothing worn by the competitors or officials at any time during the Tournament. Nor shall Initials or name of country be lettered on clothing. (*This applies also to Field Archery Championships and Olympic Games.*)

    (vi) Competitor's target number to be worn on the middle of the back and to be visible at all times while shooting is in progress.

D. Shooting Field at World Championships

Congress accepted in principle that the shooting field should be an open field and not an arena.

E. National Flags at World Championships

Congress agreed that the flags of all Member Associations should be flown during all World Championships.

F. Archers' Identification Badges

Congress accepted the principle that archers competing in World Championships should be issued with a name badge to be worn during the period of the Tournament for the better identification of each other.

G. Shelter for Archers

Congress recommends that at World Championships, Organizers should provide where possible, behind the waiting line, sufficient shelter against the weather for the protection of archers.

H. Spectators

Congress was of the opinion that Team Captains, who know own Archers as well as appointed Officials, should cooperate to ensure that spectators (tourists) do not enter and mix with the competitors, but remain behind barriers in spectators' stands or grounds as provided.

N.F.A.A. REGULATIONS

ARTICLE VII
General Rules for Field Archery Games

A. Terms:

UNIT—A 14 target course, including all official shots.

ROUND—Two such units, or twice around one.

DOUBLE ROUND—Two complete rounds.

OUT—First unit to be shot in a round.

IN—Second unit to be shot in a round.

STAKE—Shooting position.

FACE—Target face.

BUTT—Any object against which face is placed.

SHOT—This term in connection with the stake number, i.e. "4th shot", shall be used in referring to the different shots on any course.

SPOT—Aiming center.

TIMBER—Warning call to other archers who may be in danger zone, announcing that you are ready to shoot.

B. Targets:

1. Faces shall not be placed over any other larger targets nor shall there be any marks on butt or foreground that could be used as points of aim.
2. All butts must be so placed that the full face is exposed to the shooter.
3. In all tournaments using official N.F.A.A. rounds, a minimum of eight 20 cm target faces must be used on butts requiring 20 cm target faces, and a minimum of two target faces must be used where 35 cm target faces are specified. More target faces may be used as required to prevent equipment damage.

C. Shooting Positions:

1. All shooting position stakes shall be numbered, but the yardage given may be optional.
2. It shall be permissible to use two or more shooting position stakes at any or all one position targets provided however, the stakes are equidistant from the target.
3. All shooting positions shall be plainly visible. When ground level markers are used in place of traditional stakes, a sign shall be posted listing the various positions for each round.

D. Shooting Styles:
 1. Bare Bow Division:
  a) Archers shooting in the barebow division will use bow, arrows, strings and accessories free from any sights, marks or blemishes.
   1) String will be made of one (1) or more strands. Strands will be of one consistent color of the archer's choosing. The center serving on the string will be served with one layer of any material suitable to use, but material will be of one consistent size and one consistent color. Placement of a nock locator on the serving will be permitted.
  b) An adjustable arrow plate may be used to control the space between the arrow and the face of the sight window.
  c) The use of stabilizers shall be permitted.
  d) One consistent nocking point only is permitted.
   1) Nocking point shall be held by one or two nock locators, which shall be snap on type, shrink tubing, thread or dental floss, tied or served on the serving No material used for nocking locator shall extend more than ¼ inch above or below the arrow nock when at full draw.
  e) No mechanical device will be permitted other than one non-adjustable draw check and level mounted on the bow, neither of which may extend above the arrow.
  f) All arrows shall be identical in length, weight, diameter and fletching, with allowance for wear and tear.
  g) The ends or edges of laminated pieces appearing on the inside of the upper limb shall be considered a sighting mechanism.
  h) No device of any type including arrow rest, that may be used for sighting may be used or attached to the archer's equipment.
 2. Freestyle Division:
  a) Freestyle—Any type of sight and its written memorandum and any release aid as defined in section E, paragraph 3 in this article is permitted.
  b) Freestyle Limited—Any type of sight and its written memorandum and release aids limited to gloves, tabs and fingers are permitted.
 3. Competitive Bowhunter Division:
  a) This division is the revised Heavy Tackle Division for those wishing to compete with equipment normally used during hunting activities. Youth Bowhunters shall not be recognized.
  b) No device of any type including arrow rest, that may be used for sighting, may be used or attached to the archer's equipment.
  c) There shall be no device, mechanical or otherwise, in the sight window except the arrow rest.
  d) No clickers or draw check will be allowed. No laminations, level, marks or blemishes may appear in the sight window, upper limb or in the field of vision at full draw.
  e) A sight window may be altered from standard configuration providing that no lamination, blemishes, protrusions, or any identifiable mark that could be used for any aiming reference is visible.
  f) String shall be one color only. A center serving of one other color may be used. One consistent nocking point only is permitted. Nocking point shall be held by one or two locators which shall be snap on type, shrink tubing, thread or dental floss, tied or served on the serving. No material used for nocking locator shall extend more than ¼ inch above or below the arrow nock when at full draw. Any marks, ties or string attachment to the string (except brush buttons and silencers properly located) shall invalidate its use in this division.
  g) One anchor point only is permitted.
  h) An archer shall hold the arrow when nocked in the traditional manner, i.e., index finger above the nock and middle finger below the nock, except in cases of physical deformity or handicap for which special dispensation shall be made.

    i) All arrows used shall be identical in length, weight, diameter and fletching with allowances for wear and tear.

    j) The Field Captain or his counterpart shall be the final authority regarding equipment and style eligibility, and may re-classify at his discretion.

    k) Brush buttons in their proper place at the recurve tip of the bow, string silencer no closer than 12 inches above or below the nocking point and bow quiver installed on the opposite side of the sight window with no part of the quiver or attachments visible in the sight window are not deemed illegal. One straight stabilizer, coupling device included if used, not exceeding 12 inches as measured from the back of the bow may be used in the Competitive Bowhunter style. No forked stabilizer or any counter balance will be legal.

    l) The following broadhead standard will be followed by the Bowhunter whenever broadheads are allowed in competition:
      1) MALE—⅞ inch cutting edge width (min.)
      2) FEMALE—¾ inch cutting edge width (min.)

    m) There shall be no restrictions on the bow draw weight in the Bowhunter Division. Hunting arrows of any material may be used as long as they are equipped with commercially manufactured, non-modified points, a minimum of 125 grains for men, 100 grains for women, which can be replaced by broadheads and of which at least ¼ inch of the length shall be a concave surface of revolution.

    n) Any device for lengthening or shortening the draw length of an archer in the Bowhunter Division shall be prohibited. All rules and regulations of N.F.A.A. which are not mentioned in the Bowhunter Division shall apply to those competing in the Bowhunter Division and same will apply to rounds shot by archers in this division.

    o) All official N.F.A.A. rounds shall be official rounds for the Bowhunter Division, all classification in the Bowhunter Division shall be based on the Field and Hunter rounds, and any further rules shall be covered in the N.F.A.A. By-laws.

4. Competitive Freestyle Bowhunter

    a) A sight with a maximum of 5 fixed reference points that must not be moved during a tournament will be allowed. Pin sights are to be of straight stock from point of anchor to sighting point, with only one sighting reference possible from each pin or reference point. Hooded pins or scopes cannot be used.

    b) Release aids will be permitted.

    c) A kisser button or string peep sight will be permitted, but not both.

    d) An archer will not be permitted to change the draw-weight of the bow during a tournament.

    e) All other competitive rules of the Bowhunter Division shall apply.

E. Archery Equipment Regulations Used in Competition:

    1. A conventional bow of any type may be used provided it subscribes to the accepted principle and meaning of the word "bow" as used in archery competition, i.e., an instrument consisting of a handle (grip) riser and two flexible limbs, each ending in a tip with string nock. The bow is braced for use by a single bowstring attached directly between the two string nocks, only. In operation it is held in one hand by its handle (grip) riser while the fingers of the other hand draw, hold back and release the string.

    2. Compound bows may be used, provided:
      a) Basic design includes a handle riser (grip) and two flexible limbs.
      b) Total arrow propelling energy is developed from a flexing of the materials employed in limb construction.
      c) Maximum reduction between peak load and release load does not exceed 50%.
      d) Bows which develop any portion of arrow propelling energy from other sources, such as compressed gas or liquid explosives, or mechanical springs, shall not be allowed. This is not to be construed to mean that compound bows which employ other sources of arrow propelling energy, not specifically listed in this paragraph, will be allowed.

Barebow field archers do not use bowsights.

e) The cables of the compound bow shall be considered as part of the string and all applicable string rules shall apply.

3. Any release aid may be used in Freestyle Division providing that it is hand operated and supports the draw weight of the bow. Releases other than gloves, tabs or fingers shall be deemed illegal in the Barebow and Competitive Bowhunter divisions.

4. The use of a Rangefinder is prohibited. At no time shall any device be allowed that would in any manner be an aid in establishing the distance of any shot. No archer may refer to any written memoranda that would aid in determining the distance to the target.

5. Any extra attachment to the bow, that would allow the draw weight of the bow to be relieved from either or both arms, at full draw, shall be declared illegal.

6. Sighting Devices, Accessories (See shooting styles, Section D of this Article).

7. Arrow rest—The apparatus on which an arrow rests as it is drawn. Any part of this apparatus extending more than ¼ inch above the arrow would be deemed illegal in Barebow and Bowhunter Divisions.

8. Arrow plate—The part of the arrow rest which is affixed to the sight window against which an arrow rides while being drawn. An arrow plate extending more than ¼ inch above the arrow shall be deemed illegal in the Barebow and Bowhunter Divisions.

F. Tournament Officials:

1. Field Captain

A Field Captain shall be appointed and it shall be his duties to:

a) See that a Target Captain and two scorers are appointed for each group.

b) Designate the order in which groups are to shoot or assign the stakes from which each group is to start, depending on which system is used.

c) Be the final authority in settling any disputes that arise over the rules or conduct of a tournament unless verbal notice of intent to protest is given and unless this is followed by the submission of a written protest to the Tournament Chairman. A $15 sectional and $25 national protest fee must accompany this written protest within one hour after leaving the range. This fee shall be refundable if the protest is upheld.

d) Report any archer in his group violating the rules set forth in the N.F.A.A. By-laws.

e) Have the option in any tournament to set a time limit, either by target or round, when such tournament must be completed.

2. Target Captain

The duty of the Target Captain shall be to order the shooting at his target and to settle all local questions. His decisions on arrow values shall be final. Other decisions may be appealed to the Field Captain.

3. Scorers

The Scorers shall keep an accurate account of every arrow that hits the target and at each target compare scores.

G. Tournament Rules:

1. Archers shall shoot in groups of not less than 3 or more than 6; 4 shall be the preferred number. No group of less than three shall turn in an official score.

2. For shooting position at the shooting stake the foursome, by mutual agreement, shall decide which two shall shoot from which side of the shooting stake.

   a) At the conclusion of each 14-target unit the archers shall change their order of shooting. Those who shot first shall shoot last and those who shot last shall shoot first.

   b) Starting with the first target an archer shall shoot from the same side of the shooting position stake for fourteen targets. At the fifteenth target to be shot those archers who have been shooting from the right side shall shoot the remainder of the course from the left side; those on the left shall shoot from the right side.

   c) No archer shall shoot from more than six inches behind the appropriate stake nor shall any archer advance to the target until all arrows have been shot by the group.

3. When shooting at butts requiring multiple faces the first 2 shooters will shoot the bottom targets. When targets are placed side by side (i.e. 50 cm) the archer on the left will shoot the left target; the archer on the right will shoot the right target. On fan and walkup positions the same applies, except each archer will shoot two arrows at each target. Any arrow striking the wrong target shall be considered a miss and may not be reshot.

4. One group shall not hold up the following groups while looking for lost arrows. Enough arrows shall be carried so that each archer may continue shooting, and return later to find missing arrows. If one or more open targets in front and two or more groups back up, the delaying group shall allow backed up groups to shoot through.

5. No archer may practice on any shot of a course to be used for tournament shooting later the same day. Special practice targets should be supplied. The first target of each round may be used as practice at the discretion of the tournament chairman. The maximum number of arrows allowable will be determined by the round being shot.

6. An archer leaving the range for any reason may be privileged to return to his group and complete the unfinished round or subsequent rounds. He will not be privileged to make up any missed in the interim.

7. In the case of an equipment failure verified by the target captain, the archer may have the needed time (45 min. maximum) as granted by a tournament official for equipment repair or replacement. Then in the presence of the tournament official be allowed to shoot the targets missed. This occurrence may not happen more than once in a tournament day.

8. No archer may shoot or compete in any one tournament more than one time unless advertised as a multiple registration tournament.

9. In case of inclement weather the tournament shall continue unless a pre-arranged signal is given by the tournament chairman. Any archer leaving the range shall be automatically disqualified.

10. No alcoholic beverages may be carried or consumed on any range or practice area during shooting hours at National or Sectional tournaments.

H. Scoring

1. Arrows must remain in the target face until all arrows are scored. They may then be withdrawn.

2. The status of doubtful arrows shall be determined before drawing any arrows from the target, and such an arrow may not be touched until after being recorded.
3. The Target Captain shall be the final judge of all disputed arrows.
4. Off ground skids or glances into the target shall not be counted. Arrows striking objects over the shooting lane may be reshot.
5. Arrows passing through the face, but still in the butt, may be pushed back and scored as a hit in the circle through which it went. This does not mean that they may be withdrawn and then stuck back through the target.
6. Arrows believed to have passed through the target may be reshot with a marked arrow, which will not be scored if the doubtful arrow is found in the butt.
7. Unsuspected pass throughs: In any instance where arrows are found to have obviously passed through in such a manner they cannot be properly scored and their location and the condition of the butt convince the target captain that the arrows did indeed pass through a scoring area, the archer may return and reshoot from the obvious distance of furthest distance involved.
8. Witnessed bounce outs, believed to have hit the target in the scoring area will be reshot.
9. In any tournament where the method of shooting off a tie is not decided in advance, ties shall be decided by shooting the first 3 targets. In any tournament where field faces are involved, field faces shall be used. If a tie still exists after three targets, continue from target to target until the tie is broken.
10. An archer who shoots arrows at the target in excess of the prescribed number shall lose the arrow or arrows of higher value in all N.F.A.A. rounds.
11. A dropped arrow is one which falls while being transferred from the quiver to be nocked on the string or in preparation for a shot. (A dropped arrow may be shot.)
12. A shot arrow is one which is propelled by the bowstring. (Such an arrow may not be reshot.)

ARTICLE VIII
OFFICIAL N.F.A.A. ROUNDS

A. Field Round:

1. Standard Unit
A standard unit shall consist of the following 14 shots:

15, 20, 25, 30 yards at a 35 cm face
40, 45, 50 yards at a 50 cm face
50, 60, 65 yards at a 65 cm face
    (for these distances—4 arrows at each)

And the following four position shots, each arrow to be shot from a different position or at a different target:

35 yards at a 50 cm target, all from the same distance, but from different positions at different targets:

30, 35, 40, 45 yards at a 50 cm target.
50, 60, 70, 80 yards at a 65 cm target.
20, 25, 30, 35 feet at a 20 cm target.

2. Targets
Four face sizes shall be used. The outer ring diameter shall be 65 cm, 50 cm, 35 cm and 20 cm. The spot shall be two black rings with white X in center ring, two white rings and two outside black rings. (X-ring tiebreakers)

3. Shooting Positions
The prescribed distances in this Section are to be adhered to without variation. Each N.F.A.A. Chartered Club with an approved field course shall have the option of marking the distances on the shooting stakes of the following N.F.A.A. Rounds: Field, Hunter and Animal. In layout out the course any order may be used as the official shooting order on any four position shot.

EXCERPTS—N.F.A.A. REGULATIONS

4. Shooting Rules
Each archer shall shoot 4 arrows at each of the 14-target layouts in a unit. In 10 cases this shall mean shooting the 4 arrows from a single stake at a single face. In the other 4 it may mean either shooting 1 arrow from each of four stakes at a single face, or it may mean shooting all four arrows from a single stake but at four separate faces.

5. Scoring
a) The scoring is 5 points for the spot, 4 for 2 white circles and 3 for outside black rings.

b) An arrow shaft cutting two rings shall be scored as being in the ring of the greater value. The outer line of the Field target is outside the scoring field. For that reason the arrow shaft must cut the line so that no color of the line can be seen between arrow shaft and scoring field before a hit may be counted. The same is true for the inner line between the 2 circles.

c) The X ring is for use in tie breaker shootoffs.

B. Hunter's Round:

1. Standard Unit
The 14 targets form a unit. Twice around the unit makes a round, or two such units laid out make a round.

2. Targets
The Hunter's Round target has two white rings with black X in center ring, and two outside black rings. (X ring used for tie breakers only). The following shows the target face sizes and aiming spot, with the yardage distances that are to be used.

Target size: 65 cm with 13 cm white spot
70-65-61-58
64-59-55-52
58-53-48-45
Target size: 50 cm target, 10 cm white spot
53-48-44-41
48
44
40
36-36-36-36
Target size: 35 cm target, 7 cm white spot
32-32-32-32
28-28-28-28
23-20
19-17
15-14
Target size: 20 cm target, 4 cm white spot
11-11

3. Shooting Positions
One feature of this round is that it takes a lot of stakes. Where one stake is used, a stake at least 18 inches above ground is recommended. On the two-stake shots use stakes that extend 12 inches above ground and stakes that are not over 6 inches above ground for the four-stake shots. Such an arrangement will help eliminate a lot of confusion.

4. Shooting Rules
In shooting the Hunter's Round the archer will observe the following shooting positions:
a) 1 stake—shoot 4 arrows from the same stake
b) 2 stakes—shoot 2 arrows from each stake
c) 4 stakes—shoot 1 arrow from each stake

5. Scoring
Scoring is 5 points for the spot, 4 for center ring, and 3 for the outer ring. X ring is for tie breaker in shootoffs only. An arrow shaft cutting two rings must cut completely through the line to be counted in the area of next higher value.

C. Animal Round:

1. Standard Unit

The 14 targets form a unit. Twice around the unit makes a round, or two such units laid out differently make a round. The one basic 14 target unit may be varied to make any number of courses that would all be different. It is simple and easy to lay out and change. Once the maximum and minimum distances are known, then the target distance can be laid out anywhere within these distances and be according to N.F.A.A. rules.

This round, its animal targets and its sliding scale system of scoring is more of a measure of the hunting archer's shooting skill than the standard Field Round.

2. Targets

a) The targets for this round are animal targets with the scoring area divided into two parts. The high scoring area is oblong while the low scoring area is the area between the high scoring area and the "hide and hair" line or "feathers", as the case may be. The area between the "hide and hair" line (including the line) to the outside of the carcass is considered a non-scoring area.

b) The high scoring area of Group No. 1 is 9 inches wide by 14½" long with rounded ends. Targets in this group are the black bear, grizzly bear, deer, moose, elk and caribou.

c) The high scoring area of Group No. 2 is 7 inches wide by 10½ inches long with rounded ends. Targets in this group are the small black bear, antelope, small deer, wolf and mountain lion.

d) The high scoring area of Group No. 3 is 4½ inches wide by 7 inches long with rounded ends. Targets in this group are the coyote, racoon, javelina, turkey, fox, goose, wildcat and pheasant.

e) The high scoring area of Group No. 4 is 2½ inches wide by 3⅝ inches long with rounded ends. Targets in this group are the turtle, duck, grouse, crow, skunk, woodchuck, jack rabbit and rockchuck.

f) In the above target groups the animals mentioned are for a general description and not to be construed as confined to the particular species. Any animal or bird which is legal game and consistent in size with a particular group may be used.

3. Shooting positions

a) The following chart gives distances and target groups:

Group	Targets	Positions	Maximum Distance (Yards)	Minimum Distance (Yards)	Spread (Yards)
1	3	3 walk up shots	60	40	20
2	3	3 walk up shots	45	30	15
3	4	4-one position shots	35	20	15
4	4	4-one position shots	20	10	10

b) The shooting distance shall be marked its exact distance but in the spread defined in Paragraph a) above for National and Sectional level tournaments and may be marked at tournaments below that level.

c) Each target in Group 1 faces is a five yard walk-up. There are three targets in the group. Select your distances between 60 and 40 yards for the first stake, move up five yards for the next stake and five more yards for the third stake.

d) Each target in Group No. 2 faces is a three yard walk-up. There are three targets in Group No. 2. Select your distance between 45 and 30 yards for the first stake, move up three yards for the next stake and three more for the last stake.

e) Each target in Group 3 faces is one distance. There are four targets in this group. Shoot all arrows from each stake as selected between 35 and 20 yards.

f) Each target in Group No. 4 is one distance. There are four targets in Group No. 4. All arrows shall be shot from each of the four stakes from distances selected between 20 yards and 10 yards.

4. Shooting Rules

A maximum of three marked arrows may be shot, in successive order, and the highest scoring arrow will count. In the case of walk up targets the first arrow must be shot from the farthest stake, the second arrow from the middle stake, and the third arrow from the nearest stake, in order to be scored.

5. Scoring

a) 20 or 16 for the first arrow
   14 or 10 for the second arrow
    8 or 4 for the third arrow

b) The arrow shaft must cut through the line to score. If an arrow shaft touches the outside edge of an animal target it does not score. If it hits the target and cuts into, but not through, the "hair and hide" line, it does not score. It must cut through this line to score a shot of lower value. To score, an arrow shaft must cut through this line.

D. 15 Target "300" Field Round:

An official classification game will consist of one 15 target round.

1. Standard Unit

A Standard Unit shall consist of the following 15 shots:

15, 20, 25, 30 yards at a 35 cm face
   (four arrows at each distance)
40, 45, 50 yards at a 50 cm face
   (four arrows at each distance)
55, 60, 65 yards at a 65 cm face
   (four arrows at each distance)

And the following four position shots; each arrow to be shot from a different position or at a different target:

35 yards at a 50 cm target, all from the same distance, but from different positions or different targets:

30, 35, 40, 45 yards at a 50 cm target
65, 60, 55, 50 yards at a 65 cm target
30, 25, 20, 15 yards at a 35 cm target
20, 25, 30, 35 feet at a 20 cm target.

2. Targets

a) Four face sizes shall be used:
1) a 65 cm face with 6.5 cm X ring
2) a 50 cm face with 5 cm X ring
3) a 35 cm face with 3.5 X ring
4) a 20 cm face with a 2 cm X ring

The spot shall be two black rings with white X in center ring, two white rings, and two outside black rings. (X ring used for tie breakers only.)

Animal targets bearing these official round faces may be used, in which case the faces need not be painted, only outlined, but aiming center or spot must be plainly visible. Spot must be painted some color sharply contrasting with the target color. This same spot and ring target is official without animal silhouette.

3. Shooting Positions

The prescribed distances in sub-section 1 of this By-Law are to be adhered to without variation. Each N.F.A.A. Chartered Club with an approved Field Course shall have the option of marking the distances on the shooting stakes of the following N.F.A.A. Rounds; Field, Hunters, Animal, Park and Fixed Distance Handicap. In laying out the course any order may be used as the official shooting order on any four position shot.

4. Shooting Rules

Each archer shall shoot 4 arrows at each of the 15-target layouts in a unit. In 10 cases this shall mean shooting the four arrows from a single stake at a single face. In the other five it may mean either shooting one arrow from each of four stakes at a single face, or it may mean shooting all four arrows from a single stake but at four separate faces.

5. Scoring

a) The scoring is 5 points for the spot, 4 for 2 white circles and 3 for outside black rings. X ring for tie breaker in shoot offs.

b) An arrow shaft cutting two rings shall be scored as being in the ring of the greater value. The outer line of the Field Archery target is outside the scoring field. For that reason the arrow shaft must cut the line so that no color of the line can be seen between arrow shaft and scoring field before a hit may be counted. The same is true for the inner line between the two circles.

E. 15 Target "300" Hunter Round: An official classification game will consist of one 15 target round.

1. Standard Unit

The 15 targets form a unit. Twice around the unit makes a round, or two such units laid out make a round.

2. Targets

The Hunter's Round target has two white rings with black X in the center ring, and two outside black rings. (X ring used for tie breakers only.) The following shows the target face sizes and aiming spot, with the yardage distances that are to be used.

Target Size: 65 cm with 13 cm white spot
64-59-55-52
58-53-48-45
58
Target size: 50 cm target, 10 cm white spot
53-48-44-41
48
44
40
36-36-36-36
Target size: 35 cm target, 7 cm white spot
32-32-32-32
32-28-24-20
28-28-28-28
23-20
19-17
15-14
Target size: 20 cm target, 4 cm white spot
11-11

3. Shooting Positions

One feature of this round is that it takes a lot of stakes. Where one stake is used, a stake at least 18 inches above ground is recommended. On the two-stake shots, use stakes that extend 12 inches above ground and stakes that are not over 6 inches above ground for the four stake shots. Such an arrangement will help eliminate a lot of confusion.

4. Shooting Rules

In shooting the Hunter's Round the archer will observe the following shooting positions:

a) 1 stake—shoot 4 arrows from the same stake.

b) 2 stakes—shoot 2 arrows from each stake.

c) 4 stakes—shoot 1 arrow from each stake.

5. Scoring

Scoring is 5 points for the spot, 4 for center ring, and 3 for the outer ring. X ring is for tie breaker in shootoffs only. An arrow shaft cutting two rings must cut completely through the line to be counted in the area of next higher value.

F. 15 Target "300" Animal Round: No classification can be made on the Heavy Tackle Round or the regular Animal Round except under the condition specified in the Heavy Tackle Division regulations.

EXCERPTS—N.F.A.A. REGULATIONS

1. Standard Unit

The 15 targets form a unit. Twice around the unit makes a round, or two such units laid out differently make a round. The one basic 15 target unit may be varied to make any number of courses that would all be different. It is simple and easy to lay out and change. Once the maximum and minimum distances are known, then the target distance can be laid out anywhere within these distances and be according to the N.F.A.A. rules.

This round with it's animal targets and its sliding scale system of scoring is more of a measure of the hunting archer's shooting skill than the standard Field Round.

2. Targets

a) The targets for this round are animal targets with the scoring area divided into two parts. The high scoring area is oblong while the low scoring area is the area between the high scoring area and the "hide and hair" line or "feathers", as the case may be. The area between the "hide and hair" line (including the line) to the outside of the carcass is considered a non-scoring area.

b) The high scoring area of Group No. 1 is 9" wide by 14½" long with rounded ends. Targets in this group are the black bear, grizzly bear, deer, moose, elk, and caribou.

c) The high scoring area of Group No. 2 is 7" wide by 10½" long with rounded ends. Targets in this group are the small black bear, antelope, small deer, wolf, and mountain lion.

d) The high scoring area of Group No. 3 is 4½" wide by 7" long with rounded ends. Targets in this group are the coyote, racoon, javelina, turkey, fox, goose, wildcat and pheasant.

e) The high scoring area of Group No. 4 is 2½ inches wide by 3⅝ inches long with rounded ends. Targets in this group are the turtle, duck, grouse, crow, skunk, woodchuck, jack rabbit and rockchuck.

f) In the above target groups the animals mentioned are for a general description and not to be construed as confined to the particular species. Any animal or bird which is legal game and consistent in size with a particular group may be used.

3. Shooting Positions

a) The following chart gives distances and target groups:

Group	Targets	
1	3	3 walk-up shots, 1 arrow each position
		Maximum yards 60, Minimum 40 yards
2	3	3 walk-up shots, 1 arrow each position
		Maximum yards 45, Minimum 30 yards
3	4	1 position
		Maximum yards 35, Minimum 20 yards
4	5	1 position
		Maximum yards 20, Minimum 10 yards

b) The shooting distance shall be marked its exact distance but in the spread defined in Paragraph a) above for National and Sectional level tournaments and may be marked at tournaments below that level.

c) Each target in Group No. 1 faces is a five yard walk-up. There are three targets in the group. Select your distances between 60 and 40 yards for the first stake, move up five yards for the next stake and five more yards for the third stake.

d) Each target in Group No. 2 faces is a three yard walk-up. There are three targets in Group No. 2. Select your distance between 45 and 30 yards for the first stake, move up three yards for the next stake and three more for the last stake.

e) Each target in Group No. 3 faces is one distance. There are four targets in this group. Shoot all arrows from each stake as selected between 35 and 20 yards.

f) Each target in Group No. 4 is one distance. There are five targets in Group No. 4. All arrows shall be shot from each of the four stakes from distances selected between 20 yards and 10 yards.

4. Shooting Rules

A maximum of three marked arrows may be shot, in successive order, and the highest scoring arrow will count. In the case of walk up targets the first arrow must be shot from the farthest stake, the second arrow from the middle stake, and the third arrow from the nearest stake, in order to be scored.

5. Scoring

a) 20 or 16 for the first arrow
   14 or 10 for the second arrow
   8 or 4 for the third arrow

b) The arrow shaft must cut through the line to score. If an arrow shaft touches the out-side edge of an animal target it does not score. If it hits the target and cuts into, but not through, the "hair and hide" line, it does not score. It must cut through this line to score a shot of lower value. To score, an arrow shaft must cut through this line.

G. N.F.A.A. International Outdoor Round:

1. Standard Unit

a) The N.F.A.A. International Round is a 20 target (ten targets per unit) variable distance round designed for use in areas where the availability of land is restricted or limited. The round is ideally suited for public parks and recreational facilities. The N.F.A.A. International Round course requires a minimum of space and can be readily constructed on any level or gently rolling plot of ground. A 20 target course will adequately handle up to 80 participants at one time.

The International Round may be laid out on a roving type range or on an established "Field Round" course, however, whenever possible it is recommended that it be laid out in a progressive order, 20 yards through 65 yards.

b) Permanent type roving ranges are subject to course approval by the N.F.A.A. Direc-tor. Non-permanent park type ranges shall not be subject to approval by the N.F.A.A. Director.

2. Targets

a) Target faces shall conform to the specifications of the N.F.A.A. Field Round.

b) Each target position shall have one target butt.

1) There shall be one or more target faces used on each butt.

2) In the use of the International Outdoor Round, the required number of faces used for camps and school shall be left to the discretion of the coaches or teachers.

c) Distances

1) The distances and corresponding target sizes for the International Round are as follows:

Distances Yards	Target size Centimeters
20	35
25	35
30	35
35	50
40	50
45	50
50	50
55	65
60	65
65	65

2) All distances must be measured to the exact yardages.

3. Shooting Positions

a) Each target shall have two shooting positions.

b) The two shooting positions shall be parallel to the target face.

c) The two shooting positions shall be the same distance from the target and shall be separated by not less than 4 feet.

    d) The distances shall be written on markers which are visible to the archer.

    e) Each distance marker shall show the number of the target and the distance to be shot.

    f) If more than one unit is needed, the shooting positions for the targets shall be numbered from one to twenty.

4. Shooting Rules

    a) The shooter must stand behind the shooting line.

    b) Three arrows are shot at each distance.

    c) All other rules for shooting the Official Field Round shall apply to the International Round.

    d) The maximum distance for youth in the International Round shall be 50 yards.

5. Scoring

    a) The scoring on the targets shall be:

        1) 5 points for each arrow in the center black spot.

        2) 4 points for each arrow in the inner 2 white rings.

        3) 3 points for each arrow in the outer 2 black rings.

        4) No points for arrows striking the background.

    b) If any part of the arrow touches more than one scoring area, the arrow is counted as striking the highest scoring area it touches.

H. N.F.A.A. Indoor Round

    1. The Standard Unit shall consist of 60 arrows, shot as 3 games, at a distance of 20 yards. Each game shall consist of 4 ends of 5 arrows per end.

2. Targets

    a) The target face shall be 40 cm in diameter and shall be of a dull blue color. The spot shall be two white rings with blue X in center ring. All inscribed scoring rings shall be white. (X ring used for tie breakers)

    b) The bullseye shall be 3.2 inches in diameter.

    c) There shall be one scoring ring 8.9 inches in diameter and not to exceed 1/32 inch in width.

3. Shooting Positions

Shooting positions will provide sufficient area to enable two archers to shoot simultaneously at one target butt.

4. Shooting Rules

    a) An archer shall stand so that he has one foot on either side of the shooting line.

    b) The time limit per end shall be 5 minutes.

    c) All other shooting rules shall apply as listed under the N.F.A.A. Indoor League Program.

5. Scoring

    a) The scoring is 5, 4, 3, 2, 1 from the spot out.

    b) All arrows will be scored and recorded before touching or drawing any arrows from the target.

    c) An arrow cutting two rings shall be scored in the ring of greater value. Scoring is determined by the position of the shaft. The shaft must cut through the line and touch the area of higher value in order to be scored as the higher value.

    d) Witnessed bounce-outs or arrows passing completely through the target will be re-shot.

    e) Hits on the wrong target will be scored as misses.

    f) When an arrow is dropped while the archer is in the act of shooting, he may shoot another arrow in place of the dropped arrow if he can touch the arrow with his bow from his position on the shooting line.

    g) If an archer shoots more than 5 arrows in an end, only the five arrows of lower value may be scored.

    h) If an archer shoots less than 5 arrows in one end he may shoot his remaining arrows if the omission is discovered before the end is officially completed; otherwise they shall be scored as misses.

I. N.F.A.A. Indoor Championship Round

1. The standard unit shall consist of 5 ends of 4 arrows per end shot at 20 yards. The number of units shot on this round is recommended as 2, but is left to the discretion of the host.

2. Targets
   a) The target face shall contain four 16 cm targets on a screened blue surface, 40 cm square.
   b) The inner scoring ring (X ring) shall be 4 cm in diameter and white in color.
   c) The second scoring ring shall be 8 cm in diameter and white in color.
   d) The third scoring ring shall be 12 cm in diameter and shall be dull blue in color.
   e) The fourth scoring ring shall be 16 cm in diameter and dull blue in color.

3. Scoring
   a) The scoring is 5 points for the X ring, 4 points for the white 8 cm ring, 3 points for the blue 12 cm ring and 2 points for the blue 16 cm ring.

4. Shooting
   a) One arrow shall be shot at each of the four targets during each end.
   b) If more than 1 arrow is shot into a target, the arrow of higher scoring value is lost.
   c) All other rules of the N.F.A.A. Indoor Round shall apply to the N.F.A.A. Indoor Championship Round.

J. N.F.A.A. Freeman Round

1. The Standard Unit shall consist of 60 arrows, shot as 3 games at distances of 10, 15 and 20 yards. Each game will include 4 ends of 5 arrows per end.
   a) The first game shall be 3 ends at 10 yards and 1 end at 15 yards.
   b) The second game shall be 3 ends at 15 yards and 1 end at 20 yards.
   c) The third games shall be 4 ends at 20 yards.
2. Targets, shooting rules and scoring shall be the same as listed for the N.F.A.A. Indoor Round, Section E. of this Article.

K. Flint Bowman Indoor Round:

1. Standard Unit

Target Number	Distance	Number of Arrows	Target Size
1	25 yards	4	35 cm
2	20 feet	4	20 cm
3	30 yards	4	35 cm
4	15 yards	4	20 cm
5	20 yards	4	35 cm
6	10 yards	4	20 cm
7	30, 25, 20, 15 yards	1 arrow each	35 cm

   a) 56 arrows shall be considered one round.
   b) Top row target centers shall be spaced 48 inches from the floor. Bottom row target center shall be spaced 30 inches from the floor.

2. Targets
The targets are standard 20 cm and 35 cm field target faces placed in two rows on each boss. The center of the upper row shall be 48 inches from the floor. The center of the lower row shall be 30 inches from the floor and directly below the upper targets.

3. Shooting Positions
   a) This round is to be shot on a 30 yard range with shooting lines marked parallel to the target line at distances of 20 feet, 10, 15, 20, 25 and 30 yards.
   b) Starting at the 30 yard line, and proceeding toward the target line, the shooting lines are to be numbered 3, 1, 5, 4, 6 and 2.
   c) There shall be a separate lane for each boss and the archer shall go from one shooting line to his next shooting line in the lane for the boss for which his two targets are placed.
   d) The targets on the boss in the second lane shall be reversed from those in the first lane. Those in the third lane shall be exactly as those in the second lane.

4. Shooting Rules
If an archer starts out on a high target, as in lane one, he shoots his second end of the low target in the same lane. The archer continues to shoot at the targets in this lane until he has shot at seven targets. For his second seven-target score, he should go to another lane in which the targets are in reverse from the one he started out on.

5. Scoring
Scoring shall be the same as the Field Round.

6. 20 Yard Flint Round
a) Because of the inability of many clubs to obtain the necessary space for a 30-yard indoor round, the N.F.A.A. has provided rules for a 20-yard round as follows:

Target Number	Distance	Number of Arrows	Target Size
1	50 ft.	4	35 cm
2	20 ft.	4	20 cm
3	60 ft.	4	35 cm
4	45 ft.	4	20 cm
5	40 ft.	4	35 cm
6	30 ft.	4	20 cm
7	60, 50, 40, 30, ft.	1 arrow each	35 cm

b) **Rules**
Rules for the 20-yard round are the same as for the Flint Indoor Round.

L. Expert Round
1. Standard Unit
A standard unit shall consist of the following 14 shots:
15, 20, 25, 30 yards at a 35 cm face
    (4 arrows at each distance)
40, 45, 50 yards at a 50 cm face
    (4 arrows at each distance)
55, 60, 65 yards at a 65 cm face
    (4 arrows at each distance)
And the following four position shots; each arrow to be shot from a different position or at a different target: 35 yards at a 50 cm target, all from the same distance, but from different positions or different targets:
30, 35, 40, 45 yards at a 50 cm target
50, 60, 70, 80 yards at a 65 cm target
20, 25, 30, 35 feet at a 20 cm target

2. Targets
a) Four face sizes shall be used:
    1) 65 cm face with 6.5 cm X ring
    2) 50 cm face with a 5 cm X ring
    3) 35 cm face with a 3.5 cm X ring
    4) 20 cm face with a 2 cm X ring
The spot shall be two black rings with white X ring in center ring, two white rings and two outside black rings. (X ring used for tiebreakers only)

3. Shooting Positions
The prescribed distances in sub-section 1 of this By-law are to be adhered to without variation. Each N.F.A.A. chartered club with an approved field course shall have the option of marking the distances on the shooting stakes.

4. Shooting Rules
Each archer shall shoot 4 arrows at each of the 14-target layouts in a unit. In 10 cases this shall mean shooting the four arrows from a single stake at a single face. In the other four it may mean either shooting one arrow from each of four stakes at a single face, or it may mean shooting all four arrows from a single stake but at four separate faces.

5. Scoring

a) The scoring is 5 points for the spot, 4 for 2nd circle, 3 points for the 3rd circle, 2 points for 4th circle and 1 point for the 5th circle. X ring is for tie breaker in shootoffs only.

b) An arrow shaft cutting two rings shall be scored as being in the ring of the greater value. The outer line of the field archery target is outside the scoring field. For that reason the arrow shaft must cut the line so that no color of the line can be seen between arrow shaft and scoring field before a hit may be counted. The same is true for the inner line between the two circles.

ARTICLE IX
THE N.F.A.A. INDOOR LEAGUE PROGRAM

A. Terms:

ROUND . . . . A type of game, Freeman, N.F.A.A. Indoor Round

END . . . . Five arrows shot consecutively by an archer during his turn to score.

GAME . . . . The divisions of a round; 4 ends of 5 arrows.

SERIES . . . . Three games shot in a round.

LEAGUE . . . . A number of teams competing against one another in match play.

TEAM . . . . The basic unit of a league composed of two or more archers and a permissible limit of alternate members.

LEAGUE PERIOD . . . . Total number of weeks a league will be in competition.

SCRATCH SCORE . . . . An archer's actual score before it has been adjusted by a handicap.

AVERAGE . . . . An archer's average computed from the average of scores of the last six games.

HANDICAP OR

MATCH SCORE . . . . An archer's score after it has been adjusted by his handicap.

HANDICAP . . . . A number of artificial points an archer or team received to adjust scoring ability to a common level.

ABSENTEE SCORE . . . . . . A score shot prior to a league match due to an anticipated absence. Absentee scores may not exceed the archer's average.

BLIND SCORE . . . . A score used for a missing member(s). Blind scores are computed by subtracting 5 points from the archer's average score.

TEAM AVERAGE . . . . The combined averages of all archers on a team.

TEAM POINTS . . . . Points a team earns by game and series wins. In league play a team earns one point for each game won. In addition, one point is awarded the team having the highest series total score.

B. League Sanction:

1. Any N.F.A.A. chartered association, club or archery lane may apply for the Indoor Archery League Program.

2. League Sanction will be granted provided:
   a) The league sessions will be conducted on an N.F.A.A. approved range.
   b) Official N.F.A.A. targets are used in Official N.F.A.A. rounds.
   c) A league sanction fee of $1.50 per archer is submitted to N.F.A.A. Headquarters.

3. The N.F.A.A., in granting League Sanction, will furnish:
   a) League Sanction Certificate.
   b) League Secretary instruction guide.

    c) League forms and stationery, including team score sheets, team standing forms, team shooting schedules and individual archer handicap or game record cards.

    d) Individual progression awards.

C. League Formation, Officers and Duties:

1. A temporary chairman should be appointed by the association, club or manager of a commercial archery lane desiring to establish the Indoor Archery League. This Chairman will conduct an election of League Officers at the initial meeting of league archers. After the election of officers, decisions must be made regarding:

    a) Number of archers on a team.

    b) Type of Round, N.F.A.A. Indoor or Freeman.

    c) Type of handicap, Team or individual.

    d) Substitution rules, Absentee and Blind Scoring.

    e) Awards, trophies, point money, etc.

    f) Shooting fees and Sanction fees and manner of payment.

2. Management of the league shall be vested in a Board of Directors, composed of team captains chosen by the respective members of their teams, and the elected officers of President, Vice-President, and Secretary. The Board shall decide any disputes or protests occurring between individuals or teams in league play, and shall render final decisions in regard to interpretation of league regulations.

3. President

The President shall preside at all meetings and shall act as Range Captain during league sessions. He shall have the authority to regulate practice shooting and competition in accordance with official rules and customs, and to maintain safety conditions. He will be the final authority in scoring doubtful arrows when requested by a Target Captain.

4. Vice-President

The Vice-President will act in the absence of the President.

5. Secretary

The Secretary is responsible for the proper conduct of the league and shall guarantee league functions in the manner as required by the N.F.A.A.; shall collect team shooting fees and keep complete records of league finances; shall compile individual and team scores and compute averages and/or handicaps as required; shall post a record of team standings; shall administer the N.F.A.A. Awards Program; shall post team schedules and make lane and target assignments for each session; shall collect and remit Sanction Fees to the N.F.A.A., and shall perform such other duties as may be requested of him/her by the President or required by the rules governing the league.

D. League Regulations:

1. League Sanction is provided for a continuous league period. Individual archers or teams may be added after the league has started, provided applicable forms and sanction fees are submitted.

2. ELIGIBILITY: League shooting will be opened to all archers. Individual membership requirements may be imposed by the host organization in accordance with regulations of the State Association to which it is affiliated.

3. TARGETS: The Official N.F.A.A. Indoor League Target shall be used in all league sessions.

4. TEAMS: The number of archers on a team will be decided by the league membership at the initial league meeting. An archer may transfer to another team with approval of both Team Captains and the Board of Directors.

5. LATE JOINING TEAMS: If necessary, teams may be added. However, in team standing, new teams will be scored as losing all previous series.

6. HANDICAP SYSTEMS: Either team or individual handicap may be selected by preference of the league membership.

    a) Team handicap will be computed at 80% of the difference in the average scores of any two teams that will compete against each other in a league series. These handicap points will be given to the lower scoring team before the series begins.

b) Individual handicap will be computed at 80% of the difference between an archer's average scratch score and perfect. These handicap points will be given to each individual before a series begins.

7. TEAM POINTS: In league play there are 4 possible points to be won in a 3 game series. One point is earned for each game won and one point is won by a team having the higher series total. When two teams have tie scores for a game, ½ point is won by each team.

8. AVERAGE: An archer's average will be computed weekly from the average of the last six games shot. During the initial league series each archer's high game and low game will be discarded and the remaining score used as the average in determining team points. The same procedure will be used during the second league series, but thereafter will revert to six game average.

9. AVERAGES FOR LATE JOINERS OR ALTERNATES WITHOUT ESTABLISHED AVERAGES will be computed in the same manner as described in paragraph 8, above.

10. HANDICAP: An archer's handicap will be computed weekly from the average of the last six games shot. 80% of the difference between 100 and the six game average will be the handicap. During the initial league series the high game and low game will be discarded and the remaining score will be used as the average in computing the handicap. The same procedure will be used during the second league series and for averages for late joiners or alternates without established handicaps.

11. ABSENT TEAM MEMBERS: A certain number of team members must be present to compete. Having fewer than the minimum required will result in forfeiting the series. The minimum of archers present for four member teams will be two; for 3 member teams, one; and for two member teams, one.

12. LEAGUE ALTERNATES: Several alternate or substitute archer procedures may be employed. The system selected is left to the preference of the league membership. Once a system has been adopted by the league there must be no variation unless a change has been voted by the League Board of Directors.
a) A list of league alternates may be on file with the league secretary. Any archer so listed will be eligible to fill in vacancies on any team in the league, or
b) Each team may carry an additional team member as an alternate. In this instance the alternate may shoot only if vacancies exist on his team.
c) A league may elect not to allow any type of alternate rule.

13. ABSENTEE SCORE: A league may elect to allow absentee scores in lieu of or in addition to its alternate rule. An absentee score must be witnessed and may not exceed the archer's average. Points above his average will be dropped.

14. BLIND SCORES: A blind score may be used for a missing archer. It will be determined by subtracting 5 points from the archer's average score. This blind score will be used for each game in the current series. Blind scores should not be used for computing future averages.

15. LATE ARRIVAL: A team member arriving before the second game has started may participate in the balance of the game but his score for the first game will revert to blind score procedure. Arrival after the second game has started will disqualify him and BLIND SCORE procedure will be used for his series.

16. DIVISIONS OF A LEAGUE: The league period will be divided into first and second halves. All teams will start the second half with zero wins and losses. Individual averages and/or handicaps will be carried into the second half.

17. LEAGUE CHAMPIONSHIP: A shoot off, one 3-game series, between the winner of the first half and the winner of the second half shall decide the League Championship.

18. FINAL EVENT TIES: Teams which are tied at the end of the last night of the league, and first and second half winner teams will shoot off the tie in a normal four end game of 20 arrows. If the tie is not broken, shooting will continue until one team shoots a better end (5 arrows) in sudden death. Averages and/or handicaps will not be re-computed for the purpose of shooting off ties.

E. Shooting Rules

1. TEAM CAPTAIN: Each team will select a team captain from its members. The Team

Captain shall be responsible for the attendance of the members of his team and for their behavior at all league sessions. He will collect all shooting fees, including those of tardy members, and submit them to the league secretary. He will direct the shooting order of his team, appoint an archer to score and pull the opposing team's arrows and another to record the scores. He shall check and initial score sheets at the end of each session and submit them to the league secretary.

2. TARGET ORDER: The score sheets will indicate which butt and lane (left or right) where each team will shoot. The first two left lane archers will shoot the top left targets and the last two will shoot the lower left targets. The first two right lane shooters will shoot the top right targets and the last two, the lower right targets. Lane assignments will be changed each week to insure a fair rotation.

3. ALTERNATION OF SHOOTERS: After the completion of six ends, teams shall change lanes and targets. Archers who shot top targets on one side will shoot bottom targets on the other side, etc.

4. TARGET CAPTAIN: Team Captains shall each act as target captains on the opposing teams shooting lane and score all doubtful arrows. His decision will be final unless immediately appealed to the Range Captain.

F. Awards

1. INDIVIDUAL ACHIEVEMENT AWARDS: All archers who shoot in a Sanctioned N.F.A.A. Indoor League will be eligible to individual achievement awards as follows:

200 patch	Women and Youths only
220 patch	Women and Youths only
240 patch	All Archers
260 patch	All Archers
270 patch	All Archers
280 patch	All Archers
290 patch	All Archers
300 patch	All Archers

The first three individual achievement awards won by an archer during a league period will be presented by the N.F.A.A. free of charge. Additional awards may be won but a charge to to cover the cost of the awards will be assumed by the league sponsor or recipient of the award.

2. A LEAGUE CHAMPIONSHIP PIN will be presented to each member of a league championship team.

3. Individual achievement awards are available for presentation to all State Association sanctioned indoor tournaments. A charge to cover the cost of the awards will be assumed by the tournament host.

ARTICLE X
CLUB CHARTER AND COURSE APPROVAL

A. Club Charter Procedures:

1. N.F.A.A. Charter and continued affiliation authorizes N.F.A.A. sanction and automatic registration of State Association approved field tournaments for all official N.F.A.A. archery games conducted by the club, provided such games are held on an N.F.A.A. approved indoor or outdoor facility.

2. An archery club may be chartered with the N.F.A.A. upon approval of the State Association and the N.F.A.A. Board Director who has jurisdiction. A club charter may be granted by the N.F.A.A. only after prior approval of the State Association. No State Association shall approve an application for charter unless the club meets minimum state requirements.

3. Application for charter will be made in triplicate, and along with the proper fees, shall be

forwarded to the State Association Secretary. After approval by the State Association all three copies will be forwarded to the N.F.A.A. Board Director for review. Upon granting his approval the N.F.A.A. Board Director will affix his signature, forward one copy to N.F.A.A. Headquarters, return the second copy to the State Association Secretary, and retain the third copy for his records. Upon receipt of the properly executed application and charter fee at N.F.A.A. Headquarters the Executive Secretary is authorized to issue the charter. Effective date of the charter will be shown as the date of approval by the N.F.A.A. Board Director.

4. A newly chartered club will pay a $10.00 fee to charter with the N.F.A.A. and meet state requirements. After establishing Charter, continued affiliation will be maintained through the State Association.

5. One month prior to expiration of club affiliation, the State Association Secretary shall provide the club with an affiliation renewal form in triplicate. Upon successful renewal of State N.F.A.A. affiliation, the State Secretary will forward one copy of the completed form to N.F.A.A. Headquarters, one copy to the N.F.A.A. Director and retain the third copy for state records. Upon receipt of the approved renewal form at N.F.A.A. Headquarters, affiliation will be extended for one additional year. Failure to renew affiliation annually shall result in a club being dropped from the active rolls of N.F.A.A. Reinstatement will require successful application for a new charter as outlined in sub-sections 3 and 4 of this section.

6. A club dropped from the N.F.A.A. due to lapse of affiliation shall forfeit its right to hold N.F.A.A. sanctioned tournaments, its N.F.A.A. Course Approval, and its N.F.A.A. Club Liability Insurance.

B. Course Approval Procedures:

1. The N.F.A.A. recognizes as official only tournaments held on N.F.A.A. approved courses and makes no awards for competition on any other courses.

2. Only clubs and associations chartered with the N.F.A.A. may request approval of their course.

3. To get a course approved, indoor or outdoor, the club secretary must contact the N.F.A.A. Board Director for that geographical area. The Director will provide the necessary forms and arrange for inspection. The inspection may be conducted by the Director or his delegated representative. Inspection forms shall be made in triplicate, with one copy being retained by the club, one retained by the Board Director, and one forwarded to N.F.A.A. Headquarters.

4. The Board Director or his delegate shall be paid 10 cents per mile by a club or association for travel incurred to inspect their course.

5. After inspection has been made and the completed forms have been reviewed and signed by the Board Director, they shall be forwarded by N.F.A.A. Headquarters, together with the $5.00 Course Approval fee. The club shall then be issued a Course Rating Certificate.

6. If Course Approval is completed within a four month period from the effective date of Charter, no fee will be required for the initial approval.

7. Course Approval shall expire two years from the date of issuance excepting when a change is made in the course or a higher rating is desired. In each instance, a new Course Approval must be obtained. Procedures as outlined in sub-sections 3 and 4 of this Section must be followed. The $5.00 Course Approval fee will apply.

8. The club or association secretary shall be notified by N.F.A.A. Headquarters four months prior to expiration of their Course Approval. If successful inspection and approval has not been completed prior to the date of expiration, the N.F.A.A. Executive Secretary shall notify the club or association secretary, the State Association Secretary, and the Board Director that the range is no longer an approved range.

9. Course approval may be withdrawn at any time when in the opinion of the Board Director, a condition falls below the standards for the rating awarded.

10. Revocation or expiration of Course Approval shall mean that no N.F.A.A. sanctioned events may be conducted on the course. It does not affect Club Charter nor Insurance.

EXCERPTS—N.F.A.A. REGULATIONS

11. N.F.A.A. Star Rating

To receive a rating of ONE STAR, a course must meet all the requirements listed in 13, below. A ONE STAR COURSE RATING represents compliance with minimum requirements. A ONE STAR course rating is not considered satisfactory for tournament competition. No tournaments can be registered and no N.F.A.A. awards allowed for any scores shot on a ONE STAR Course.

A TWO STAR COURSE rating will require compliance with 12. and 13. below plus the requirements of 70 BONUS points from 14. below.

A THREE STAR COURSE rating will require compliance with 12. and 13. below plus the requirements of 190 BONUS points from 14. below.

A FOUR STAR COURSE rating will require compliance with 12. and 13. below plus the added requirement of 250 BONUS points below.

A FIVE STAR COURSE rating will be granted to any FOUR STAR COURSE provided there is at least one 14 target unit which readily lends itself to TV filming. 300 BONUS points.

Course rating of TWO, THREE, FOUR and FIVE STARS makes the course eligible for tournament competition, registration, and N.F.A.A. awards.

The optional Club and Animal Round shooting positions as well as Youth shooting positions, when present, must be up to standards and become a regular requirement of the inspection program.

12. Course Layout Requirements

   a) Distances used shall be those given in the current edition of the N.F.A.A. By-laws.
   b) All distances shall be correct and no deviation is permitted. Inspectors will check any distance in question with a tape or other means. The clubs shall tape all targets from shooting position to target butts.
   c) All butts must be stable so there is no danger of tipping. If such a chance exists, then they must be braced or anchored.
   d) Shooting lanes must be cleared so that the lightest bows can shoot an arrow to the target without being deflected.
   e) Any person, regardless of height, must have a clear view of the full face of the target.
   f) If the target is not back-stopped, one-half the target distance shall be cleared behind the butt. If back-stopped, or ditched, then the area to such back-stop shall be cleared so that arrows may easily be found.
   g) Area one-fourth the shooting distance shall be cleared in front of the butts.
   h) Paths between targets should be clearly marked and clear enough for easy walking with no obstruction, preferably so that archers can walk two abreast. If the inspector has any difficulty finding his way, this must be remedied. Paths should preferably be at the side of the shooting lane.
   i) Shooting position shall be marked with target numbers, or separate target number marker shall be present and shooting stake color uniformity; Field-White, Hunter-Red, Animal-Yellow, Cub Division-Black, Youth-Blue.
   j) Bales or butts must not leak arrows. They shall not be reinforced with any material which will damage arrows.
   k) The course shall provide appropriate rest room facilities. It is most desirable that these rest rooms should meet the minimum requirements provided by the laws of their state or townships. Such requirements can be obtained from the local County Board of Health. Due to the condition of many of these facilities, City or County Board of Health affidavits should be required. A privy law is on the books of every state of the nation. Each city, county and township also has its own requirements and very often are more strict than the state's. There is no alternative but to have the course inspector check the requirements in his area and a Board of Health certificate should be attached to every N.F.A.A. application.

13. Safety Requirements

   a) No course shall receive approval until all safety hazards, in the opinion of the inspector, are removed.

b) No paths leaving target shall go directly behind butts.

c) If target butt is situated so that any path, target, road, or building is behind at any reasonable distance, then the target must be provided with an adequate backstop.

d) Practice area must be placed so that no paths or roads pass a reasonable distance behind practice butts. Practice area shall be treated as a giant-sized target, and so cleared and backed.

e) A minimum ranging from 25 feet to 50 feet must be provided between any paths or shooting lanes paralleling another shooting lane. This minimum range permits tolerance to be used, depending upon terrain, length or shot, and any distance used must preserve absolute safety.

f) Distance on either side of a target to be free from archers shall range (depending upon conditions and length of shot) from 15 to 30 degrees from the shooting position. Example: For a 40 yard target; 120 feet, tangent 30 degrees, equals 120 X (0.57735) equals 68 feet clear distance on each side of the butt (about 23 Yards). (If 30 degrees is used, then factor is always 0.57735). This does not mean all clear, but only that no shooting positions, waiting areas, etc., be located in this area.

g) No target shall be situated on top of a hill where a miss becomes virtually a flight arrow.

14. Bonus Points

Clubs having more than one 14 target field range meeting the requirements of paragraphs 12 & 13 will receive additional bonus points of 5 points for 2—14s, 10 points for 3—14s, 15 points for 4—14s, and 20 points for 5—14s or more 14s.

a) GROUP I:

1) Cleanliness. If range and all facilities are clean and neat, and provided with trash disposal cans, fresh paint, etc.—10 points.

2) If range paths wide; cleared and mowed—5 points.

3) Road. Passable the year round—5 points.

4) Practice Area. Balanced to size of club: especially set-up, cared for, and provided with good shootable bales and backing—5 points.

5) Camping Area. Specially set up and designated—5 points.

6) Parking Area. Specially arranged so that it is more than just open area (leveled, signs, etc.)—5 points.

7) Picnic Area. A picnic area shall consist of mowed area, 1 picnic table, 1 grill or fireplace, and trash-can.—10 points.
(Two points for each additional picnic table and/or grill).

8) Extra directional signals, signs, etc., on range and ground—5 points.

9) Club entrance sign—10 points.

10) 50% of club membership N.F.A.A. members—15 points.

11) 100% of club membership N.F.A.A. members (10 members or more)—20 points.

12) Shooting stake color uniformity—10 points. (Field—White; Hunters—Red; Animal—Yellow; Cub Division—Black; Youth—Blue).

13) Shooting lanes wide enough to accommodate 4 shooting positions, so 4 archers may shoot at one time on all targets—20 points.

b) GROUP II:

1) Children's play area separated by fence, etc.—5 points. Swings, 2 points each; Sandboxes, 2 points each; Slides, 2 points each.

2) Club bulletin regularly published—10 points.

3) Club signs and decorations at the entrance—5 points.

4) Safe drinking water—15 points.

5) PA System—5 points.

6) N.F.A.A. approved instructor—10 points.

7) Club or dealer arrangement for selling equipment—5 points.

8) Regularly scheduled club events, shoots, parties, picnics, etc. Allow one point per activity with a maximum of 10 points.

9) Regularly scheduled Junior Program (Junior Olympics), etc.—5 points.

10) Club owned land—20 points.
   1 point for every two acres.
11) N.F.A.A. Liability Insurance—10 points.
c) GROUP III:
   1) Kitchen facilities (building)—10 points.
   2) Separate broadhead range. Sand-banked—20 points.
   3) Bow racks on range and general area—5 points.
   4) Benches and seats on range, ¼ point per target—7 points.
   5) Double toilet facilities, over and above the minimum requirements. Neat, clean, and sanitary—10 points.
   6) Paid caretaker—15 points.
d) GROUP IV:
   1) Storeroom. Building for supplies—5 points.
   2) Running water in facilities—5 points.
   3) Club house at range—20 points.
   4) Club house heated—10 points.
   5) Electricity to facilities.—10 points.
   6) Extra shooting facilities. Short course (children's course or practice course)—5 points. Mechanical targets (moving targets, etc.)—5 points.
   7) Electrically lighted: Practice area—5 points. One 14 target unit—15 points. Parking, picnic area, etc.—5 points.

ARTICLE XI
JUNIOR DIVISIONS

A. General

1. Archers covered under this Article XI are considered an amateur and may not compete for, advertise for, nor obtain rewards except as outlined herein under Article XXIII (Amateur Rules).
2. No archer under Article XI may compete with or against archers or another section of Article XI in any official National or Sectional championship rounds.
3. Handicaps and divisions established on the proper course prior to April 4, 1974 shall stand, except: archers not in the correct age group may return to the proper division as outlined herein providing they have not submitted a signed N.F.A.A. waiver form, in which case the waiver must apply.
4. Archers under Article XI may elect to compete in any higher division with written parental consent. An N.F.A.A. form in triplicate shall be provided for parental or guardian signature. These forms will be submitted as follows: 1 copy to the archer, 1 copy to the State Secretary, 1 copy to N.F.A.A. Headquarters. Once in a division in this manner he may not revert back.
5. The youth and young adult archers only are eligible for 20 pins and other awards in the same manner as adult division.
6. There shall be no competitive bowhunter style recognized under Article XI.
7. Archer's date of birth must appear on his official membership card.
8. All division under Article XI shall provide championships by sex and accepted shooting styles.

B. Cub Division

1. A cub division is established for archers under 12 years of age at Sectional and National Tournaments and is optional at state level and below.
2. An archer may waiver the cub division by completing an N.F.A.A. waiver the same as paragraph 4 above.

3. Cub divisions official target units shall consist of:

Yardage	Field	Hunter	(Animal) Group	International
20 Ft.	20 cm	20 cm	4	—
10 Yds.	35 cm	35 cm	4	—
10 Yds.	35 cm	35 cm	4	35 cm
10 Yds.	35 cm	35 cm	4	35 cm
10 Yds.	35 cm	35 cm	3	35 cm
15 Yds.	50 cm	35 cm	3	50 cm
18 Yds.	50 cm	50 cm	3	50 cm
20 Yds.	50 cm	50 cm	3	50 cm
20 Yds.	50 cm	50 cm	2	50 cm
20 Yds.	50 cm	50 cm	2	65 cm
20 Yds.	65 cm	50 cm	2	65 cm
25 Yds.	65 cm	65 cm	1	65 cm
30 Yds.	65 cm	65 cm	1	
30 Yds.	65 cm	65 cm	1	

4. Cub shooting positions shall be marked with black stakes.
5. The cub's handicap must be established entirely on the cub course and is not applicable to or from any other course.
6. The cub division archers shall receive distinctive 50 point progressive merit patches. They shall be awarded on official 28 target rounds for consecutive 50 point increment scores between 50 and 550. Applications for cub merit patches shall be made to the State Association Secretary free of charge by the N.F.A.A.

C. Youth Division
1. The youth division is established for archers age 12 through 15.
2. The handicap must be established entirely on the youth (50 yard maximum) course and is not applicable to or from any other course.
3. Any and all official N.F.A.A. units or rounds shall not contain shots over 50 yards. Group 1 animal faces shall be shot from the closest walk-up animal stake only.
4. Youth official target units shall consist of and be the same as the adult rounds with the following exceptions:

Adult Field Round	Youth Yardage	Face
55 Yards	40 Yards	65 cm
60 Yards	45 Yards	65 cm
65 Yards	50 Yards	65 cm
80, 70, 60, 50 Yards	50 Yards	65 cm
Hunter Round		
60, 65, 61, 58 Yards	50 Yards	65 cm
64, 59, 55, 52 Yards	50 Yards	65 cm
58, 53, 48, 45 Yards	45 Yards	65 cm
53, 48, 44, 41 Yards	41 Yards	50 cm
International Round		
55 Yards	50 Yards	65 cm
60 Yards	50 Yards	65 cm
65 Yards	50 Yards	65 cm

5. An archer may waiver the youth division to a higher division by completing an N.F.A.A. waiver, see paragraph 4A.

6. The youth archers shall receive distinctive 50 point progressive merit patches. They shall be awarded on official 28 target rounds for one consecutive score of one 50 point increment between 50 and 550. Applications for youth merit patches shall be made to the State Association Secretary, free of charge by the N.F.A.A.
7. The shooting positions for youth archers shall be marked blue.

D. Young Adult Division

1. The young adult division is provided for archers 16 and 17 years of age, and for those younger who have waived into this division.
2. The young adult must establish his handicap entirely on the 80 yard (adult length) course and it is not applicable to or from any other course.
3. An archer may waiver the young adult division into an adult division, never to return, by completing an N.F.A.A. waiver, see paragraph 4A.

ARTICLE XII
THE N.F.A.A. HANDICAP

A. Purposes and Definitions:

1. Essence of the N.F.A.A. System

Handicapping is the great equalizer among sportsmen of differing abilities. The national system of handicapping must meet two main requirements:

a) Simple enough for operation by the small modestly equipped club as well as the large state associations.

b) Thorough enough to produce fair, uniform handicapping the country over.

The National Field Archery Association presents this Archery Handicap system in the conviction that, when faithfully operated, it results in equitable handicaps no matter where archers live and play. The handicap system does not exclude the use of both handicap and/or scratch shooting in the same tournament.

2. Handicap Name

The Handicap produced by this system is termed a "N.F.A.A. Handicap". Such a handicap should be identified on a card or elsewhere as a "N.F.A.A. Handicap" or as "Computed under N.F.A.A. Handicap system".

3. Purposes

Among the purposes of the N.F.A.A. system are to:

a) Provide fair handicaps for all archers, regardless of ability.

b) Reflect the archer's inherent ability as well as his recent scoring trends.

c) Automatically adjust his handicap down or up as his game changes.

d) Disregard freak low scores that bear little relation to the archer's normal ability.

e) Make it difficult for the archer to obtain an unfairly large handicap increase at any revision period.

f) Make a handicap continuous from one shooting season to the next without need of adjustment.

g) Encourange the archer to keep his game near its peak.

h) Establish handicaps useful for all archers, from championship eligibility to informal games.

i) Make handicap work as easy as possible for the handicapper.

B. Definitions:

1. Style

Style is the method that an archer uses to shoot a bow, i.e., Bare Bow. Freestyle.

2. Division

Division is the separation or archers by style, i.e., Amateur, Competitive Bowhunter, Youth, Men and Women.

3. Class

Class is the division of archers within a division.

4. Net or Scratch Score
Net or scratch score is an archer's actual score before it is adjusted by his handicap.
5. Gross Score
A gross score is an archer's score after his net score has been adjusted by his handicap.
6. Handicap
A handicap is the number of artificial points an archer receives to adjust his scoring ability to the common level of perfect.
7. Handicap Differential
A handicap differential is the difference between an archer's net score and perfect.

C. Establishing a Handicap:
1. An archer's handicap shall be computed on the official N.F.A.A. field and/or hunter round, and shall be computed by the following table:

Best score of 2 scores	80% of average differential
2 best scores of 5 scores	80% of average differential
3 best scores of last 7 scores	80% of average differential

The first and second methods shall be computed only for those archers who have not recorded the minimum of seven scores needed for a full handicap.
2. An archer's handicap shall be derived only from those scores shot within the last twelve (12) month period.
3. All handicaps must be established during any tournament held on official N.F.A.A. targets, approved N.F.A.A. 2 Star Ranges or higher, and any tournament where official N.F.A.A. field or hunter rounds are shot.
4. The differential is the difference between the actual average and perfect. (Example: Last 7 scores: 430, 415, 440, 440, 450, 460 and 410; the best 3 scores are 440, 450 and 460—average 450—560 minus 450 equals 110; 80% of 110 equals 88, which is the handicap.)

D. Handicap Procedure:
1. A new archer or one who holds an expired handicap card, shall be issued a handicap card in the most expedient manner upon the payment of established fees, and must shoot two official scores to establish handicap.
2. No archer shall be permitted to compete in a N.F.A.A. registered tournament or any tournament in which any official N.F.A.A. rounds are shot unless he/she holds a valid handicap card, or has made proper application, except in a closed club shoot.
3. No archer shall be issued a handicap card unless the archer is a member in good standing of the N.F.A.A. and the State Association chartered and recognized by the N.F.A.A.
4. If a person shoots more than one style, he/she must be handicapped in each style, in accordance with the items listed in Section B.

E. Handicap Cards:
1. All official handicap cards shall be printed by the N.F.A.A. and shall be made available, free of charge, to affiliated State and Foreign Association. The card shall have provisions to indicate N.F.A.A. State and Club membership, all styles of shooting, and shall provide space for recording scores for all recognized styles of shooting.
2. Handicap cards shall be issued by the Association which has granted membership as provided under Constitution Article III, Section A., sub-sections 3 and 4.
3. Handicap shall be concurrent with membership, i.e., expiration of membership in the N.F.A.A. shall void handicap.
4. No handicap card shall be issued by the N.F.A.A. in conjunction with direct N.F.A.A. membership applications, provided an affiliated State or Territorial Association exists in the area where the archer resides.
5. The handicap and membership card shall carry the full name, address and social security number of the archer.
6. Handicap and membership cards of military personnel in transit or on temporary duty shall be recognized.

F. Scores to Be Recorded on Handicap Cards:
1. All scores recorded on the handicap cards shall be the actual scores for the field and/or hunter rounds.
2. All scores shot in tournaments using field and/or hunter rounds shall be recorded.
3. All recordings on the handicap card shall be on the basis of each 28 targets, i.e., a tournment of 28 targets field and 28 targets hunter . . . each score is to be recorded. Fourteen field and 14 hunter . . . the combined total shall be recorded. Twenty-eight field and 14 hunter . . . the round that is completed shall be recorded. No fractional round shall be recorded.
4. Tournament officials shall be responsible for the recording of actual scores on the handicap cards of all participants. Violation shall be cause to suspend club charter and/or recognition of the State Association.

G. Lost or Misplaced Handicap Cards:
1. An archer who has been handicapped but cannot submit a handicap card or statement from his club secretary showing his/her true handicap, is required to compete without handicap for that tournament.
2. An archer may not submit club secretary evidence of handicap to the state handicap officer or N.F.A.A. board member for more than 14 consecutive days. The archer must apply for the replacement handicap and membership card. The application must be accompanied by the fees established by the N.F.A.A. and the State or Territorial Association. The replacement card shall run concurrent with their previous card as recorded in the records of the State Association and/or records of the N.F.A.A.

H. Administration of Handicaps:
1. Handicap shall be administered through the State or Territorial Association chartered and recognized by the N.F.A.A. If no chartered or recognized association exists, the N.F.A.A. shall administer the system.
2. The State Association shall maintain a satisfactory central control to insure that handicap is properly administered.
3. The State or Territorial Associations shall agree no archer is denied a handicap card upon proper application and payment of fees, regardless of race, creed, or color.
4. The State or Territorial Association shall agree that no member in good standing with the N.F.A.A. is denied a handicap card.
5. State or Territorial Associations may not impose additional requirements for handicap and membership in the N.F.A.A.
6. The State or Territorial Association shall furnish the N.F.A.A. with a current list of handicap card holders in a form satisfactory to N.F.A.A. This information will be furnished at the same time as membership and handicap cards are forwarded to the archer.
7. Non-compliance with these requirements shall be grounds for immediate suspension or recognition by the N.F.A.A. The State or Territorial Association must submit within 30 days a brief, showing cause why the offending Association's charter and recognition should not be revoked by the N.F.A.A. Board of Directors Council.
8. The use of non-official targets shall not be construed as a permissive to negate the provisions of the handicap article.

ARTICLE XIII
Rules Governing the 20 and 15 Pin Awards

A. These awards may be won in the N.F.A.A. Field, Hunter or International Round, or portion thereof, with a distinctive pin and set of bars for each round.
B. QUALIFICATIONS: Only members of the N.F.A.A. are eligible and the archer must have his score card signed by two witnesses. Application for the 20/15 bar shall be submitted within 30 days, by the archer eligible for the award, accompanied by a $1.00 fee, sent to the

State Association Secretary or Awards Chairman. The same procedure is followed for the 20/15 pin award. The accompanying fee for the pin is $2.00.

C. RULES: An archer shall become eligible for these awards upon shooting a 20 score on any field or hunter target or upon shooting a 15 on any International target on any officially approved N.F.A.A. course using official N.F.A.A. targets while competing in any of the following tournaments:

1. The Annual National Field Archery Association Tournament.
2. Any National Field Archery Association Mail Tournament.
3. Any registered Club or Association Tournament.
4. Only clubs and associations chartered with N.F.A.A. shall be permitted to register tournaments as 20/15 Pin Tournaments.
5. Members of N.F.A.A. may earn yardage bars to attach to the 20 Pin Award for scoring a 20 on the 6; 12; 18; and 24 inch targets and under the rules set up for the 20 Pin Award. The bars shall have the distance shot marked on the bar.
6. Members of N.F.A.A. may earn yardage bars to attach to the 15 Pin Award for scoring a 15 on the 14, 22 and 30 inch targets and under the rules set up for the 15 Pin Award. The bars shall have the distance shot marked on the bar.
7. Upon receiving the pin and entire series of bars in any one style of shooting, the N.F.A.A. Perfect Pin shall be awarded an archer upon application and verification of achievements through the State Association Secretary. Perfect Pins are available for the Field, Hunter and International Rounds. No fee is involved in this award.
8. Members of N.F.A.A. may earn an Animal Perfect Pin by shooting a 280 on a 14 target unit at a registered tournament. The cost of the pin shall be $2.00 and shall be paid for by the archer.

ARTICLE XIV
BATTLE CLOUT

A. Distance: 200 yards.
B. Target: 12 feet diameter center. Rings: 6 feet wide.
C. 36 arrows shot in ends of 6.
D. Arrows must weigh 425 grains, or more, and have Broadheads not less than 7/8" wide.
E. Score—Center, 9 points; Rings, 7, 5, 3 and 1.

ARTICLE XV
ART YOUNG AWARDS

A. **GAME AWARDS OF THE NATIONAL FIELD ARCHERY ASSOCIATION:**

1. There shall be two: The "Art Young Big Game Awards" and "Art Young Small Game Awards".
2. PURPOSE: The purpose of the Art Young awards is to promote interest in hunting with the bow and arrow, to encourage good sportsmanship and to give recognition by the organized field archers to their members who obtain game with the bow.
3. RULES:
   a) All animals must be taken in accordance with the laws of the State, Territory, Province, or County, whichever is appropriate, and in accordance with the rules of fair chase.
   b) In order to be eligible for awards, all animals must be reported within 90 days of the date taken. A handling fee of 50 cents must accompany each application.
   c) The hunter must have taken possession of the animal to receive credit for the award.
   d) It shall be the responsibility of the hunter himself to know the legal status of the species hunted. National Headquarters is responsible only to the extent of verifying whether a species is, or is not protected, since this is the basis of acceptance.
   e) Animals specified as big game by the N.F.A.A. are not eligible for credit in the Art Young Small Game Awards system.

f) Members who willfully take game out of season, take protected animals or otherwise violate game laws, falsify a claim or deliberately witness a falsified claim shall be expelled from the N.F.A.A. and all its programs. An expelled member may petition the N.F.A.A. for reinstatement after one year. The Bowhunting and Conservation Committee shall rule on the petition.

g) An additional award shall not be given for game previously accepted under a prior awards system. (Persons who have amassed a combination of seven or more pins under the original program as of July 1, 1973, and have so requested by January 1, 1974, shall be allowed to continue the original program. The same animals used in claiming any portion of the original Master Bowhunter Award may not be used again for awards in another program).

h) Any game taken from areas where they are officially designated as "rare" or "endangered" shall be ineligible for awards.

B. ART YOUNG BIG GAME AWARDS:
1. DEFINITION OF BIG GAME:
   a) All species of American bears. For lack of confusion the "Alaskan Brown Bear" will be considered a grizzly (now so recognized by most modern taxonomists).
   b) Big cats including mountain lions or cougars.
   c) The deer family, including elk, moose, caribou and various species of native deer.
   d) All other native hoofed animals including pronghorns, sheep, goats and javelina.
   e) All feral (gone wild), swine (boars), sheep and goats if recognized as "game" by the local conservation department.
   f) Allow sub-species of deer including whitetail, mule, blacktail, coues, sika and fallow recognized as big game by the responsible Conservation Department are eligible.
2. ELIGIBILITY: Eligibility for "Art Young Big Game Awards" is limited to members of the N.F.A.A. at the time of the kill. There shall be no geographical restrictions, either as to residence of the claimant or to the location in which the game is secured.
3. CLAIM OF AWARD: Any member of the N.F.A.A. wishing to claim the Art Young Big Game Pin, or the subsequent awards will apply to the N.F.A.A. Headquarters for an application blank, supply the information and evidence called for, and mail it to N.F.A.A. Headquarters.
4. AWARDS:
   a) Art Young Big Game Pins shall be given for only the first example of each species taken with the bow and arrow according to the N.F.A.A. rules.
   b) Cloth patches for additional examples of each species taken with the bow and arrow according to the N.F.A.A. rules will be awarded.

C. ART YOUNG SMALL GAME AWARDS
1. DEFINITION OF SMALL GAME: All eligible small game species will be shown on a master list maintained by N.F.A.A. headquarters office and shall be available to member so requesting. Recommendation for additions or deletions to the master list shall be reviewed by the Bowhunting & Conservation Committee at each annual N.F.A.A. meeting.
   c) A particular species may not be claimed more than once by any bowhunter participat-
2. ELIGIBILITY: This shall be the same as for the "Art Young Big Game Award". If several species are taken within such a 90 day period, they may be held and reported at one time. However, no species may be reported more than 90 days after taking.
3. AWARDS:
   a) The Art Young Small Game Arrowhead Pin shall be given upon taking the first six species of small game.
   b) For each additional four species taken by a member an additional award in the form of a bar with the number 4 shall be presented to the hunter. There shall be no limit to the number of bars which may be earned, but all game must be legally taken.
   c) A particular species may not be claimed more than once by any bowhunter participating in the Art Young Small Game Program, except in states which have fewer than 3

species designated legal small game for bowhunting. At least one of the animals claimed must be considered "game" by the local conservation department.

D. BOWHUNTER AWARDS:
1. There shall be three classes of Bowhunter Awards:
   a) Bowhunter Pin
   b) Expert Bowhunter Pin
   c) Master Bowhunter Medal
2. ELIGIBILITY:
   a) A person may be awarded the Bowhunter Pin when he has earned the Art Young Small Game Arrowhead Pin and one Four bar, and two Big Game Arrowhead Pins.
   b) A person may be awarded the Expert Bowhunter Pin when he has earned the Bowhunter Pin plus one additional Four bar and one additional Big Game Arrowhead Pin.
   c) A person may be awarded the Master Bowhunter Medal when he has earned the Expert Bowhunter Pin plus three additional Four bars and three additional Big Game Arrowhead Pins.
3. CLAIM OF AWARDS:
   a) All applications must be made to the N.F.A.A. Headquarters. Verification that all species, to the best of his knowledge, were legally taken must be made by another N.F.A.A. member. No application will be accepted by N.F.A.A. without such verification.

E. DIAMOND BUCK AWARD:
1. The Diamond Buck Award will be given for the largest example of mule deer, whitetail deer and blacktail deer based on antler measurements. The antlers must be scored by Pope and Young Club or Boone and Crockett methods and verified by one of these club's official measurers. Applications shall be available from N.F.A.A. Headquarters and from Sectional Officers of the N.F.A.A. in charge of Bowhunting.

F. APPLICATION DISAPPROVAL:
1. In the event of application is disapproved the hunter has the right to petition the N.F.A.A. Bowhunting and Conservation Committee. The petition must be in writing and must state the facts of the claim. It shall be the responsibility of the review committee to study the applicable game laws and the petition and make a recommendation to the Bowhunting and Conservation Committee. The Chairman shall appoint the three-man committee to rule on the claim and act on the claim within 60 days.
2. The results of the petition shall be kept confidential, but the ruling shall be sent in writing to each member of the committee, the N.F.A.A. Headquarters and the petitioner.

ARTICLE XVI
RULES FOR COMPTON MEDAL OF HONOR

A. The N.F.A.A. Medal of Honor shall be known as the Compton Medal of Honor, and it shall be bestowed sparingly and only in recognition of outstanding and unselfish contributions to archery in any of its phases.
B. To the end that the Compton Medal of Honor shall for all time retain its place as the most highly esteemed award in all archery, the safeguarding of its future will be entrusted to a committee of three N.F.A.A. members who must have been members for ten years and one former Compton Medal of Honor recipient selected by the President. The members will be appointed to 3 year terms, with one new member being appointed each year.
C. The Medal of Honor Committee shall be free of all restrictions as to their choice of recipients except (1) that the Compton Medal of Honor shall not be bestowed upon any elected officer of the association during his tenure of office, and (2) that their deliberations shall be held in inviolable confidence.

D. The President of the N.F.A.A. shall be the Honorary Chairman of the committee, with the following duties and authority:
   1. He shall appoint from among the committee members an acting chairman to serve in that capacity for one year, thus providing for rotation of the acting chairmanship.
   2. He shall have the sole authority to decide for, or against, such candidate only as may be reported to him by the acting chairman as having a majority, though less than unanimous, support of the members of the committee.
   3. He shall accept a unanimous recommendation by the committee as mandatory upon him to order the bestowal of the Compton Medal of Honor.
   4. He shall prepare, or have prepared, a citation in accordance with the committee's unanimous choice, or with his affirmation of the committee's majority recommendation, as the case may be.
E. In conjunction with receiving the Compton Medal of Honor the recipient will automatically be awarded an Honorary Life Membership.
F. The Secretary-Treasurer shall be responsible for the custody of the dies for the Compton Medal, and shall pay out of the treasury the costs of the striking and engraving or such replicas of the Compton Medal as, and when, directed by the President to do so.
G. A copy of these regulations shall appear in each issue of the N.F.A.A. Constitution and By-Laws booklet.

ARTICLE XVII
RULES GOVERNING THE AWARD OF THE MEDAL OF MERIT

A. The N.F.A.A. Medal of Merit shall be bestowed sparingly and only in recognition of unselfish contributions to field archery and its closely allied activities. The inscription, "Opera, Artes, Honor" (Works, Skills, Honor) which appears on the medal, shall serve as the measure.
B. To each of the States and each of the Sections comprising the N.F.A.A. is given the privilege of nominating worthy members of the N.F.A.A. as candidates for the award. The State through its N.F.A.A. Director; the Section through its Councilman shall, after receiving instructions from their respective memberships, submit nominations to the N.F.A.A. Executive Secretary. Qualification and endorsements shall accompany every nomination.
C. An individual may be awarded only one Medal of Merit for all time.
D. The N.F.A.A. Executive Secretary shall furnish all available information on all nominations to the Board of Directors Council, which, after discussion and investigation, may vote on the issue. A two-thirds yea vote shall be required to affirm the award. The Executive Secretary shall forward the medal to the State or Section for presentation.
E. The Executive Secretary-Treasurer of N.F.A.A. shall be the custodian of the dies for the medal and the archives of the award. The initial cost of design, striking and engraving shall be paid out of the treasury of the N.F.A.A. The unit bestowing the award (State or Section) shall pay a suitable fee to the N.F.A.A. for the medal.
F. The name of the unit (State or Section) making the award shall be engraved on the award.
G. A copy of these regulations shall appear in each issue of the N.F.A.A. Constitution and By-Laws booklet.

ARTICLE XVIII
THE ORDER OF THE BONE

A. Members of this order shall receive an award pin and a membership card.
B. Members shall be chosen by a committee to be appointed by the President of the N.F.A.A.
C. Requirements for Membership:
   1. Be a member in good standing of the N.F.A.A.
   2. Pull a conspicuous "boner" pertaining to archery hunting.
   3. Write or cause to be written a full account of events leading up to and following said "boner" in publishable story form. At least one article will be selected each month to be

published in Archery Magazine, although you may win the award and not have your article published because of lack of space. Stories should be mailed to N.F.A.A. Headquarters and should include the date the boner was committed.

ARTICLE XIX
FELLOWSHIP OF ROBINHOOD

A. Any member who telescopes an arrow, previously lodged in the highest scoring area of a target shall be eligible for recognition in the Fellowship of Robinhood.
B. The award shall consist of a certificate in Old English text.
C. Applications shall be made to N.F.A.A. Headquarters.
  1. Applicants shall describe the general circumstances of the shot, including the date and name of one witness.
  2. Application blanks shall be supplied by N.F.A.A. Headquarters upon request.

ARTICLE XX
500 Club and/or Perfect Patch

A. Any member who records a score of 500 or more, from the adult stakes, on an N.F.A.A. Field Round or N.F.A.A. Hunter Round or combination of 14 Field 14 Hunter, shall be eligible to join the N.F.A.A. 500 club. The feat must be accomplished on a N.F.A.A. approved course.
B. Any member who records a perfect score from the adult stakes on an N.F.A.A. Field Round or N.F.A.A. Hunter Round, or combination of 14/15 Field 14/15 Hunter, or the International Round, shall be eligible to join the N.F.A.A. Perfect Club. The feat must be accomplished on a N.F.A.A. approved course, at a registered tournament.
C. Any member who records a perfect score on any N.F.A.A. official indoor round shall be eligible to join the N.F.A.A. Perfect Club. The feat must be accomplished at a registered tournament.
D. The award shall consist of an appropriate certificate. An embroidered 500 club patch or perfect patch is also available for a fee.
E. Application for membership in the 500 Club or Perfect Club shall be made to N.F.A.A. Headquarters.
  1. Application shall be accompanied by the applicant's score card. The date, location of the course and signatures of two witnesses shall appear on the card.
  2. Application blanks shall be supplied by N.F.A.A. Headquarters upon request.
F. Design a new 500 patch for the metric target.

ARTICLE XXI
N.F.A.A. Service Pins

A. Continuous membership in the N.F.A.A. shall be recognized by the awarding of an appropriate lapel pin.
B. Periods of membership indicated shall be 10, 15, 20, 25, 30, 35, 40, 45 and 50 years.
C. The pins shall be awarded by N.F.A.A. Headquarters upon application through the state association secretary, or directly to N.F.A.A. Headquarters.
D. Eligibility for service pins shall be determined on the basis of available membership records at N.F.A.A. Headquarters and/or those of the affiliated state association, or any other proof of continuous membership.

ARTICLE XXII

The By-laws may be amended or revised by a two-thirds vote of the Board of Directors as voted at the annual meeting or by mail ballot.

ARTICLE XXIII
THE N.F.A.A. OUTDOOR LEAGUE PROGRAM

A. Terms:

ROUND........................... A type of game, Field, Hunter or International, Round.

END .... four arrows in Field or Hunter, 3 arrows in International Round.

GAME........................... The divisions of a round; 14 Field, 14 Hunter, 10 International.

SERIES .... Two games shot in a round.

LEAGUE......................... A number of teams competing against one another in match play.

TEAM .... The basic unit of a league composed of two or more archers and a permissable limit of alternate members.

LEAGUE PERIOD .... Total number of weeks a league will be in competition.

SCRATCH SCORE............. An archer's actual score before it has been adjusted by a handicap.

AVERAGE....................... Use regular Outdoor Field Handicapped System.

ABSENTEE SCORE........... A score shot prior to a league match due to an ancitipated absence. Absentee scores may not exceed the archer's average.

BLIND SCORE.................. A score used for a missing member(s). Blind scores are computed by subtracting 5 points from the archer's average score.

TEAM AVERAGE.............. The combined averages of all archers on a team.

TEAM POINTS.................. Points a team earns by game and series wins. In league play a team earns one point for each game won. In addition, one point is awarded the team having the highest series total score.

B. League Sanction:
1. Any N.F.A.A. chartered association, club or archery lane may apply for the Outdoor Archery League Program.
2. League Sanction will be granted provided:
   a) The league sessions will be conducted on an N.F.A.A. approved range.
   b) Official N.F.A.A. targets are used in Official N.F.A.A. rounds.
   c) A league sanction fee of $1.50 per archer is submitted to N.F.A.A. Headquarters.
3. The N.F.A.A., in granting League Sanction, will furnish:
   a) League Sanction Certificate.
   b) League Secretary instruction guide.
   c) League forms and stationery, including team score sheets, team standing forms, team shooting schedules and individual archer handicap or game record cards.
   d) Individual progression awards.

C. League Formation, Officers and Duties:
1. A temporary chairman should be appointed by the association, club or manager of a commercial archery lane desiring to establish the Outdoor Archery League. This Chairman will conduct an election of League Officers at the initial meeting of league archers. After the election of officers, decisions must be made regarding:
   a) Number of archers on a team.
   b) Type of Round, N.F.A.A. Field, Hunter or International
   c) Type of handicap, Team or Individual.
   d) Substitution rules, Absentee and Blind Scoring.

e) Awards, trophies, point money, etc.

f) Shooting fees and Sanction fees and manner of payment.

2. Management of the league shall be vested in a Board of Directors, composed of team captains chosen by the respective members of their teams, and the elected officers of President, Vice-President and Secretary. The Board shall decide any disputes or protests occurring between individuals or teams in league play, and shall render final decisions in regard to interpretation of league regulations.

3. President:
The President shall preside at all meetings and shall act as Range Captain during league sessions. He shall have the authority to regulate practice shooting and competition in accordance with official rules and customs, and to maintain safety conditions. He will be the final authority in scoring doubtful arrows when requested by a Target Captain.

4. Vice President:
The Vice-President will act in the absence of the President.

5. Secretary:
The Secretary is responsible for the proper conduct of the league and shall guarantee league functions in the manner as required by the N.F.A.A.; shall collect team shooting fees and keep complete records of league finances; shall compile individual and team scores and compute averages and/or handicaps as required; shall post a record of team standings; shall administer the N.F.A.A. Awards Program; shall post team schedules and make lane and target assignments for each session; shall collect and remit Sanction Fees to the N.F.A.A., and shall perform such other duties as may be requested of him/her by the President or required by the rules governing the league.

D. **League Regulations:**

1. League Sanction is provided for a continuous league period. Individual archers or teams may be added after the league has started, provided applicable forms and sanction fees are submitted.

2. ELIGIBILITY: League shooting will be opened to all archers. Individual membership requirements may be imposed by the host organization in accordance with regulations of the State Association to which it is affiliated.

3. TARGETS: The Official N.F.A.A. Outdoor League Target shall be used in all league sessions.

4. TEAMS: The number of archers on a team will be decided by the league membership at the initial league meeting. An archer may transfer to another team with approval of both Team Captains and the Board of Directors.

5. LATE JOINING TEAMS: If necessary, teams may be added. However, in team standing, new teams will be scored as losing all previous series.

6. HANDICAP SYSTEMS: Regular N.F.A.A. Outdoor Handicap System.

7. ABSENT TEAM MEMBERS: A certain number of team members must be present to compete. Having fewer than the minimum required will result in forfeiting the series. The minimum of archers present for four member teams will be two; for three members teams, one; and for two member teams, one.

8. LEAGUE ALTERNATES: Several alternate or substitute archer procedures may be employed. The system selected is left to the preference of the league membership. Once a system has been adopted by the league there must be no variation unless a change has been voted by the League Board of Directors.

   a) A list of league alternates may be on file with the league secretary. Any archer so listed will be eligible to fill in vacancies on any team in the league.

   b) Each team may carry an additional team member as an alternate. In this instance the alternate may shoot only if vacancies exist on his team.

   c) A league may elect not to allow any type of alternate rule.

9. ABSENTEE SCORE: A league may elect to allow absentee scores in lieu of or in

addition to its alternate rule. An absentee score must be witnessed and may not exceed the archer's average. Points above his average will be dropped.

10. BLIND SCORES: A blind score may be used for a missing archer. It will be determined by subtracting 5 points from the archer's average score. This blind score will be used for each game in the current series. Blind scores should not be used for computing future averages.

11. LATE ARRIVAL: A team member arriving before the second game has started may participate in the balance of the game but his score for the first game will revert to blind score procedure. Arrival after the second game has started will disqualify him, and BLIND SCORE procedure will be used for his series.

12. DIVISIONS OF A LEAGUE: The league period will be divided into first and second halves. All teams will start the second half with zero wins and losses. Individual averages and/or handicaps will be carried into the second half.

13. LEAGUE CHAMPIONSHIP: A shoot off, one 3-game series, between the winner of the first half and the winner of the second half shall decide the League Championship.

14. FINAL EVENT TIES: Will be handled the same as ties are broken on Outdoor Field Rounds.

E. **Shooting Rules:**

1. TEAM CAPTAIN: Each team will select a team captain from its members. The Team Captain shall be responsible for the attendance of the members of his team and for their behavior at all league sessions. He will collect all shooting fees, including those of tardy members, and submit them to the league secretary. He will direct the shooting order of his team, appoint an archer to score and pull the opposing team's arrows and another to record the scores. He shall check and initial score sheets at the end of each session and submit them to the league secretary.

2. TARGET ORDER: Round will be shot according to Outdoor shooting, as per Round shot.

3. TARGET CAPTAIN: Team Captains shall each act as target captains on the opposing teams and score all doubtful arrows. His decision will be final unless immediately appealed to the Range Captain.

F. **Awards:**

1. INDIVIDUAL ACHIEVEMENT AWARDS: All archers who shoot in a Sanctioned N.F.A.A. Outdoor League will be eligible for individual achievement awards as follows:

120 patch	Women and Youths only
140 patch	Women and Youths only
140 patch	All Archers
160 patch	All Archers
180 patch	All Archers
200 patch	All Archers
280 patch	All Archers
Perfect patch	Field, Hunter, International game

The first three individual achievement awards won by an archer during a league period will be presented by the N.F.A.A. free of charge. Additional awards may be won but a charge to cover the cost of the awards will be assumed by the league sponsor or recipient of the award.

2. A LEAGUE CHAMPIONSHIP PIN will be presented to each member of a league championship team.

3. Individual achievement awards are available for presentation to all State Association sanctioned outdoor tournaments. A charge to cover the cost of the awards will be assumed by the tournament host.

NATIONAL FIELD ARCHERY ASSOCIATION
POLICY

1. Dues for the National Field Archery Association shall be $10.00 per person and shall include the N.F.A.A.'s official publication. Dues for additional family membership shall be $2.00 per person. The total membership fee for a family shall not exceed $14.00, effective April 1, 1975. There shall be no charge for additional family members in excess of three.

2. Dues for the National Field Archery Association paid through an affiliated Foreign Association shall be $4.00 per person. Dues for additional family members shall be $1.00 per person. The total membership fees for a family shall not exceed $6.00, effective January 1, 1971. Said membership is provided only for a citizen of the country in which the Foreign Association is located.

3. Military personnel on transient basis who are not located within the jurisdiction of an affiliated body shall pay a fee of $5.75 per person for N.F.A.A. dues. Dues for additional family members shall be $2.00 per person. These military persons shall be serviced from N.F.A.A. headquarters.

4. N.F.A.A. membership dues in states not affiliated with the N.F.A.A. shall be $16.00 per person. Dues for additional family members shall be $5.00 per person.

5. A N.F.A.A. Bowhunting Defense Fund shall be established for funding of legal counsel in defense of bowhunting rights in the United States and for development & promotion of hunter information and education programs to combat anti-hunting efforts. The Bowhunting Committee Chairman recommends the expenditures to the President and is approved by the President before expenditure is made. Income for the fund will be derived from a portion of the N.F.A.A. Bowhunter Membership.
    a) Initial fee shall be $10.00 per year with $3.00 to be deposited in the Bowhunter Defense Fund.
    b) Additional family membership shall be $2.00 per year with $1.00 to be deposited in the Defense Fund.
    c) That N.F.A.A. Executive Board give a complete accounting of the Bowhunters Defense Fund annually, monies taken in, monies spent and what it was spent for.

6. The N.F.A.A. Bowhunter Membership benefits shall include:
    a) 12 issues of the Official N.F.A.A. Publication.
    b) Big and Small Game Awards Program.
    c) Landowners guarantee.
    d) Eligibility for all hunting award contests sponsored by the N.F.A.A.

7. The N.F.A.A. Bowhunter membership fee and distribution to the Defense Fund may be adjusted by the Board of Directors, subject to recommendation of the N.F.A.A. Bowhunting Committee.

8. The Board of Directors Council shall have the right, as surplus money becomes available, to apply it on other items of the budget if it becomes necessary.

9. Dues to the N.F.A.A. becomes effective January 1, 1966 and thereafter, during each fiscal year.

10. Payment of dues shall coincide with payment of state dues.

11. Archery magazine shall be the official publication of the federation of states and the N.F.A.A.

12. All annual sectional meeting material that is developed for the National Meeting agenda and that is intended to change, add to, or delete from the N.F.A.A. Constitution or By-laws, shall be prepared in resolution form and in the language of the Constitution and By-laws.

13. All action taken by the Board of Directors shall carry an effective date of sixty (60) calendar days from the close of the annual meeting, or the termination of voting in the case of mail sessions, unless an individual action includes an effective date.

14. The annual budget shall be the first item of business of the second day of the annual meeting.

15. All clubs shall receive changes in the Constitution and By-laws within 60 days of action to change.
16. Upon completion of issuing a Professional Division membership the State Secretary involved and the Professional Sectional Representative involved will be promptly notified of the name and effective date. This will also apply to the N.F.A.A. Bowhunter Associate Members.
17. The Youth and Cub range shall be as near to tournament headquarters, at National Tournaments, as possible, well marked, good paths and well supervised.
18. If for any reason the Vice President is unable to complete his term of office, the unexpired term will be filled by an election at the next annual meeting by the Board of Directors. Nominations may be made by a Board of Directors Councilman or a member of the Board of Directors. Until the election, the immediate Past President assumes the dual role of Vice President Pro-tem and immediate Past President. In the event that both the President and the Vice President are unable to complete their terms of office for any reason, the immediate Past President assumes the dual role of President Pro-tem and immediate Past President and the Councilman receiving the most yes votes from the Board of Directors will serve the dual role of Vice President Pro-tem and Councilman for his/her section.

PROFESSIONAL DIVISION CODE OF ETHICS

1. Professional Division Code of Ethics
   a. The professional archer should conduct himself at all times in a manner that will bring respect and honor to himself, archery, and the N.F.A.A.
   b. A professional archer shall make every effort to comply with all tournament rules and regulations both as published and intended.
   c. A professional archer shall not allow his name or likeness to be used in such a manner as to misrepresent any product, nor shall he make claims that tend to misrepresent any product and mislead purchasers as to the actual value or quality of such products.
   d. A professional archer shall make every effort to protect the amateur standing of amateur archers.
2. Professional Dress Code
   a. General
      The professional archer shall present himself in clean, neat attire, acceptable to public view.
   b. Recommended
      1. Men
         Slacks, shirt with collar and appropriate footwear.
      2. Women
         Slacks or skirt with blouse and appropriate footwear.
   c. Not acceptable
      1. Swimming suits
      2. Cut offs
      3. Obscene or vulgar slogan or pictures on clothing.
3. Professional Disciplinary Action
   a. Action may be taken by any current N.F.A.A. member through the tournament chairman.
      1. The following items are subject to immediate disqualification from the tournament and may be subject to immediate disqualification from the tournament and may be subject to further disciplinary action.
         a) Obvious witnessed intoxication while shooting on the range is in progress.
         b) Verified cheating.
         c) Blatant violation of code of ethics or dress code.
   b. Protests must be in writing, signed and submitted to the tournament chairman within one hour of completion of shooting for that day's round.
   c. Additional Disciplinary action
      1. Refer to Article III, Section A, paragraph 10, page 3.

4. Professional Guidelines
   a. Trophy awards:
      1. Refer to Article VI, Section E, sub paragraph g, page 17.
      2. An N.F.A.A. Pro may compete for trophy awards at the state level with the open shooters, providing there is no pro division recognized at that tournament.
   b. Recognized Division:
      1. The N.F.A.A. Pro Division recognizes all adult shooting styles.
5. Tournament Sanction
   a. Refer to: Article VI, Section E, sub-paragraph e, page 17.
   b. Approved Tournament:
      Purpose is to allow a tournament promoter to accrue a guaranteed purse with co-operation of N.F.A.A.
   c. Must be negotiated with N.F.A.A. 180 days prior to shot date.
   d. All entry fees will be collected and maintained by N.F.A.A. Headquarters.
   e. All archery manufacturing booth fees will be collected and maintained by N.F.A.A. headquarters.
   f. Thirty days prior to the shoot date a sanction will be issued by N.F.A.A. with a purse guarantee equal to the funds on deposit or a pre-agreed dollar amount which ever is the lessor.
   g. The control of these funds will remain with the N.F.A.A. and will be disbursed by the Executive Secretary or his agent.
   h. Upon sanction, a notice will be sent to the Pro Division membership.
   i. The fee will be $50.00.
   j. The decision to negotiate an "approved tournament" will be at the discretion of the Executive Secretary, Pro Division Chairman and N.F.A.A. President.
6. Sectional Representatives
   a. Election and Term of Office
      1. Article VI, Section E, sub-paragraph c, page 17.
      2. Additional clarification
      a) The term of office for representative of the Southwest, Mid-Atlantic, Great Lakes, and Southern Sections shall end December 31 of even numbered years.
      b) The term of office for representatives of the Northwest, New England, Midwest, and Southeastern Sections shall end December 31 of even numbered years.
      c) In the event an individual comes into office other than January 1 or the beginning of a 2 year term an election must still be held as stipulated above.
   b. Duties
      1. Shall chair and conduct a Pro division meeting at each sectional.
      a) Purpose is to elect new representatives when applicable.
      b) Maintain minutes for agenda items to be presented at National Pro meeting held during N.F.F.A. Field Championships.
      c) Assist the tournament chairman at the sectional championship on pro division matters as requested.
      d) Compute the awards for the pro division.
         1) Give list to tournament chairman and forward copy to N.F.A.A. headquarters.
         2) Issue vouchers to each professional who wins money.
         3) Carbon copies of these vouchers will be sent to headquarters where in turn a check will be issued and sent to each winner within 30 days.
      e) The $10.00 additional registration fee will be included in the regular sectional tournament report and mailed along with the total amount due the N.F.A.A.
      f) Act as mediator for pro division problems in his section.
      g) Should a problem arise the sectional representative will contact the N.F.A.A. director of the involved state.
7. Purse Allocation
   a. By shooting style
      1. The total purse for each shooting style shall be determined by the registration of that style at a sanctioned event unless decreed otherwise by the tournament sponsor.

a) Example: Should Pro Bowhunter registration equal 12% of the total Pro registration then 12% of the total purse would be assigned to that division.

b) Should only 1 archer register in a given style, he (she) will be awarded their percentage of the purse providing he (she) finishes the tournament.

8. Purse Division

   a. General Guidelines

      1. Note: These guidelines are made available as a reasonable and acceptable method to distribute winnings. They are not mandatory.

Shooter	Places	Distribution in %
1	1	100%
2-3	2	65-35
4-7	3	50-30-20
8-12	4	50-25-15-10
13-16	5	45-25-15-10-5
17-20	6	40-20-15-12-8-5
21 or over		1 place for each 3 entered

9. National Ranking

   a. Each period will last for one year and commence on January 1.

   b. Every N.F.A.A. Pro sanctioned shoot must be sanctioned with N.F.A.A. Headquarters at least 30 days prior to the shoot. A copy of the sanction shall be sent to the pro representative in that section.

   c. Pro points can be earned only at N.F.A.A. Professional Division sanctioned events.

   d. The State, Sectional and National Championships are automatically sanctioned events. (Points may be earned only at a state field and/or state indoor championship tournament.)

   e. In the event that a state championship tournament does not recognize a pro division, pro members will earn the point value applied to the position finished in the open division.

   f. No tournament will be awarded a greater number of points than assigned to the National Championships.

   g. A pro member may earn no more than 25 pro points in "5 point" tournaments in a ranking period.

   h. The following schedule of point values shall apply.

      1. NATIONAL CHAMPIONSHIP—100 possible points.
         Points distributed to the first 20 places. Decrements of five. (100-95-90-85 etc.)

      2. SECTIONAL CHAMPIONSHIP—50 possible points.
         Points distributed to the first 10 places. Decrements of five. (50-45-40-35 etc.).

      3. STATE CHAMPIONSHIP—25 possible points.
         Points distributed to the first 5 places. Decrements of five. (25-20-15-10-5)

      4. OTHER N.F.A.A. PRO SANCTIONED TOURNAMENTS
         Points will be awarded based upon the guaranteed cash amount in the championship flight of the event. The following schedule will apply and points will be distributed in decrements of five:

Cash	Points	Places	Distribution
$ 100 to 999	5	1	5
1,000 to 1,999	10	2	10-5
2,000 to 2,999	15	3	15-10-5
3,000 to 3,999	20	4	20-15-10-5
4,000 to 4,999	25	5	25-20-15-10-5
5,000 to 5,999	30	6	30-25-20-15-10-5
6,000 to 6,999	35	7	35-30-25-20-15-10-5
7,000 to 7,999	40	8	40-35-30-25-20-15-10-5
8,000 to 8,999	45	9	45-40-35-30-25-20-15-10-5
9,000 to 9,999	50	10	50-45-40-35-30-25-20-15-10-5
$10,000 and above			Point values will be negotiated

9. Guarantee Fund
   a. Funds are accrued in the N.F.A.A. Professional Division guarantee fund to stimulate professional archery competition.
   b. Tournament sponsors wishing support from this fund shall contact the Pro Division Sectional Representative, Pro Chairman or N.F.A.A. Executive Secretary at least 90 days prior to the event.
   c. Generally, subject to negotiation, the fund will guarantee up to 50 percent of net losses for prize money pay-off incurred at a sanctioned event.
   d. All net losses for prize money pay-off may be guaranteed from the fund for the National N.F.A.A. Professional Indoor Championships in that it is an event for N.F.A.A. Pros only.
10. Tournament Default
   a. In the event of a default of a sanctioned event, the fund shall guarantee payment of prize money to N.F.A.A. Pros only.
11. Pro Bonus
   a. In sanctioned events allowing open shooters to compete with pros, it is recommended that a bonus equal to 20 percent of their winnings be paid to N.F.A.A. Pros.

Addresses, State/Province Game Departments

THE FOLLOWING IS a complete listing of the addresses of the game departments in all 50 states and the Canadian provinces.

ALABAMA
  Department of Conservation
  64 N. Union Street
  Montgomery 36104
ALASKA
  Department of Fish and Game
  Subport Bldg.
  Juneau 99801
ARIZONA
  Game and Fish Department
  2222 W. Greenway
  Phoenix 85023
ARKANSAS
  Game and Fish Commission
  State Capitol
  Little Rock 72201
CALIFORNIA
  Department of Fish and Game
  1416 Ninth Street
  Sacramento 95814
COLORADO
  Division of Game, Fish and Parks
  6060 Broadway
  Denver 80216

CONNECTICUT
  Board of Fisheries and Game
  State Office Bldg.
  Hartford 06115
DELAWARE
  Board of Game and Fish Commissioners
  Box 457, North Street
  Dover 19901
FLORIDA
  Division of Game and Fresh Water Fish
  620 S. Meridian
  Tallahassee 32304
GEORGIA
  Game and Fish Commission
  270 Washington Street, S.W.
  Atlanta 30334
HAWAII
  Division of Fish and Game
  530 S. Hotel Street
  Honolulu 96813
IDAHO
  Fish and Game Department
  600 S. Walnut, Box 25
  Boise 83707

ILLINOIS
Department of Conservation
102 State Office Bldg.
Springfield 62706
INDIANA
Division of Fish and Game
608 State Office Bldg.
Indianapolis 46204
IOWA
State Conservation Commission
State Office Bldg., 300 4th Street
Des Moines 50319
KANSAS
Forestry, Fish and Game Commission
Box F
Pratt 67124
KENTUCKY
Department of Fish and Wildlife Resources
State Office Bldg. Annex
Frankfort 40601
LOUISIANA
Wildlife and Fisheries Commission
400 Royal Street
New Orleans 70130
MAINE
Department of Inland Fisheries and Game
State Office Bldg.
Augusta 04330
MARYLAND
Department of Game and Inland Fish
State Office Bldg.
Annapolis 21401
MASSACHUSETTS
Division of Fisheries and Game
100 Cambridge Street
Boston 02202
MICHIGAN
Department of Natural Resources
Mason Bldg.
Lansing 48926
MINNESOTA
Division of Game and Fish
301 Centennial Bldg., 658 Cedar Street
St. Paul 55101
MISSISSIPPI
Game and Fish Commission
Game and Fish Bldg., 402 High Street
Jackson 39205
MISSOURI
Department of Conservation
P. O. Box 180
Jefferson City 65101
MONTANA
Fish and Game Department
Helena 59601

NEBRASKA
Game and Parks Commission
State Capitol Bldg.
Lincoln 68509
NEVADA
Department of Fish and Game
Box 10678
Reno 89510
NEW HAMPSHIRE
Fish and Game Department
34 Bridge Street
Concord 03301
NEW JERSEY
Division of Fish and Game
Box 1809
Trenton 08625
NEW MEXICO
Department of Game and Fish
State Capitol
Santa Fe 87501
NEW YORK
Conservation Department
State Office Bldg. Campus
Albany 12226
NORTH CAROLINA
Wildlife Resources Commission
Box 2919
Raleigh 27602
NORTH DAKOTA
Game and Fish Department
103½ S. Third Street
Bismarck 58501
OHIO
Division of Wildlife
1500 Dublin Road
Columbus 43212
OKLAHOMA
Department of Wildlife Conservation
1801 N. Lincoln
Oklahoma City 73105
OREGON
Game Commission
Box 3503
Portland 97208
PENNSYLVANIA
Game Commission
P. O. Box 1567
Harrisburg 17120
RHODE ISLAND
Division of Conservation
83 Park Street
Providence 02903
SOUTH CAROLINA
Division of Game and Freshwater Fisheries
Box 167, 1015 Main Street
Columbia 29202

SOUTH DAKOTA
  Department of Game, Fish and Parks
  State Office Bldg.
  Pierre 5750
TENNESSEE
  Game and Fish Commission
  Box 9400, Ellington Agricultural Center
  Nashville 37220
TEXAS
  Parks and Wildlife Department
  John H. Reagan Bldg.
  Austin 78701
UTAH
  Fish and Game Division
  1596 W. N. Temple
  Salt Lake City 84116
VERMONT
  Fish and Game Department
  151 Main Street
  Montpelier 05602
VIRGINIA
  Commission of Game and Inland Fisheries
  4010 W. Broad Street, Box 11104
  Richmond 23230
WASHINGTON
  Department of Game
  600 N. Capitol Way
  Olympia 98501
WEST VIRGINIA
  Department of Natural Resources
  1800 Washington Street, East
  Charleston 25305
WISCONSIN
  Division of Fish, Game and Enforcement
  Box 450
  Madison 53701
WYOMING
  Game and Fish Commission
  Box 1589
  Cheyenne 82001

CANADA
  Canadian Wildlife Service
  400 Laurier Ave., West
  Ottawa 4, Ontario
ALBERTA
  Department of Lands and Forests
  Natural Resources Bldg.
  Edmonton 6, Alberta
BRITISH COLUMBIA
  Fish and Wildlife Branch
  Parliament Bldgs.
  Victoria, B.C.
MANITOBA
  Department of Mines and Natural Resources
  808 Norquay Bldg.
  Winnipeg, Manitoba
NEW BRUNSWICK
  Fish and Wildlife Branch
  Fredericton, New Brunswick
NEWFOUNDLAND
  Department of Mines, Agriculture and Resources
  Confederation Bldg.
  St. John's, Newfoundland
NOVA SCOTIA
  Wildlife Conservation Division
  Box 516
  Kentville, Nova Scotia
ONTARIO
  Fish and Wildlife Branch
  Parliament Bldgs.
  Toronto 5, Ontario
QUEBEC
  Fish and Game Branch
  Parliament Bldgs.
  Quebec City, Quebec
SASKATCHEWAN
  Wildlife Branch, Department of Natural Resources
  Government Administration Bldg.
  Regina, Saskatchewan

Excerpts—
Safety in Archery (NSC)

Introduction

1. Archery is one of the fastest growing sports today for several reasons. First, many people are recognizing it as a wonderful outdoor, leisure time activity—one in which the entire family can participate. Second, the rapid advancements in producing good equipment at a reasonable cost have made this sport possible for many persons as well as school, recreation and camp programs. Third, many school and recreation centers with limited facilities for including other individual activities realize its value in helping to fulfill a need

for individual sports. Fourth, archery offers real possibilities for providing an activity which the handicapped boy and girl can do well and from which they gain much pleasure and satisfaction.

2. It is difficult to report the accident incidence resulting from target shooting. However, as the popularity of this sport increases, the need for instruction in safety education becomes more apparent. The bow and arrow falls into the same category as the firearm. Both could be weapons, and both used unintelligently and without proper precautions can cause serious injuries.

Types of Injury

3. There are two main types or classifications of injuries occurring from shooting:

a. Injury to oneself brought about by improper shooting techniques, lack of proper protection and poorly selected and maintained equipment. For example—

(1) Bruises of the bow arm and scraping of the chest and breast are the result of improper position of the bow arm and body. The former injury is very common while the latter is more serious but occurs less frequently.

(2) Sore fingers are often the result of inadequate finger protection.

(3) Cuts and scratches on the bow hand are frequently due to the fletchings (feather) being put on the arrow improperly or the arrow being improperly nocked.

b. Injury to others, of course, is the most serious type of accident which could occur and is caused when the arrow actually strikes another person. Such injuries happen when:

(1) Archery ranges are not marked and roped off correctly.

(2) Participants fail to use a definite shooting line.

(3) Signals are not used for beginning and ending shooting.

(4) Participants do not confine their shooting to the limits of the range.

(5) The bow and arrow is treated as a toy.

Administrative Controls

4. Before attempting to conduct an archery program of any kind, certain policies and procedures should be cleared with the appropriate administrative authority. Provision should be made for:

a. Adequate space for a range, i.e., protected area, free from passers-by.

b. Adequate space for the safe storage and maintenance of equipment. Under no circumstances should equipment be kept in places where people could reach it and use it without proper supervision.

c. Good leadership is an absolute essential. Archery should not be a part of any program unless directed by qualified, competent and experienced personnel.

d. The size of the class or group shooting should be small enough to enable good supervision at all times. To specify an exact number of participants is difficult for so much depends on the skill and experience of the group. However, when the number exceeds 15 persons shooting at one time, under the direction of one person, good supervision becomes difficult. In this case, a rotation system could be used with designated groups shooting and retrieving in a definite order.

Facilities

5. **Backstop**— Probably the most ideal backstop for outdoor shooting is a well maintained terrace or hill directly behind the targets. Such a terrain provides a natural backstop for arrows. Breakage and damage to arrows are kept at a minimum. However, many programs must be carried on in a "flat" or open space. Bunkers of straw placed in back of the

targets and stacked high enough (9 ft. to 10 ft.) will prevent arrows from overshooting the area. If it is not feasible to erect straw bunkers, an area 20 yards in length should be roped off behind the targets and the area clearly marked.

6. For indoor shooting, bunkers of straw as described above or a heavy, durable, canvas backdrop may be placed directly behind the targets. Also, heavy cardboard eight inches wide and 30 inches long works out very well for backstops. While there is little danger of an arrow rebounding from a wall and causing injury, there is the problem of damage to the arrow which may eventually lead to injury.

7. **Enclosing the range**— Some provision must be made for enclosing the range to prevent passers-by from walking across the range or getting too close to either the targets or the shooting line. The most practical solution to the problem is to rope off the area and post signs warning that shooting is in progress and prohibiting people from walking across the area. For indoor archery, doors leading onto the range should be either locked or posted with warning signs.

8. **Marking the range**

    a. The minimum width range for one target is 6 yards. At least 3 yards should be allowed between targets.

    b. Shooting lines should be clearly marked off across the entire range with lines running parallel to one another and distances from the targets indicated. White chalk or lime as used in marking off athletic fields is the most desirable. Where targets are the kind that can be moved without too much difficulty, some instructors recommend staggering the targets at varying distances and using only one shooting line. In other words, two targets might be placed at 100 yards, two at 60 yards, two at 50 yards, etc.

Index